The Accidental Stripper

Public nudity, skydiving, flying and other extreme sports

By

Dean Ricci
"The Fuckin' Pilot"

Forward

This book is a re-working of a book that I attempted to write many years ago about my life as a professional stripper turned skydiver and eventually pilot. In each attempt I have previously made, and there have been many, I tried as hard as I could not only to stick truthfully to the events that unfolded in my life but to tell it as a seamless story from start to finish.

After working now for eight years as a monthly columnist for Blue Skies Magazine I've learned a few things about my writing; The first of which is that my initial attempts at writing this story were completely and utterly unreadable, and if I'm being brutally honest, boring as all fucking hell. I mean really, who wants to hear about bad relationships and shitty jobs? Everyone has their own version of that story to tell! Which led to the second lesson; Get down to the meat and bones of the story. So, I decided to change things around quite a bit and go with the style I've become much more accustom to after my years writing for the magazine.

In the pages that follow are a series of, for lack of a better description, short stories. Short stories that are based on actual events in my life. They most certainly follow along in a chronological order, but you'll notice as you read that there are more than a few spaces that seem to skip over large periods of time. That's basically because during those times, not one fucking thing worth writing about or wasting your time with happened. Luckily for me, very little of my life has been what you might refer to as "normal".

Now when I say "Based on actual events in my life", I mean it. Most of the borderline insane situations contained within have actually been a very real part my life. BUT... The level of truth in each of the following stories is directly proportional to the legality of the story in question. In other words, if it was or is illegal and I can in any way be held accountable for my actions in the past, I totally made that shit up. Never happened.

Enjoy!

Dean Ricci
"The Fuckin' Pilot"

The accidental Stripper
Public nudity, skydiving, flying and other extreme sports

Fuckin' Liar

I can trace my entire adult life back to just one moment. One girl. One lie. If you were to ask me now why I told the lie I did, I'm really not sure I could answer the question. Actually that's not true; basically I told the lie to get laid. It's why I told that particular lie that I can't quite explain.

I'll see if I can back up here just a little bit and fill you in. I had ended up working as a banquet waiter at the Holiday Inn in Downtown Sacramento after a failed attempt at securing my star on the Hollywood walk of fame in LA. In the City of Angels, I'd managed to get hit on by a talent scout and a rather high end producer (both men), go broke quite quickly working retail in Santa Monica and bust myself up pretty good in a motorcycle accident before leaving with my tail tucked between my legs and a cast on my foot.

After about a six month stay at my mothers in Seattle where I celebrated my 21st birthday with Mom at a Chili's restaurant, I'd taken the time to heal up enough to head back to Northern California where a substantial amount of traffic tickets needed to be dealt with before I ran the very real risk of ending up in jail. My only form of transportation at the time was a twelve speed road bike (as I had no car and no license) housing care of my grandmother was a shitty little basement apartment about five miles from the house I was raised in, and at the time the only thing I had less of than money was pride.

Within a few weeks I'd managed to get the banquet gig which was at least putting a little (very little) cash in my pocket, and within a few months I'd managed to get myself into a bit of a groove; and by groove I mean a pretty miserable existence all and all, with just a few notable exceptions. One, I'd started hanging out on the weekends at a local dance club called the Yucatan Liquor Stand (a.k.a the Yucatan Hooker Stand) where I'd ended up meeting and becoming friends with a great group of guys. And two, I had fallen head over heels in lust with one of my female co-workers from the Holiday Inn.

Now I'd always considered myself to be a pretty good dancer, and this was around the time when guys would happily go out dancing on their own in public, (or in groups no less). It was not just acceptable, but actually pretty badass. When I'd met the group that would eventually become my very close friends, they had all been perched precariously on a 20 inch rail which ran the length of the Yucatan's dance floor, stepping in time with some clearly choreographed moves to a Boyz II Men song, both women and men alike watching their every move.

The truth is, it didn't really even cross my mind that I shouldn't hop up and give it a shot right along with them, and perhaps that's just why it worked. By the end of that first night of dancing, I'd managed to learn the majority of the "steps" they'd been doing, and Price, Craig and Jay had decided that I was welcome to try and keep up with them again sometime. That sometime of course became every weekend for quite some time indeed.

Over the course of the next few months I managed to spend a fair bit of my free time hanging out with Price and the boys both in and out of the club, and had passionately cultivated lusting after my work crush when at work or even at home. Of course I not only hadn't made any progress toward fulfilling the multitude of fantasies I had by then worked up over Kasey, but was pretty sure that she didn't even actually know my name.

The night it happened started out like most other nights working the banquet hall at the Holiday Inn. Shitty. The crew I was working with that night were all the girls from the department, and I was the only guy, which I'll admit at least made for interesting eve's dropping, but to my surprise, a few of the girls were going out of their way to get me into the conversation. I talked briefly about being from Sacramento originally, about having moved down to LA and why (although I skipped over the only being hit on by guys part), and basically tried to make myself sound at least a touch cooler than I looked on paper.

Then Kasey asked me a question. A pretty simple question to answer really. "So, what were you doing for work down in L.A.?" The answer should have been the straightforward truth that I'd worked retail for a bit and then bailed after my motorcycle accident, but the answer that I actually gave was more along the lines of "Well I worked a few part time gig's here and there while I was going to auditions, and spent the weekends working as a stripper." Wait, what?

The looks I got from the ladies was one of surprise and amusement for sure, but before any of them had the chance to let it sink in and start asking me questions I had no fucking chance to answer, the banquet broke up and we were ushered in to clean the place up. By the time we'd managed to finish the job a few hours later, it seemed that my bullshit had been forgotten and everyone said goodnight without mentioning it at all.

When more than a week had gone by, I was relatively sure I'd gotten away with it. I still to this day have no idea why I thought telling them I moonlighted as a damn stripper would make me look in the least bit cool, nor can I fathom why I thought that they would for even one second believe it. I was all of about 165 pounds, with no real upper body to speak of and even though I had quite muscular legs from all the cycling, the fact that I was pasty white negated any positive effects a built set of legs might have had. I actually still remember the physical relief I felt each night as I walked into work and not one of the girls that had been there that night said a thing about my verbal vomit attack.

"DEAN!! I've been looking all over for you! You just have to do me the biggest favor… I will SO OWE YOU!" Kasey looked so damn good as she came bounding up to me as only a 20 year old blonde with large breasts can do that it flat out didn't even cross my mind that this favor might be bad for me!

"SO… it's my sisters birthday next week. It was my job to try and plan out something amazing for her cause it's her 21st, but I screwed it all up!" I quite literally went cold inside and felt the hair on the back of my neck stand on end. It was kind of like in the movies when a ghost walks in the room and all the sudden you can see your breath. "You just have to help me out and dance for her! It would be so amazing! And since its what you use to do, I figured it would be super easy for you!"

Clear as a bell I could instantly hear the answer. "I'm sorry Kasey, there's just no way I can do that. It's been quite a while since I danced so I'm way out of practice and to be honest, when I quit it was cause I was just over it and I promised myself I was done." It was a rational and easily understandable way to decline, and one in which although Kasey might be a bit disappointed, she would easily get past it. it was exactly what I knew I had to say, when in actuality what I said was "Sure!". Fuck.

She bounced up and down for a solid minute before she dove at me and gave me a glorious hug. A hug that made me acutely aware that her boobs were even larger and firmer than I had imagined (and I had really imagined…), and almost made me forget that I had just agreed to take off my clothes in front of her and god knows how many other women in public. The body heat from her was still warming the front of my shirt and my mind was already feverishly trying to think of ways to get out of it, but somewhere in the back of my mind that little troll inside me was only thinking about boobs. All he was thinking was that if by some miracle I managed to do this I had a solid chance of getting to see those beauties firsthand, and I was already mentally warming up my engine for a solid motorboat session.

The next week was complete and utter shit. The terrible anticipation, bordering on sheer dread was all but overwhelming, and my upcoming date with public nudity was nearly all I could think about. I had not one clue what I was going to do. I had never seen a stripper in my life, either male or for that matter female, and I couldn't possibly conceive how to go about it. Clearly it involved music, and of course some kind of outfit to take off, as I couldn't imagine trying to strip off a pair of blue jeans with any amount of style, so those two tasks became my first two orders of business.

Just as I had known he would be, Price was the perfect person to go to for advice and assistance. He was by far the most stylish of the group as well as the de-facto leader, and if anyone was going to be able to help me in the least it was him. As it turned out, the outfit was by far the easiest problem to solve to my surprise. Price had managed to hang on to his pea-green U.S Air Force jumpsuit just like the pilots wore in Top Gun, and even though he was a good six inches taller than me, it fit well enough that nobody would notice it was a bit too long in the legs. The fact that it fit well, and the fact that to take it off only required one zipper made it the absolute perfect outfit. the downside to both the suit and his help with the tunes was that I don't believe Price actually stopped laughing even once while I was at his place. What are friends for but to help accentuate the negative!

"DA DA DA du du-du du DA DA DA du du-du GET READY FOR THIS! DA DA DA...". I hated it right away, but I and everyone else had heard the tune in the clubs enough for it to be instantly recognizable, and in my estimation the music was most likely to be the only part of the show the ladies would enjoy, so I let Price put my tape together so at least something for that night was done correctly. Once he'd finished it off and handed me the cassette, there were really only a couple of things that needed to be taken care of before I would be ready for what I was sure would be the worst night of my life.

Fredrick's of Hollywood is probably the tackiest ladies lingerie store ever, but I can assure you personally that the stock they have for women is of the utmost class and elegance compared to the two small racks of so called "mens apparel" in the back corner. in less than thirty seconds I knew which thong I'd be buying for the show. How you ask? Well, it's the only one that wasn't some type of animal head, like the elephant with the trunk, or the lion with its tongue sticking out, or as an alternative, the leopard spotted neon pink print.

Never in the history of the statement "One size fits all" has there been a more gross misrepresentation of reality. as I stood in front of the mirror sporting my not overly bright purple speckled thong, it looked more as if it would serve better as an elongated fanny pack than a fucking sexy piece of clothing, and I had never felt more emasculated or inadequate. Now I'm hung like the average guy. Not too big, not too small, and have been happily satisfied with what genetics provided me, with the exception of that very moment. It looked to me as if someone had tossed a tater tot and a couple of chick peas into a purple Ziplock freezer bag. You knew something was in there, but you just could't quite tell what. Luckily for me, I'd been raised by a women who was beyond amazing with a needle and thread, and I sat down for what was one of the strangest evenings I'd had up till that point. Watching shit T.V. on my own, I sat for about two hours stitching my way into a thong that eventually just about looked like it fit me. When it was all said and done, it was readily apparent that in my hand stitched purple banana hammock was an actual cock and balls. Exactly the effect I was going for.

The only thing I had left to do was try and get a bit of color on the all too white lack of a build I was sporting, but with only two days left before the show, there was no way that was gonna happen outside. In my first ever attempt at using a "self tanning" cream, I failed to adequately read the instructions, the proof of which were my darkly stained hands and the happy sunny orange glow I ended up with.

As the day loomed closer and closer, I proved beyond a shadow of a doubt that a weeks worth of furious push-ups may do a bit for your confidence, but it'll do little for your build, and make it extremely difficult to lift your arms. When I arrived at Price's place on the evening of the show, I was still orange, still wasn't built, still terrified at what was about to happen, and could blame nobody but myself.

As it turned out, Price lived in the same apartment complex as were the party was taking place so it was only a short stroll with flight suit on and boom box in hand before I approached the dreaded door marked "181". Straight down for another round of push-ups I went, convinced that this time if I could manage to cram in enough of them in to one go, I'd have a chest for the next 30 minutes.

The wave of terror that shot through my body as I realized Price had just knocked on the door to cure his impatience to witness my destruction was almost indescribable. It was total fight or flight at that instant, and if they hadn't opened the door so quickly, I do believe I would have tackled that asshole! The moment that door opened though, all thoughts vanished from my mind. The roar of female voices that cascaded from the apartment was overwhelming, and I couldn't wrap my head around that much noise coming from inside one little apartment.

With a hand on my back ushering me in, my worst fears were immediately realized. In the most brightly lit room I believe I've ever been in were crammed more than forty screaming drunk women, all looking directly at me. Nothing I could have done would have prepared me for the image that is to this day still burned into my brain. The "birthday" girl was seated in an armless chair in the center of the room with a look on her face that was somewhere between amusement and embarrassment and as she made eye contact with me, I could tell that just like me, she knew it was gonna be a little work to get through this unscathed. I decided she was my only friend in the room. Especially when without cue and without me being the least bit ready, Price decided to reach up to the boom box and push "Play". Fucker.

It must have been the flight suit that kicked me into autopilot. I can't actually say I recall walking further into the room. I can't quite recall starting my dance either. It wasn't quite a blackout; more of a brownout in my estimation, but I snapped back into myself just in time to realize that I was straddling the guest of honor and giving just a bit of a wiggle back and forth. Not really a stellar performance to wake up to!

Once I seemed back in control of my own faculties I can't actually say I did all that much better though, because I didn't even make it to the second song before I had the flight suit down around my ankles in a horrible case of premature de-cloaking. As it turned out, the flight suit was too damn easy to take off, because by all of about minute three I was down to my custom thong and out of ideas, acutely aware that terror of the magnitude I was currently suffering through has just about the same effect as diving into a freezing cold pool.

So, I did the only thing I could think of. I turned to face the birthday girl, squatted down on to her lap and dry humped her leg like a Sheppard in heat. Within a minute or two of this tactical move I discovered yet another downside to that fight or flight instinct, that being an incredible amount of sweat literally pouring from my skin. I vividly remember thinking that if I were standing under the shower at that very moment I probably wouldn't have as much water running off me as I did sweat right then.

It felt simultaneously like two minutes and two hours. Time stretched out in a way that I had never experienced before, and as the last of the three songs Price had put down for me came to and end, it looked as if both the birthday girl and I had spent the last twenty minutes running through the sprinklers. Other than looking a bit shell shocked, the guest of honor was smiling and hooting with the other girls in the room, but I wasn't doing nearly as well. The insides of both my thighs were rubbed a bit raw from sliding up and down her blue jean covered legs, I was light headed and a touch sick to my stomach from dehydration and nerves and quite frankly couldn't be bothered to locate my shoes before I grabbed the flight suit and headed for the front door. I actually had Price collect not only the boots I'd left behind but my money for me as I stood next to the door, hastily dressing and ready to make my escape.

As I walked barefoot back towards Price's apartment, the only thing I could manage to say over and over again was "Fuck that... FUCK THAT! fuck...that". It had been just as bad as I had imagined, if not even worse. I had gone about making the biggest ass out of myself that I ever could have, and would live with the shame of that so called "show" for at the very least the rest of this lifetime. The first thought that crossed my mind once I managed to stop saying "Fuck that" was "Oh my god.... I have to work with some of them!" This would haunt me for the rest of my days. Self inflicted Karma had been quick on this one and I'll be damned if it didn't get me good.

Club Onyx

"Hey…. Can I speak to Dean?" If I'm being honest, my first reaction was to say there was no Dean at this number. Somewhere along the line I started assuming that people I didn't know calling for me was a bad thing. "This is Dean…?" I said, listening to myself make it sound more like a question that a statement.

"My name is Mark, and I got your number from Trisha. She told me I should give you a call." "Okay…" I said, having no idea who the fuck Trisha was or how she had my phone number. "So Trish was at your show last week and said I should give you a call cause you could help me out."

I must admit that I'm not always as fast on the uptake as I'd like to think, and this was most certainly one of those times. For at least a solid minute I couldn't figure out what show this "Mark" guy was talking about or why the hell he'd be calling me for help. Then of course the terrible truth dawned on me.

The previous week had seen what was to me the most horrifying day of my life thus far. I had suffered through what could only be described as self inflicted mental torture of the greatest degree and looking back now was clearly suffering from PTSD, having almost hourly flashbacks of my splotchy pasty white/orange ass dripping sweat in buckets all over some poor unsuspecting twenty-one year old who had started the day only wanting to enjoy herself with her friends. Since the party, I had done my best to avoid anyone and everyone associated with that bone chilling event, and was actively trying to block it from my mind with every fibre of my being. It wasn't working.

Between the Post Traumatic Stress, and my conscious attempt to banish that evening from my memory, the phrase "at your show" just didn't register at first. As Mark kept talking, the blossoming memory of my entertainment debut started to filter its way into my higher brain functions, and I came back from another momentary brownout just in time to get the gist of why this Mark fellow had called.

As it turned out, Mark was the owner of a strip tease telegram company based in Sacramento. He'd been running the place for a few years, and had managed to get himself a pretty successful business going. The companies name was "Masquerade", and was one of only two such companies operating in Sacramento at the time.

"So like I said" Mark continued, "He canceled on me last minute, and I'm really in a corner… So, what do you think?" I had to get him to back up a bit and start again with his request, as the involuntary twitching that his request had kicked off had kept me from hearing him properly. "Say again?" I said. "My boy Darren backed out of the show I've got tomorrow night, and I've gotta get a fill in for him or the club owner is gonna be pissed! I promised him six guys this time and after the last mess I had, I need to come through, so what do ya say? Are you good to dance tomorrow?"

OH FUCK! No no no no fucking way! The phrase "Fuck that fuck that fuck that" was literally ringing in my ears as I actually voiced my answer this time instead of just thinking it. I was very much in the middle of saying "No way can I dance tomorrow man! Theres just…." But he cut me off mid sentence with "It pays $500.00 cash plus tips, and it'll only be about four hours total by the time we're back in town." Oh fuck….
Lets face it. I was broke as hell. I rode a bicycle as my only form of transportation. On the evenings I spent hanging out with Price and the guys at the club I could only afford to get one, maybe two Sprite's in an evening, I had no romantic life what-so-ever, and the money he was offering for his show would go a long way toward at least helping out with one or two of my more pressing issues. "Fuck it. Sure Mark, I can dance tomorrow."

During the rest of our conversation, I explained to Mark that I had no way of getting to his show as I didn't have a set of wheels. I also let him know that I didn't really have much of an "Act" so to speak, and that I could manage the "Hip Hop" type dancing that I'd gotten pretty good at after all my time with Price at the Yucatan, none of which seemed to be any issue at all for him. He took down my address and directions on how to get to me, gave me a time to be ready and let me know it would be a bit of a drive to the club as it was in Fresno. He didn't really tell me much about the show though, and I had a rather odd feeling about it all. More odd that is than the fact that my dick was pulling the "cold water" routine just thinking about it. He said he'd be able to bring me up to speed on what his show's were all about on the drive down, as it would take about an hour to get there. But, as he put it, a "white guy" dancing Hip Hop would go over really well with the crowd. Ahh, white guy? Hmmmmm...

This time I didn't have to come up with music, as Mark had a DJ/MC on staff who he said would have anything I could possibly need. All I needed to do was tell him either what songs or what style and he'd sort me out. As far as the outfit went, he asked for me to just bring something that fit in to the "club" scene. Since I didn't really have an act to go along with the Air Force jumpsuit, he thought it would just work better if the "white boy" just came out and got at it.

I once again blame the PTSD from my first so called show. I was still so shell shocked from the previous week that I just wasn't putting all the clues together, but it seemed I was just like the people who saw "The Usual Suspects" and figured out who Keyser Soze was just as Kevin Spacey stopped limping and slid on his gold watch; but as the large black Lincoln Navigator pulled in to the parking lot of my building, it clicked. Well, at least some of it did.

As I walked through the lot towards him, the drivers side door open the most massive set of Timberland boots I believe I'd ever seen hit the pavement. Mark, as it turned out was aptly named "Big Mark", and fuck me running he was! He had to be at least 6'3 and 250 pounds naked. He was about as imposing a black man as I'd ever seen, and certainly the most imposing I'd ever marched up to intentionally, but that image disappeared like a fart in the wind as soon as he smiled and offered his hand. He instantly became one of the nicest guys I'd ever met, and as I climbed into the Lincoln beside him for the drive, I felt decent about the whole thing for the first time. That feeling unfortunately didn't last all that long.

The "white guy" comment was ringing in my ears about the time we pulled on to the highway, and my worst fears were confirmed about the time we cross the Sacramento City limits. Masquerade had managed to become semi-successful in Sacramento and the outlying area for one reason; they had a real niche market. They were the only all black strip troupe in California at the time. Well, they were the only all black troupe that performed stage shows as well as the more personal "telegram" service that made the real money. When It came to the telegram service, Mark had a few "token" white men and women working for him as well, but none of them did any of his stage shows.

As it turned out, I would be the very first man of *non*-color ever to perform in a Masquerade stage show, which by Mark's estimation was quite an honor. "Honor" wouldn't exactly have been the word I would have used to describe the situation, but considering Mark had already handed over five hundred bucks cash in good faith, I was willing to let it go.

Pulling into the club parking lot didn't do much to help me feel one way or the other about the show. There were only about half a dozen cars in the parking lot, and the club itself looked as thought it had been an old Denny's restaurant that had been converted over to be a wannabe Fresno hot spot. All the windows had been blacked out, the exterior had been painted black with pink trim, and the sign, a mix of neon pink, gloss black and silver trim loudly proclaimed that you had arrived at "Club Onyx".

Entering through the service entrance as we did, I really didn't get a chance to take a look around the place but I figured I had a pretty good idea of the decor just from the exterior. I expected to see a whole lot of black lacquer and a lot of pink lights; but just as I was dwelling on my surroundings, we entered the back stage area that served as the dancers "dressing room". In it, in various stages of undress were five of the most built black men I had ever seen. Like Holyfield built! Fucking shredded, each and every one of them; although the baby oil they had all generously slathered all over themselves assisted in seriously amplifying that fact. I was clearly not the man for this job, and I was fucked.

Now that whole myth about black guys.... Well, If these gentlemen were any indication, it's not a fucking myth! These were the guys that those horrible thongs in Fredrick's of Hollywood had been designed for, and they strutted around that room in complete comfort. Then again, If I had a cock anywhere near as big as theirs appeared to be I would have had that thing out in church! If one of those had belonged to me, it would have been black too, cause it would have been out in the sunlight every damn moment of every damn day! It was somewhere right around that time that it just clicked, again. It dawned on me that pride was a completely overrated commodity, and that quite obviously I had no use for it. Might as well get on with the show…

I'd had a chance to peek out from behind the curtain a few times as people started to enter the club, but really hadn't paid attention to them other than in passing. The last time I looked before the show began there had been perhaps forty women in the crowd, which made me feel great considering there had been almost that many for the telegram I delivered, and It had been in a tiny brightly lit apartment. This at least was an appropriately lit club, so all the myriad of imperfections I was sporting wouldn't be nearly as apparent. If it stayed the same until I was out there I might not make much it tips, but I wasn't too concerned as I wasn't expecting to make much of a killing anyway.

With the way Mark had his show set up, the easiest way according to him, was to leave the order of performers just the way it had been. I'd be taking the slot that "Lightning" usually occupied, which as it turned out had me hitting the stage fifth. As you can imagine, waiting my turn was excruciating. I spent the majority of that time in limbo in the darkest corner of the room, watching as the other performers who had clearly worked together for some time go out and back, returning from the other side of the curtain looking as if they were wearing Hawaiian grass skirts made from dollar bills. Every one of them came back with a smile on their faces and sweat running down their bodies, and well as a polished air of ease. I hated each and every one of those fuckers.

Then, it jumped up and bit me. I honestly was paying attention, like seriously waiting, and even though I knew I was "up", hearing the "DA DA DA" of the very same song I'd started with once before caught me completely off guard. But hey, fuck it, I didn't know any of these people. I was in a town an hour away from where I lived and I knew that other than being "The white guy", not one of the customers or even the dancers for that matter was gone remember any other thing about me.

Well perhaps that wasn't exactly true. They would probably remember the acid washed blue jeans (yes, it was that long ago). They would probably hang on to the image of the black cowboy boots with the silver tips (yes, I know…), and more than likely they would always link the white boy stripper with paisley considering the shirt I had on, but what is it they say? No such thing as bad press?

As I stepped through the curtain it physically felt like I got punched in the face. The crowd had, well it had become a real fucking crowd! If I had to take a ballpark guess, there were between two hundred fifty to three hundred women in the audience, completely loosing their shit. As I hip-hopped my way onstage and then around, and back and forth using every single step I'd learned from Price, Jay and Craig, It dawned on me in-between spins that there was not a single white face looking back. As it turned out, I was not only the only white dancer in the troupe, I was the only white person in the club! And I was dancing hip-hop. In acid washed blue jeans. Fuck…?

They went completely insane. I don't know if it as shock at seeing a white guy, shock at seeing a white guy dancing the way I was, shock at the horrible choice of outfit or what, but before I even managed to unbutton my shirt there was a bill in every hand I could see. It was daunting really! I actually remember thinking how much work It was gonna take to collect every one I was looking at and I almost started laughing! Then as I hopped my way out of the jeans and boots and found myself in the middle of a huge crowd of women in my self-tailored purple thong having hit the floor to collect my tips, I had the strangest realization.

As soon as I was off the stage and among the tables, chairs, outstretched hands and dollar bills, I was completely at ease. I found almost instantly that as soon as I was wading through the very enthusiastic ladies all around me, I didn't feel the least bit self conscious. The club itself wasn't brightly lit, and even though the "disco" lights were blasting like solar flares, they never focused on one spot for more than a second at a time. "Boom!" I thought, I wasn't naked at all! I was clothed from almost every side by the damn crowd itself! Unless you were following me around while crouched down and dodging elbows you more than likely couldn't see more than just a silhouette, and because of it I slid easily between the tables, snatching bills as I went, with just as many being deposited in my thong, almost as if by magic.

Ass grabbed a hundred times, balls even brushed once or twice, and even a mild bite or two, but as I headed backstage while the M.C. called a close to my so-called act, I crossed through the curtain with a lot more money left on the floor than I could have possibly collected in a reasonable amount of time. Dizzy would be a damn good description of how I felt as I put my clothes back on, and I had to admit to myself that It could not have gone any better. It didn't matter to me that I probably only made money because I was a novelty. It didn't matter that I was the least qualified guy dancing that night, and it sure as fuck didn't matter that I'd been terrified.

All tolled, I'd managed to collect nearly four hundred dollars in cash during my four song set; That plus the pay upfront being almost a full months pay at the Holiday inn. As I finished counting up my tips on the drive home, still feeling as if the entire experience was beyond unreal, I took the time to give Mark a heart felt thanks for the opportunity.

"I gotta tell you, when I picked ya up tonight I wasn't too sure about you, but you did a damn good job man. How would you feel about coming to work for Masquerade doing telegrams?"

"Really?" I responded "You want be doing telegrams for you?" I wasn't exactly shocked by the offer (shocking me at that moment would have taken fucking taser with new batteries), but it certainly wasn't what I'd been expecting when the day started.

"You know, I wasn't too sure about all of this either, but after tonight? Yeah, I think I could work for you. Sure!"

And just like that, I was a fucking stripper. Never in my life would I have ever imagined that this path was even an option, and yet here I was, having just agreed to go to work for a mostly black strip troupe in the capitol of California and my home town. What could possibly go wrong?

Training Day

Amy was her name, and for lack of a better word she was to be my tutor. Stripper tutor that is. Taking into consideration the fact that my first "show" had been in my estimation a complete and total failure, confirmed and punctuated by the fact that not one of my co-workers who had been there had ever mentioned it even in passing, made me feel like an even bigger fraud than I was. I believed (and still do) that if something was so embarrassing that even the spectators couldn't bring it up, it had to be really fucking bad.

I felt, sitting shotgun in the Lincoln as Mark drove us back to Sacramento, that mentioning that I had no damn clue how to do a "Stripper Telegram" would be a really good idea seeing as how he had just hired me to do exactly that. I ended up spilling pretty much the whole story of how that first show came about, and once he stopped laughing (which took a while), he told me not to worry and that he'd sort something out.

A few days later, I found myself in the offices of Masquerade Strip Tease Telegrams having a Polaroid head shot taken to add my face to the book of entertainers which potential customers could come look through to choose their dancer (no, they couldn't just go online and browse the dancers profiles, as there were no profiles, and in fact, no online. Yes, that long ago!). Once my photo was added, I was one of only three white guys in the book, and they were about as opposite to me as could be. The first I saw was straight out of Conan the Barbarian; long dark hair, arm bands above his substantial biceps, eye liner and all. It actually made me feel a bit better to be honest, as there was no way in hell that anyone who liked the look of this guy was ever gonna want me. The second, well he looked like a blonde, smaller version of Conan only he was wearing a cowboy hat with a cigarette hanging from the corner of his mouth (an homage to the Marlboro Man I suppose).

Cue Amy. While flipping through the ladies section to kill time I came across the few white and one asian girl that Mark had working for him. The first thing that was apparent was that he required a much more, shall we say outgoing set of pictures from them than he did from the men. Besides the head shot that each of the guys had, each of the ladies also had a picture or two of them in costume, as well as a picture or two of them out of costume. Completely out. As I heard the office door open behind me, I tried with a bit of difficulty I might add, to pry my eyes away from the adorable little naked brunette staring up at me from the book, pouty face, hard nipples and all.

"Damn! She's fucking hot!" Came from just behind me, and I turned rather startled at the comment to find the same set of eyes looking back at me from both the book and the doorway. Of course the very first thing to cross my mind was that the same nipples I had just been staring at would also be attached to this person as well…

"So you're gonna go with Amy tonight to one of her shows so you can see how we deliver a telegram. Gonna be a little bit different than what you'll do of course, but you'll get the basic idea of how shit goes anyway." Nipples.

"Cool!" She said, seeming honestly excited at the prospect, although I had no idea why she would be. She talked fast and moved even faster, snatching the paperwork that gave her the customers information off the counter along with the garter band that apparently was to be worn by the dancer to give to the recipient.

"I'm Amy, but for work they call me Jasmine. I like Jasmine a lot more! Sounds sexy as fuck don't it? Who are you anyway? Whats your name? New dancer are you? Good choice Mark, he's cute! We need more white guys! So whats your name again? Alright! You'll meet me and I'll show ya.... Gotta go! See ya later!"

I don't believe I saw her take a breath even once. She must have asked me half a dozen questions all in one shot, not waiting to get an answer to a single one. Without ever even learning my name, she told me to meet her on the corner of Sunrise and El Camino near where her show was at 8 o'clock sharp, and she'd show me what was what. With that, she gave Mark a peck on the cheek and was out the door in a flash!

She couldn't have been in the office more than four minutes total. "Yeah" said Mark, "she's kinda just like that. Ton's of fuckin' energy! Probably why the customers like her so much. They probably just imagining her in the sack!" While he was speaking, I was looking down at her photos again. I was still a bit stuck on the nipple thing to be honest, but I was most certainly picturing them in action, so I guess I agreed with him. So with that, I was set.

I was in the book, I had a tutor, I would learn what I needed and would simply wait until either someone went in the office to choose me for their special occasion, or as Mark said happened quite often, they wouldn't chose a specific guy but instead simply say what type they wanted, in which case it was up to him. What that meant more than anything he said, was who ever the hell was available at the time was who got the gig.

Six-thirty found me sitting on the corner of Sunrise and El Camino, crazy early as I'd had to bum a ride from Price because as of yet I still lacked any form of self propelled transportation. It was another huge hurtle I was gonna have to overcome if I were to be able to do the job for which I'd been hired, but I figured it would be at least a little while before I got an actual gig, so as was my usual M.O. I waited. Craig had told me in passing that his cousin was selling an old beater car for cheap if I was interested, and I had made a mental note to follow up with him on it.

As 8 o'clock rolled around, with me still standing on the street corner looking like a douche, that old specter "Self Doubt" started creeping in again. Who in the hell did I think I was to try something like this? I clearly had to be off my fucking rocker to believe there was a chance in hell this was gonna end well for me, but as soon as I started really getting into a good self loathing groove.... Nipples.

She drove like she spoke. Fucking fast and erratic! I watched her doing at least five things at once other than driving the car, and it knocked anything and everything else out of my mind.

"Can be a real pain in the ass trying to read the map, figure out who in the hell you're suppose to talk to, what outfit you're suppose to be in..." eyes in the mirror, applying bright red lipstick while hanging a rather aggressive right turn in front of oncoming traffic with a map flopping around on her lap. Looking back I thank the powers that be that "Smart Phones" weren't a thing then as had there been, you can damn well bet she would have been chatting and texting with someone or looking through selfies or some such shit.

Amy was literally just one big ball of manic energy, and I couldn't imagine what the hell her show was gonna be like. As we got closer to the destination she was, while driving of course, trying to show me the order form she had picked up from the office which gave her all the pertinent details of the show. The name of the person who hired her, the name of the recipient, the address, the occasion, the outfit she was to wear.... According to the form, for this show she was to come in a nurses outfit, and just about the time it dawned on me that she looked nothing like a nurse in her Nine Inch Nails T-shirt, she took it off! Nipples.

Now topless and driving down the road like a blind epileptic, not looking where she was going because she was arched back with her right arm in the back seat trying to grab her costume top, I should have been seriously fearing for my life, but it never even crossed my mind. Her very perky tits, adorned with what were clearly perpetually hard nipples were coming dangerously close to brushing up against my arm, and I didn't give a fuck about her not watching where she was going.

If she had noticed that I hadn't looked at anything but her chest since she took the shirt off she didn't give any indication, and clearly she didn't give a fuck anyway or she wouldn't have tossed Nine Inch Nails in the back seat in the first place. The next thing I knew, we had come to a screeching halt in front of a relatively nondescript house in a relatively nondescript neighborhood, and she was somehow miraculously dressed from head to toe as an old fashion nurse, cap and all. Amazing.

Once we were out of the car and at the door, things went a lot like I had expected them to I guess. The brother of the birthday boy answered the door, laughed when he saw the nurses outfit, and by laughed I mean gave one of those pervy giggles people give, then gave me a quizzical look which "Jasmine" quickly dealt with as she pawned me off as her escort for the event. "Company policy" she said.

Once inside, the man of the hour was as you would assume. He was quickly grabbed by his friends and wrangled into the chair which had been hastily set in the center of the room; and then without any further fanfare, the music kicked in and his happy horny nurse strutted from around the corner and into view.

No fucking way was this the same girl. This Jasmine chick sauntered across the floor with about the sexiest strut I had ever seen. Smokey eyes, shoulder and hips thumping and rolling to the beat of the song, she never once took her eyes off the guy in the chair. Not one damn thing about her was erratic or out of control. On the contrary, she seemed to be not only in control of herself but of everyone else in the room, ladies included!

About the time the heel of her stiletto was pinned against the birthday boy's chest, I realized I could never EVER do what she was doing. If she hadn't taken a single thing off, it still would have been up till that point in my life the sexiest thing I had ever seen in person. By the time she had given the birthday boy his garter (and by given I mean forced him to his knees to remove it from her leg with his teeth), read the happy happy message scrolled on his certificate and posed, nipples against his cheek for a quick snap shot with the birthday boy I knew beyond the shadow of a doubt that I was fucked. I had no idea what she could possibly do to help me.

"So lets go practice!!!" She was back. Jasmine had fucked off back to wherever she had magically appeared from, and Amy was once again in full effect, clearly ready it seemed to begin my lessons.

"Practice? What, you mean have me dance? For you? NOW?" She looked at me like I was a total idiot, which I suppose in the current context wasn't too far off the mark. "Hell yeah now! It's not like we're gonna have weekly classes or something, right? I mean there's really not all that much you're gonna need to know. I'll just see what you're doing, give you a few tips and you'll get out there and shake that shit! Plus, now is one of the only times I have, so c'mon! Tell me how to get to your place and lets go!"

My place? Ahh…. Fuck! I had no idea anything like this was gonna go down, and was brutally unprepared for this turn of events; but then again, she made perfect sense. It wasn't like this was ever going to be some in depth tutorial on how to delve deep into the sexual psyche of my clients. It was how to drop your drawers in an entertaining way, grab some cash and run.

As I snatched a chair off the pool deck across from my apartment, I couldn't help wondering what a strange turn my life had taken. As I opened the door and watched Amy bounce through while I got the damn chair stuck trying to get in behind her, I realized that it was 10pm, and I was bringing a working stripper home so that she could watch me dance for her. So so strange.

Same songs flowing out of the speakers of my boom box. Same flight suit I wore that first night and the same terror creeping back up on me again, because unlike Club Onyx, there was simply nowhere to hide. She wasn't saying a word. She was sitting as still as I'm sure it was possible for her. No smile, no expression at all really. Just her eyes clearly watching every single move I made. Silently watching in such a crazy uncomfortable way that it was everything I could do not to run out the front door and dive in the pool. Then…

"Wait…. You're not taking the jumpsuit off already are you? You gotta dance more. Its strip tease, not strip quick! More hips. Try something a little more sexy…. It's okay to touch me some ya know! Like maybe kneel down and look all sexy in front of me… Damn! Its not that hot in here is it? Yeah, so you can take something off now. Don't just yank it off… You gotta make me want it. Like really WANT!"

As soon as her silent appraisal of me had ended, she started kicking out a seemingly never ending stream of "tips" that had me scurrying around like a sixteen year old trying to hide the Playboy's (Playboy, for those too young to know, is a *magazine, which features slightly less than politically correct articles and photo shoots highlighting beautiful naked women. It was my generations version of PornHub. *Google <u>magazine</u> for further information.). It was getting worse and worse by the minute, and about the time the sweat really started to kick in, she suggested that I just go ahead and get naked.

Once again sporting the purple thong (which had yet to be washed because as with both occasions I hadn't expected to be using it again) I dropped the jumpsuit and let Mr. Perfectly Average fly. As before, I went straight for burring my dick against her stomach and bumping away, but she was having none of it. She grabbed me by the hips and pushed me back, telling me it was a hell of a lot sexier if I kind of "slid up from her knee and kept it slow and sexy". As I gave the whole slow and sexy thing a shot, she began doing what she said was what a lot of the customers I'd dance for might do, which was to get really fucking handsy….

"You'll have to learn pretty quickly how to tell them to fuck off if they get too carried away! You know, shit like this!" And reached out and grabbed a handful of cock and balls, giving a tug or two for effect. My physical reaction was almost instantaneous, but my reaction mentally never really caught up with the pace. Her recognition of events on the other hand was lightning quick, and as I tried to play the part she'd given me and swat her hand away, she tightened her grip ever so slightly and grinned up at me in what I can only describe as a very male way.

"You probably won't want to let anyone get away with this in a show, and you probably won't want to be getting hard all over town either!" she said with a sinister tone, "but I guess that depends on the show…" The laugh that barked out of her told me she thought she was absolutely hilarious, but even while she laughed, she didn't let go. Not only did she not let go, but she was now quite obviously stroking me to the beat, while I, not having a clue what to do, simply kept bouncing around like a jackass, watching Amy, or was it Jasmine now, giving me a surprise hand job wrapped in purple.

I was so clearly not in control of the situation that it wasn't even funny. I pulled back just a little bit, intent on trying to at least get my bearings. It wasn't like I was a fucking virgin or anything, and this was far from the first sexual situation I'd ever been in, but the fact that she was suppose to be giving me tips on how to handle a strip tease had me really off balance. Was she fucking with my head in an attempt to show me how to take control of a customer? was she actually making the move on me it appeared she was? Was she just waiting to see if I tried to do anything to her before she pushed me off of her and yelled "Gotcha!"? All of these questions and a hundred more were bombarding my brain all at the same time, right up until she reached into my thong with one hand, pulled it down as far as she could with the other, and wrapped her mouth around me like a Ball Python who hadn't eaten in a month. Well, if nothing else, the first few seconds of her blowjob told me beyond a shadow of a doubt that the lesson, at least for the moment, was over.

"Fuck! I gotta go! It's God damn 3 o'clock!" Amy, very clearly Amy, dove out of my bed and started stomping around the apartment collecting her clothing from around the room. The surprise head she shocked me with had led to a full blown fuck fest, and after my initial reaction or should I say lack of, the guy in me took over, and I actually managed to make a pretty decent showing for myself. By the time she was digging around for the last of her clothing we'd gone at it three or four times, and we'd both clearly had our fun. A fact that hadn't escaped me regardless of my clear confusion with it all.

"Oh by the way" she yelled back as she was walking out the front door, "You're gonna want to come up with some kind of a gimmick, cause you're just not built to be a stripper! I mean cute as hell, but Dude, go to the gym!" And with that, she was gone. Fuck.

Half a Steering Wheel and Spidy

So I still didn't have an act and I still didn't have a car, but I sure as fucking hell had a booking, and was once again under a major crunch to come up with the other two in short fucking order! I had all of about forty hours before I was expected to show up at the private home of Mr. J. Jacobs to dance for his daughters 18th birthday. I actually had to read the "occasion" line multiple times, as I couldn't quite get my head around a father hiring a stripper for his little girls 18th birthday, but the house was located deep in North Sacramento which was at the time very much the California cowboy redneck part of town, so I thought that might have a little to do with it.

The act that I was still desperately lacking was unfortunately for me not creating itself, but in all honesty I wasn't exactly putting a lot of thought into it either. I think I'd almost resigned myself to having to suffer through some serious on the job training, which I had no doubt was going to be one seriously painful process. The transportation thing on the other hand was something that I could actually do something about.

As I mentioned before, my buddy Craig had a cousin that lived in Sacramento as well, and had a little two door Fiat convertible that was described to me as "running". When Price took me out to give the thing a look, "running" was about the only positive thing that could be said about it. It was a convertible, yes, or at least it was before the top stopped going up, which meant it was simply a roofless Fiat. It had the most horribly mis-matched set of tires I'd ever seen, all of them in various stages of decomposition. It was half a dozen different shades of primer grey, had more dents in it that smooth spots, and half a steering wheel. When I say half, I mean it had 180 degrees of the wheel. Not 360, not 270. Literally half a circle. The asking price was $250 bucks, and the moment I pulled $200 out of my pocket it was mine.

As I drove away, followed closely by Price who would make sure I didn't get stranded if the fucking thing blew up, I was completely and totally in love! It was the first time I had driven a car in well over a year, and the first time I'd driven a car that belonged to me on over 3, so it literally could have been a three ton pile of shit with four wheels and an engine (It was as close to that as running automobile could be) and I would have loved it.

The numerous problems I faced with said automobile were as follows:

1. I couldn't register it as my drivers license was currently suspended.
2. If I were to get pulled over while driving it I would most likely go straight to jail.
3. Not registering it meant that Craig's cousin was still the legal owner of the car, and still technically responsible for it.

Here is where I'll clue you in on something that you've most likely already picked up on. I'm kind of an asshole. I'm not really sure where I gained the capacity to be one, or when I decided (or as an asshole would, simply didn't think about it) that being an asshole was okay, but here I was. Happily motoring around town with no drivers license and no insurance in a vehicle some poor lady assumed was no longer her fucking problem because she'd sold the thing to me. I knew it was wrong not in the back of my mind, but in a completely conscious way, yet had decided that my needs simply outweighed the risks, so fuck it. Asshole.

Day of the show. Car…check! Music…check! Costume… Check? (They hadn't requested an outfit, so I was wearing baggy pants and a dress shirt cause they came off easy). Act…Nah. Like I said, sink or swim!

So, there I was… Driving around town in my half steering wheel permanent convertible trying to find the house on the order form. I'd swung by my fathers house the day before to snatch the Thomas Brothers Guide (an actual book of street maps for a specific town which required intense concentration for self navigation… remember folks, this shit was way before Google Maps!) but even with an extremely detailed map I was having one hell of a time finding the place. Luckily for me, I'm chronically early absolutely everywhere I go, so I'd given myself almost an hour to make what should have been no more than a fifteen minute trip. As it turned out, that was just about exactly as much time as it took.

When I finally pulled up in front of the house, I'd made more than a dozen wrong turns, and had been driving so erratically because of it that if a cop had seen me, it was as close to a sure thing that I'd get popped as could be. For a change though, luck had been on my side, and the police was the one problem that drive didn't give me.

As I turned the key and set the emergency brake, I finally had a chance to survey my surroundings. "Holy fuck me" was about all I could think. This place was a dump! I mean wow! There was a chain link fence surrounding half the yard, but it stopped cold on the left side of the gate. Everything to the right side of the gate was lying on what was left of the grass, the triangle shape of the metal burned into the turf from what had to be years of scorching NorCal valley summer sunshine heating the metal and killing the blades that sprouted sparsely in between.

The house itself seemed to be pretty much intact, but if you were to ask me what color it was I wouldn't have even able to tell you, as It clearly hadn't been painted since the day the very first coat went on. Two of the three sets of windows on the front of the house had bedsheets up as curtains, one set sporting the very faded image of Spider Man climbing up and or swinging from something, and the other bearing something that looked more like the Shroud of Turin than anything else.

Two broken-down refrigerators sat side by side on the concrete patio, next to what appeared to be a running washing machine, and more children's toys in various stages of misuse than I could take in at a glance.

I really didn't want to be a stripper. I really didn't want to go in that house. I really didn't think I'd made any wise choices in my life thus far, and was in all honestly very close to starting up the car and running when I heard "HEY JOHN! I THINK THE STRIPPER IS HERE!" Well then, that's that. On with the show I guess.

As I climbed out of the Fiat and was reaching in my back seat to pull out the boom box with my music along with the order form and the garter, good 'ol John came walking out the front door, Miller beer in hand and a wide grin on his face. "Awe she's gonna love you!" John was drunk. John had an ever so slightly detectable Southern drawl to him. John walked up and gave me a solid handshake and a slap on the shoulder. John was a good fucking guy. I was immediately okay with pretty much the whole situation.

After giving me the break down and letting me know that he was pretty sure his daughter had caught on to the fact that Daddy had someone coming for her birthday as well as confirming that she was indeed turning all of eighteen years old, he attempted to sneak inside the house with my boom box but failed miserably when he tripped over something just inside the door, coming to a very audible crash somewhere within.

Two minutes later I heard the whistle that was my signal to come on in, and that's exactly what I did. Suffice it to say that this was a very liberal family. John may have had a Southern accent but he and the rest of the gang had quite clearly gotten very comfortable with California ways. There was a layer of pot smoke in the living room about six feet off the ground that was so thick, if you stuck your head through it you'd most likely loose sight of the floor. The dozen or so people in the living room and kitchen were all so clearly either baked or drunk off their asses that they were having trouble visually tracking me as I walked into the room, and the birthday girl...

Well the birthday girl was seated in the middle of the room in a chair as I had requested, a beer in one hand, a fat joint in the other, some type of paper crown on her head and the most bright red cheeks I had ever seen in my life! How she was actually sitting up in the chair was beyond explanation, and I feared that she and half the crowd might pass out before I even got started!

I don't know if it was the fact that these folks had "hot boxed" an entire house, I don't know if it was because they were all clearly off their asses or if I had just managed to up my own personal dose of fuck-it, but there were zero nerves firing off in me. I strutted up to the birthday girl like I actually had a plan. I plopped down in her lap, looking down directly into her eyes and asked "So... You're the birthday girl?"

The fucking room exploded in laughter, and something in me clicked. I mean it actually clicked! These shows had nothing to do with the guest of honor. Dad didn't hire me to get his little girl all humid and ready to go, he hired me so the rest of the family could laugh their asses off at her. I had it! I had my show, my gimmick, my hook.

Everything I did in that very first Masquerade telegram I did to make people laugh. The way I took my pants off with my ass directly in the birthday girls face. The way I sat back in her lap and slapped my own ass with her hands. The way I tied her hands around my waste with my belt and only let her out by sliding her hands down my body, basically dragging my ass across her face. They fucking loved it, and if truth be told, so did I!

When the show was over and I was standing outside once again with John, he not only handed over the $70 bucks for the cost of the telegram, but another hundred (in small bills) as a tip! I don't think I'd ever seen someone grin so much over something I had done in my life. John and the family had been hooting and hollering through all fifteen minutes of my show, and in all honesty I had just about as much fun as they did.

As I pulled the Fiat back onto the highway, secretly praying that I wouldn't see any cops that would fuck up my amazing mood, I had the show I had been looking for. I would still need to bang out a few of the details, and had a very long way to go before my physical self image wouldn't haunt me, but I'd cracked the puzzle of how I could manage to do this for a living. Make 'em laugh, and they'll forget about everything else. It really was just that simple. The not so simple part was gonna be trying to learn what in that context would always make 'em laugh…

Rollercoaster

As has been the overwhelming theme in my life, for every two steps forward, I end up taking at the very least, one step back.

Mark and Masquerade were doing there best to try and send as much work my way as he could, but as with all things it seems, the outward impression he and the company were giving wasn't quite on the level. As it turned out, Mark was doing really well in two different areas with his business. He was keeping the ladies consistently working every week, and he was managing to crank out a decent number of out of town stage shows for the gentleman, but that was about it.

The demand for Mark's male telegram services just wasn't where he thought it was going to be when he started working with the guys, and one of the reasons he brought me on in the first place was to see if a new "white, clean cut pretty boy" face might not help out some. Unfortunately, in the month or so that I'd been onboard it hadn't really made a difference at all.

After the Spiderman curtain show I'd done an additional 5 shows for Mark, all with varying degrees of success, but none that could be considered bad. My confidence, if not high, had grown at least by a factor of ten, and by the time I had delivered my sixth telegram I no longer felt like a complete fraud. I had figured out how to deliver an entertaining strip tease without making a complete fool of myself, and the feedback that I'd gotten from each had been pretty positive. The tips hadn't sucked either!

So when Mark sat me down in the office to give me the straight skinny on how the guys side of the business was going I was pretty bummed. He explained it all, and I completely understood, but it still sucked as I was really hoping the extra money I was pulling in would just continue to increase. I even asked him about the stage shows, but as it turned out, "Lightning" was back in full effect, and he really just didn't have a spot for me in the "Troupe" right then. He would of course continue to get as much work for me as he could but didn't want me to get my hopes up, as he had to spread the love amongst all his crew…

Meanwhile, back at the Holiday Inn… I had never been more miserable at a job. (Totally not true, but that's how it felt at the time). I was still riding my bike back and forth downtown, as I was trying to keep the Fiat off the road as much as possible. That cars appearance, coupled with its expired tags made it a lot like driving around as if it had a big flashing light and a neon sign that read "Fuck the Police". "Drive it too much and its only a matter of time" was what I thought every time I looked at it, So I parked it, except to get to and from my shows.

The ladies at the Holiday Inn had still never spoken to me about the travesty I'd performed for them, and curiosity finally got the better of me. When I finally grew the balls and asked my "crush" about about it, she simply smiled politely and said "yeah… It was fun. Thanks!" Confirming without a doubt that the very first so-called-show had been just as bad as I thought it was. (For those still wondering, of course I didn't get laid. No boobies, no nothing. If I'd had a chance in hell of fucking her before the show, that chance ended up running down her sisters blue jeans in the form of sweat. Pussy potential gone one salty drip at a time.)

Every time I would clock in to work at the hotel, all I could think about was the fact that I could manage to make more in one fifteen-minute show for Mark than the hotel was paying me for a day and a half worth of work there, and I resented the hell out of it! By the time I'd gone a full week without hearing from Mark, I knew I had to do something to fix the situation.

Take-It-Off telegrams had been around in Sacramento for more than 15 years at the time, and business for them was booming. They'd been providing strip tease and joke telegram services all around Northern California with a crew of over 20 dancers, all of whom used the service as their primary source of income.

The first time I heard about them was actually at one of the shows I performed for Mark, and it was the client that told me of them. "I was gonna go with that Take-it-Off company, but you guys were good bit cheaper, so I went with you". The name stuck in my mind I guess, because as I sat in the back of the house waiting for a banquet to break it popped into my head. The next day I was on the phone trying to see if they were looking for people.

"We are always looking for good dancers" said the female voice on the other end of the line. "If they're attractive and have experience of course". She then went on to explain what it was they expected from their "entertainers", and asked a bit about my experience. I lied.

I explained to her that I'd been working locally with another company, but that they weren't currently fulfilling my needs. I also told her that I had worked previously with an outfit down in Los Angeles, you know, part-time and for extra cash (yeah, I know... I guess I didn't learn my lesson the first time I used that lie). As I hung up the phone, I couldn't help but grin. I'd managed to get myself an audition in a few days time, and if it went well.... The Lady I had spoken with would be getting back to me the next day with all the details of when and where, as their way of auditioning new people was to have them come deliver a telegram for them to see.

"Okay" I said, "Peppermill on Sunrise at 7pm tomorrow night!". I was to show up dressed in whatever outfit I chose, meet a Mr. Rick Scuttle, the Owner of T.I.O telegrams, perform for the woman he would be with, and see what he thought. He was the final say on new staff, so this was my one and only shot. I could totally do this!

6pm found me in the parking lot of the Peppermill. The place itself was an attempt at a bit of a theme restaurant and bar, with a massive fire pit in the middle that was burning year round, a very 70's feel to the decor and in all honesty, tacky as fuck. It was the type of place where you expected to see the older man/younger woman thing, and that's pretty much exactly what you'd find.

By the time 7o'clock rolled around, I'd managed to get myself pretty nervous, but I'd been doing that to myself so much lately that it almost felt like a completely natural state to be in. Standing out front, boom-box yet again in hand, dressed in the now familiar flight suit unwittingly donated to the cause by Price I was getting a bit concerned as 7:15 rolled around still with no sign of Mr. Scuttle. By the time I felt a tap on my shoulder and turned around to greet him, I had assumed he was going to be a no-show.

Rick, as he asked me to call him, had been inside the Peppermill the entire time, having dinner with the young lady that I would be entertaining for. My first impression of the guy wasn't exactly great if I'm being honest. He had that unusual weasel quality that some guys seem to have, and was exactly the type of guy you would expect to own something like a strip-tease company. Not a terribly attractive person, sporting a widows peak and a thick salt and pepper 70's porn star mustache, he just gave off that slimy vibe that makes you feel a little dirty for simply having spoken to them. But the fact was, this was the guy that could get me the hell out of the Holiday Inn, so who gives a fuck if he was a little "off".

"She's gonna be in a booth over on the left hand side of the bar, so you shouldn't miss her. Pretty blonde girl. You can just go up and start your act when you're ready and we'll see how you do."

Well simple enough really. I had yet to give a telegram in a public place like this before, but I always knew that it was a real possibility as Mark had told me it happened quite often with his company. It simply hadn't happened till now. I took a few minutes outside to try and compose myself and had already decided that the flight suit looked enough like a maintenance jumpsuit that I could just start my so called "act" by pretending to work on the building or some shit. I mean lets face it, I wasn't gonna get hired because of my Oscar level acting skills!

As soon as I walked in, I was a little confused. The bar was in the round, as was the entire restaurant, so left of the bar was a relative statement! Go far enough to the right and you end up left... Shouldn't be a problem though. I'll just look for the attractive blonde in one of the booths, see Rick there as well, and off to the races! And just like I thought, there she was.

She was an attractive, all-be-it not show stopping blonde, sitting in the booth by herself, clearly looking bored a bit out of place. I tried not to let the nerves kick in too heavily by waiting around and just marched on over to her to get started. Setting the boom-box on the back of the high back seat that ran a semi-circle around the table, I then gave her a quick hello, and explained that I was maintenance for the Peppermill, and needed to get to the light fixture that was on the wall just behind her head.

Now remember, I had decided ever since Spiderman that the road to stripper success for me was paved in laughter, so everything I did was in an attempt to illicit a giggle from those in attendance. Keeping that in mind, I didn't wait for her to slide over and give me room to get to the light in question, I simply hopped up onto the back of the booth, sliding almost directly over a very confused looking woman, and pretending to fix an obviously working light.

All of 30 seconds into my "repair" of the working fixture, I reached over to the stereo and pushed "Play". As the music kicked in, I went from standing on the booth, to straddling her legs by stepping over and slowly sliding down into her lap in time with the beat. I'd gotten into the habit of sitting in my customers lap, making firm eye contact with them, and saying nothing more than "hello" as I would take their hands and put them firmly on my ass. It had yet to fail to get the response that I wanted, and this time was no different, as I heard laughter from both of the booths to either side of us, and a bit of a shocked squeal from the girl.

Then she giggled alright! She also asked, after I had been dancing on and in front of her for about a minute, exactly what was going on… "Is this a joke or something? Did Eric put you up to this? I really (giggle giggle giggle) don't understand whats happening right now!" She was turning bright red, and looking around as if to attempt to find understanding from somewhere else in the restaurant.

About the time the top half of the jumpsuit was sliding off my back, I heard a "Oh WHOA! Hey ahhh, Ddd, Dean?!? Hey, ahh you got the WRONG GIRL there my friend!"

What? The fuck. Did I just hear? I stood half naked over the lady for whom I THOUGHT I was suppose to be dancing for, frozen like a deer caught in the glare of oncoming headlights.

"Miss…" Said Rick, "I am SO sorry!" He looked like he was about to go into an epileptic seizure as he spoke. "He's suppose to be auditioning to do strip tease telegrams for my company here tonight, but its suppose to be for that woman over there!" And pointed firmly to a different booth and a very attractive blonde on the other side of the bar who was hysterically laughing. "I am so so sorry for the misunderstanding!" By this time, people from all around the place had turned their full attention to the show happening, and were clearly enthralled by the slow motion train wreck that they were now witnessing.

I was horrified. Rick was stifling a laugh to my surprise, the girl I was actually suppose to be dancing for was simply looking at the whole scene with her mouth open and tears streaming down her face; and the poor unsuspecting blonde? She flat out shocked us all by not missing a beat an saying "well hell, then audition away!"

Rick looked at her. Rick looked at me. Rick looked at his blonde two tables away. Rick looked back at her. Rick looked back at me, laughed loudly and said "well then... On with the show!"

The boom-box, which hadn't picked up on the fact that there was any problem at all had happily continued to play music throughout the whole misunderstanding, and as Rick was telling me to go ahead and get on with it, the final song on the tape was just beginning. Thankfully for me, the Peppermill had the habit of keeping their place very well air condition because of the fire pit that had burning year round, so the gallons of sweat that would have normally started to flow after having made such a catastrophic blunder were kept to a minimum.

I continued on, at a slightly increased pace to make up for the music I had lost while the wheels were busy coming off the bus that was my life, and got down to Mr. Purple Thong in short order. The crowd was most certainly laughing, the "Customer" was grinning ear to ear, my potential employer seemed pleased, and I managed to make it to the end of the music without doing anything else too stupid. As the last beat finished and the "show" came to a close, I would have normally wished the guest of honor a "happy birthday" or some such, but instead I simply pulled the garter I'd ripped the Masquerade button off of from around my arm, presented it to her as a gift and yelled "SURPRISE!!"

The crowd, having by now realized the enormous mistake I'd made absolutely roared with laughter and as I collected my clothing, my stereo, and a kiss on the cheek from my mistaken victim, I couldn't help but laugh just a little myself. I'd once again managed to up my personal level of fuck-it, and it felt pretty good really. It seemed at least so far being an idiot wasn't fatal.

"So, you'll need to go to the office next week to get things sorted. I'll need for you to get all the standard costumes that all our dancers are required to have, but the more outfits you can come up with, the more I can market you to potential customers, so come up with as many gimmicks as you can."

Both of us were standing outside the Peppermill chatting, but behaving a bit like a couple of members of a team mulling about after a game they hadn't really expected to win.

"Well... Pretty damn sure I've never seen an audition quite like that one; and especially after you screwed up like that... Oooof! But the way you handled it and kept on going after how badly it could have gone was great. God knows in this job you've got to be able to roll with the punches!"

This was epic fucking news! And he was right... what could and should have ended up a huge failure because of my mistake had ended up bringing the house down so to speak, and had been the very reason I was being offered the job. How strange is this fucking life!

"Oh, one piece of advice though…. If you're gonna make any real money doing this, you really should get yourself in the gym."

Badges, Velcro and Spotlights

It's actually amazing what you could buy back then. I walked in to the uniform shop in Downtown Sacramento half assuming that Rick was playing a joke on the new guy. I'd been told to head on down there to order, get fitted for and purchase my Police Officer costume/uniform. As I walked up to the counter, I assumed as soon as I asked for the outfit, the lady would ask for my Police I.D. or some such, but instead she simply asked if I were actually on the force or if it were for another reason.

"Well, it's actually to use as a costume for a telegram company" I said. Once again, I expected her to just laugh and tell me I was clearly in the wrong place, but what she instead said without a blink was "so we can't put the Sacramento PD patch on the uniform for obvious reasons, but what I can do is put California Highway patrol ones on there, and just stitch over the the emblem so it's not official. Nobody will be able to tell the difference anyway!". The next thing I knew, she had measured me, I'd paid, and was walking out the door, having been told that I could come back in 2 days to pick it up. What I did walk out with was a police issue duty belt, an actual cop baton, a set of stainless steel handcuffs with the belt case and two sets of keys.

After having picked up my new costume and tried it on, the average person would at a glance never suspect that I wasn't real PD. If they looked closer, the boyband tall crunchy hair and the too flashy boots would give it away, but otherwise I looked like a young fucking cop. Between the Police uniform, the Air Force jumpsuit a cheap looking business suit, a club outfit and a US Navy uniform, I had managed to put together a pretty decent list of costumes that Take-it-Off could market me for. When the time came to head back into the office to take a set of photos for them, I was pretty sure Rick would be able to manage to at least get me a little work. Holy shit was I unprepared!

A bunch of snapshots later and a quick rundown of what was expected of me, Rick slid over a stack of order forms that he told me was my weekends work. 'Hope you've got a full tank of gas, cause I ended up being a little short staffed this weekend, and you, well you've been saddled with a whole lot more than I would have normally given a new guy. Roll with the punches though, right?"

All tolled for the weekend he had booked me, he had handed over 8 shows for me to perform on Friday, and 11 on Saturday! I couldn't quite wrap my head around what was coming. $45 bucks a show multiplied by eight on Friday, and eleven on Saturday was more money coming to me in a weekend than I was gonna make in a month at the Holiday Inn. The only stop I made on my way home after seeing Rick was by the Holiday Inn to fucking quit!

Funny enough, the hardest part of the weekend wasn't the shows. It wasn't having to deal with the embarrassment of being 98% naked in public, it wasn't having to navigate all the different personalities not only of the girls I was dancing for, or the people that hired me. Funny enough, the hardest part was simply making it to the damn shows on time! Luckily for me I have a real thing about being late, and had tried to at least to map out each of the different locations I was supposed to go to but with that many shows, just trying to find the different locations in my Thomas Brothers was a big job all on its own. I drove to or through every single neighborhood in the Sacramento Valley that first weekend. Some of them two and even three times. The timings for the shows left absolutely no wiggle room in between, which meant that if I ran late for one show, there was no way I wouldn't be running late for all the rest to come that night, and I hate being late with a passion. So, I drove way too fast, dressing while driving, reading maps and order forms... Shit, the only thing I wasn't doing that Amy had was put on lipstick!

The other thing that bothered me almost instantly (and would continue to do for as long as I worked telegrams) was the fact that my schedule was invariably linked to the readiness of the client. On each of the order forms was listed the contact person who had either ordered the telegram or was the one to make sure I made it to the right person, which meant that even if I managed to make it where I was suppose to be when I was suppose to be there, I could still end up late because of someone else.

Without trying to make it sound as if I were living in the stone ages (although looking back it certainly feels like it), cellphones were around, but they most certainly weren't in every pocket, which especially if the show was taking place in say a restaurant, meant that you had to rely on and hope that the person you were suppose to meet would actually be where they should be. That first weekend I think I managed about a 50/50 ratio. I, by some fucking miracle made it to all 19 shows on time, but spent way more time than I was comfortable with standing around with my dick in my hands just waiting. Bar none the worst part of the job.

The following Tuesday found me walking back into the Take-it-Off offices to hand in my paperwork and money from the weekends shows.

"Well theres the Superstar now" said Rick's assistant. "I think you're the first person ever to make it to all his shows on time! I was betting you'd have at least one cancelation cause you'd be running that late!" Rick, sitting at his desk behind her looked up with a smile.

They'd checked up on me! I don't know why it didn't cross my mind that they would, but until she told me they had called the contact from all nineteen of my shows for a review the idea never entered my mind. She said that each and every client had nothing but good things to say about my performance; The major theme being that I was really funny, and kept everyone laughing and comfortable the entire time. Great to hear I can tell you! And it was then I had yet another little minor epiphany.

Some of the girls I danced for fell right into the groove, hooting and hollering, laughing and having a good time. Some clearly just tolerated the event, not really wanting it, but dealing with it for the benefit of whoever had set the whole thing up. And then there were the ones that were horrified. The ones that looked as if they might lace up their running shoes and sprint out at any given moment, and those, those I felt really fucking bad for! It might have been me that was getting naked in public, but they were certainly the most embarrassed, and in some cases flat out humiliated. It was for those that I ended up catering all of my shows to, and it was that approach that turned out to be my best quality. It was the main reason why I was now standing in front of the counter with Rick and his assistant telling me that I'd received the best feedback any new guy ever had.

"Damn good job this weekend Dean! I'm impressed!" Rick continued "So... I know I told you that this wouldn't be an option for you nearly this soon but you're in luck. Keep Thursday night clear from 8 o'clock on please, and come up with something for the stage, cause I'm gonna need you at the El Dorado for the show."

"Seriously? Ahh, okay, sure Rick! I'll figure something out..."

Another stage show, and this time not some traveling one either. This one everyone in city knew about. I had been told by Rick that there wasn't a chance in hell I'd see the stage of the El Dorado for a really long time for a number of reasons. The El Dorado Saloon was one of the most popular scenes for the younger crowd in the valley by far. It was an 18 and over establishment which had on Thursday nights, been hosting Take-it-Off's male review for more than six years. I'd heard of the show long before ever tossing my junk in a thong, and knew that it was popular not only for the ladies because of the show, but for the men who would go afterward to try and work the girls who'd just spent the last few hours watching a bunch of naked men strut around the place. The dancers that worked there were the most senior of Ricks staff, and not everyone who delivered telegrams for him would stand under those lights.

The fact that I was not just new, but the newest guy there and was already booked to perform at the El Do was crazy, or at least that's what Rick's assistant said. She also filled me in on the fact that the guys who had been working the show for ages might not be all that receptive to the new guy, but that I shouldn't let it get to me too badly.

"They're all great guys really, but they aren't big on change, so don't be surprised if they give you the cold shoulder at first. You probably won't do more than this one show for a long while though so just do your best and have fun."

I'd seen all the guys photos in the book, and knew just at a glance that this show was gonna be night and day different (No pun intended) than that of the Club Onyx gig. Other than the fact that I was probably 15-20 pounds lighter than all of them, we all looked very similar in appearance, which really wasn't good for me at all.

K.C, the MC of the show was the oldest in the troupe at the ripe old age of 38, and had been on that stage since the shows conception. He was about as old school as a male stripper could get (Think Swayze/Farley on Saturday Night Live). Slicked back jet black hair and sporting the bow-tie collar and cuffs like the Chippendale's boys use to do, Spandex pants and a set of ankle high shiny black boots, he was a sight. Jason was the big boy of the group weighing in at probably 240 pounds of nothing but muscle, and although he did the Conan style thing he was short haired an clean cut as well. They had a cowboy who sported a solid 5 o'clock shadow and never took his hat off, a fire eater, who funny enough was the only one with long hair, and a tuxedo sporting Rico Suave type, all who performed every week as the core group of the El Do's entertainers. The rest were telegram guys like me, who would be told a week or so in advance if they were to perform.

The El Do gig wouldn't make you much money really, as Rick only paid dancers $50 to perform in a show that lasted 2 hours long. You only had two chances during the entire thing to go out and get tips from the audience, each only a couple of songs long, so financially you were better off if you never ended up on stage; but all the guys wanted the El Do for one simple reason. Pussy.

It wasn't an "if" you could manage to get laid from dancing there, it was "when, and how much", and not one of the guys that worked for Rick wasn't willing to give up a decent paying night for consistent pieces of "strange". Of course this hadn't crossed my mind yet as I still hadn't even seen the club let alone performed there, but it was the exact reason why not too many of my co-entertainers were gonna like me very much.

In what turned out to be another crazy lucky break for me, none of Ricks El Do entertainers were really what you'd call dancers. Entertainers yes, but you simply never saw one of them doing more than a few steps here or a few steps there before they picked up some prop, struck some pose, or did something else that kept them from maintaining a beat for very long. And there in lie my next "catch". I could dance, and I knew it.

The club outfit that I'd put together for my telegrams was a pair of slacks and a jacket of the style that was popular at the time. Think Vanilla "Ice Ice Baby" or Boyz II Men and you're getting warm, and it was perfect for what I had in mind. I'd almost decided to take the slacks to a seamstress to have them toss the obligatory "velcro" to them to make the whole flashy rip 'em off move part of the act, but then I remembered that for me taking it all off slower was much better than faster, as although I had started going to the gym the only person that could tell a difference was me; but I had a way around that as well...

Just as Rick's assistant had said, I got the coldest attitudes of my life from those guys. You seriously would have thought I was the new hot chick in the sorority or something, because everyone from K.C. on down was acting like a little bitch, clearly whispering and talking shit in the corners like snippy little girls. K.C, having to organize and run the show had to at least deal with me on a slightly more cordial basis which was a plus, but he didn't seem all too happy about it.

"So you're on first. You get four songs total, and you're expected to stay on stage for the first two. When I announce you on stage, get on the fucking stage. Once the last song is done you go straight to the dressing room, no matter how much money is being offered to you. Don't make me call you down twice. Don't kiss any of the girls, don't grab any tits or ass. They wanna grab you, let 'em, but I don't want to see your cock in anybody's hands but your own. Clear?"

Fuck me. I told him yeah, he was being crystal clear. There would be no problem from me on any of it. When he asked what my act was and I responded that I'd be dancing mostly hip-hop, he was even less enthusiastic. I don't think he could quite wrap his head around the fact that all I intended to do was dance. Who the fuck did I think I was had to be what he was thinking, but I could also tell he assumed this would be the only time he'd have to deal with me, so he brushed it off and proceeded to ignore me along with the rest of them.

By the time the show had started, and the troupe of core entertainers had gone out and done their opening act to the music of "Grease Lightning" (yeah, it was fucking really old even back then!) I was in the back, dressed and nervous as fuck, but ready to go. There were about 100 women in the crowd by my estimation, but the place was huge, so it still felt a bit on the empty side to me. I was just trying to figure out how I was gonna get back and forth across such a large floor to collect tips, when I heard the name "Dean, Dean the Dancing Machine" come booming from the speakers, followed only seconds later by "DA DA DA du du du du", so... off I went!

Although I'll be the first to admit that all the dance steps I had learned with Price, Craig and Jay looked a hell of a lot better performed as a group than as a solo act, a white boy with rhythm dancing in what was a very popular style at the time, even all on his own still worked well. To my great relief, the ladies in attendance that night whole heartedly agreed! I have no doubt that part of it was that I was the new face. I'd been told that a lot of the girls that came to the El Do show attended almost every week, and a new face to them, even if it wasn't all that great, was still exciting to see. But I also knew that the way I was dancing was something none of them had never seen on that stage before, and if the screams from the ladies was any indication, they clearly had no aversion to change.

The whole first song I forced myself to do nothing but dance. I went through every routine that the boys had taught me at least three times each, only changing up the order of the steps to try and make sure it didn't look to repetitious. As the second song kicked in, I tossed the jacket to the side of the stage and then did something completely unheard of from a stripper. I took off my pants. I hadn't really even planned it to be honest, but as I was up there dancing away, it dawned on me that if I did the standard shirt off strut that the other dancers did, the girls would flat out fail to be impressed, and I may lose the momentum I had going from my dancing; so I turned around, back to the crowd, and slowly straight leg bent over to drop my slacks to the floor and step out of them. Best move I could have possibly made!

By the time I took my shirt off, the third song was rolling, and I was once again safely in the crowd, snatching tips from table to table, happily obscuring most of the ladies views, only adding to their excitement at the prospect of my making it to their table. It was awesome!

As I saw K.C. picking up the microphone out of the corner of my eye, I was already heading back to the stage to collect my clothes and bail. By the time he asked them for a round of applause for me, the only thing left to see was my ass walking back to the dressing room. I had no intention of pissing him or any of the other guys off that night, and in keeping with that plan, as soon as the show was over I shook the hands of those who would and ran, opting to leave instead of sticking around to flirt with the girls. I figured the worst thing I could do after already having stepped on toes by daring to perform there was to stick around afterward and try and pull women.

I'd only managed to make about a hundred dollars from the show, and certainly not any friends, but I still considered the night a success and went home to bed that night alone, but quite happy with the way things had turned out. My first official week with Take-it-Off telegrams had gone a thousand times better than I ever would have imagined the week before, and I had to admit that for the first time in quite a while I was pretty excited to see what might come next.

Political Maneuvering

It had taken a while, no doubt about it, but I had finally managed through trial and error to refine my show into something that I could do almost without thinking about. I'd put together elements of all the situations I regularly found myself in and had figured out how to make them work for all of the shows I performed.

Over the six months that I had been working for Take-it-Off I had been pretty steady about hitting the gym, and had finally gotten to the point where other people that knew me not only noticed, but would occasionally comment that they saw a difference in my physique, which was wonderful! Although due to the insecurity about being physically qualified for the job from the start, I'd worked hard to come up with a couple of pretty ingenious ways around it.

First, as I'd done with my first appearance on the Stage at the El Dorado Saloon, the last thing I took off before hitting the crowd was my shirt, not the first. Having decided that once my ass was prominently displayed in my client/victim's face, the fact that I didn't have body builder pecks and bone crushing biceps wouldn't really be all that much of an issue (I hoped). Also to help stretch out the "Strip" part of my strip tease during the telegrams, being shows where a bunch of high energy dancing around simply wasn't an option, I had taken to wearing a button up club style vest under whatever shirt I might have on. It simply gave me another layer to take off, while still leaving my rather anticlimactic chest reveal until the very last moment.

on my very first telegram for Masquerade I had stumbled across another gimmick that was now using in every show as well. After having purchased the handcuffs for the police outfit, I decided that using them in all my shows was a great way to score serious laughs. I'd have the girl I was dancing for stand up and put her arms around my waist from behind me. The handcuffs would magically appear from a pocket and end up around her wrists, cuffing her in a permanent hug. After a few bump and grinds from me, I'd do the last thing anyone expected, and I'd drop my pants.

From there I could spin around, joke about where her hands could and couldn't go, walk around the room with her in tow…. You get the idea! The best part was always the last though. The keys to the handcuffs would always be left in the pants that I would make sure were just too far out of reach for me to get, leaving only one option to free my captive. Facing away from her with her still standing, I would make my victim slide her arms down the length of my body so that when she was finally bent down low enough, I could simply step out from her arms to go and retrieve the key. This of course meant there were multiple amazing photo opportunities as the poor girls face was basically dragged across one or both butt cheeks while maneuvering to let me out. Never failed to get the proper reaction!

The rest of each of my shows was then almost exactly as you would expect… I'd dance a bit, loose the shirt, leaving me in a thong and a vest. Dance a bit more, lose the vest but end up plopped in her lap facing her. Stare uncomfortably in her eyes for long periods of time (Something I discovered actually made everyone a little uncomfortable, but uneasy in that giggly way) and take her hands and slowly slide them onto my ass, then back again when she'd almost inevitably moved them. And again…. Considering eighty percent of the shows that I did were simply fifteen-minute telegrams, just that routine alone would get the job done nicely. Quick, easy and clean! It had turned out to be a perfect recipe for me, and in the now decent amount of time I'd been dancing it was my go-to routine with only ever so slight variations that I performed time and time again. Of course there are always exceptions, and always a show here and there that would catch you completely off-guard, but usually nothing so off the rails that you couldn't make it work. Usually.

On one of the rare day-time shows I ended up doing, I found myself in by far the most public venue I could have ever imagined, and it caught me completely by surprise. I had on a few different occasions ended up being hired to dance in an office building for an employee during hours, and of course a few bars and restaurants as well, and even once in a park, but this particular show had me going into the business offices of Arden Fair Mall at about two o'clock on a Saturday afternoon, which was certainly a bit out of the ordinary.

Not really anything all that noteworthy stood out until I met the customer who hired me, and was informed that in fact the show wasn't to take place within the safe confines of the offices upstairs but was actually to be performed in the middle of the malls substantial god damn food court! To add even more of a jolt, they actually had me give them my music cassette so that they could, on my cue have them start my tunes over the entire mall's PA system so that everyone could hear! Arden Fair Mall was and is fucking enormous, and at the time was newly renovated and a wildly popular place on a Saturday, so as you can imagine, holy shit did I have an audience!

I don't remember anything particularly unique about the show itself, other than looking around as I performed, seeing the faces of old folks, little kids, teens and the like all wondering, laughing and sometimes gasping at something they had clearly never expected to see in the mall. I do on the other hand remember getting dressed as quickly as I could, and getting to my car with the utmost haste as I was pretty sure that I'd violated at least one or two decency laws in California with that one. One thing was for certain I thought, I was sure I'd never have another show come close to being embarrassing on such a grand scale as that; but as is usually the case in my life, the more sure I am…

Another Friday night, another fat stack of telegrams. I'd gone through and mapped everything out when I picked up the order forms as was my habit, and figured out the best way to get to each. When I flipped through them a second time to make sure I hadn't missed anything, something about my third show stood out. I just couldn't quite put my finger on what it was.

Cop outfit, fiftieth birthday party, downtown Sacramento in a pretty fancy restaurant/bar called the Brown Derby (actually known to be a political hot spot as it's just down the street from the state capitol). Husband is the customer, name of Willie Brown who will meet just outside in the parking lot at 8 O'clock sharp. Easy. But Willie Brown.... That name was sparking something somewhere, but I must have been distracted by something shiny, because I didn't bother to follow the thought to it's conclusion.

As show number two wrapped up I had a rare extra bit of time on my hands, and once I knew the coast was clear I changed into most of the police outfit on the street just outside my last gig. The name "Willie Brown" kept rolling around in the back of my head while I was dressing though, and once I was driving toward downtown I was actively trying to think of why.

Pulling into the Brown Derby parking lot should have been enough to really having me wondering what the fuck was going on, but as I rolled past the channel 3, 10, 13 and 40 news vans, broadcast booms up and ready, I only remember thinking some big political to-do must be happening in the area if all the local stations were here. Out of the car I got, putting on and buttoning up my cop uniform with pride. Boom box out of the back seat and in hand, I started heading toward where I was suppose to meet Mr. Brown, a glance at my watch telling me I was about 5 minutes early, and that was great.

Then, like a drunk in the huge pick-up truck that fly's through the red light and T-Bones the fuck out of some poor unsuspecting little car, it hit me. At that same moment, out the front doors strolled the one and only Mr. Willie Brown. A name I should have known instantly.

My grandmother was a very political women. She was a staunch Republican that voted along party lines no matter what. An extremely intelligent person, she had graduated almost at the top of her class at Stanford University at a time when very few women went to college, let alone excelled. She had managed to take what was at the time a pretty decent sized inheritance from my Great Grandfather, and turn it into a nice respectable fortune, and there in lie her allegiance to the "Money" party in the United States. As if it weren't bad enough, besides being a rich Republican she was also a bit of a racist. All of those factors, as strange as it may seem are exactly why I should have known who the fuck Willie Brown was.

When I met Willie Brown in the parking lot of the Brown Derby that evening, he was the sitting Speaker for the California State Assembly (he went on to become a very popular and charged Mayor of San Francisco). Speaker in the State Assembly was and is arguably the most powerful position in that political arena. After 30 years in the Assembly all tolled, he'd made quite a reputation for himself as being not only incredibly powerful but controversial, flashy and very well publicized, and for that reputation and a few other reasons my grandmother fucking hated him.

Willie Brown was not only a Democrat, but he was arguably the most powerful politician in the state my grandmother loved, and to add insult to injury for her, it just so happened Wille Brown was black. Top that little treat off by crowning it with the fact that he had a white wife, and he could have cured cancer and she wouldn't have been able to stand him. The reason I'd known the name and the man (without actually knowing) was because I'd heard my dear old grandma talk shit about the guy for as long as I could remember. And now here I was shaking his hand. Which to me didn't matter in the least, until it dawned on my why all the damn news vans were in the parking lot!

I was trying as hard as I could to act as if this were any other show, but I was so caught off guard not only by the recent revelations of my customers identity but by my odd link to him, that when one of the local reporters who was in attendance to cover the newest of Willies antics asked me what my name was, I gave it to him. My full fucking name. Because I'm stupid.

The show itself was exactly as I've described. From the handcuff's to the hands on my ass, I didn't change a thing. The reaction the show got on the other hand, was on a whole different level. People in the entire place had stopped everything to watch my antics, and were gasping, blushing, and laughing their fucking asses off as if they'd been scripted and paid to do so. When the show came to and end, and the music stopped, I don't think one person in the room didn't join in loudly to sing his dear wife a raucous "Happy Birthday". And all the while the cameras had been rolling.

The rest of my night, completely uneventful. My grandmothers night on the other hand…

The only member of my family who was aware at the time that I was actively working as a stripper was my mother. She and I had always been much closer than I was to anyone else in the family, and to her credit, she was just glad I was making honest money and not getting in any trouble! She had supported if not the stripping, at least me from the very start. The rest of them though; my father, sister, grandparents, aunts and uncles had no idea that little Dean was working as an exotic dancer though, and even though I didn't put a lot of thought into it, I liked them not knowing.

I could picture the scene. She would have just finished up with whatever random chores she had to take care of. More than likely shuffling through ledgers and paperwork to keep up with all the money people would have owed her and her loan brokerage firm. She'd be in a ridiculously outdated house coat and slippers, her feet sliding across the carpet that was worn down from more than 30 years of traffic, and would have climbed the stairs past my grandfathers room (more than likely with a shitty look on her face if he dared to make a sound as she passed) and into her own little sanctuary. Being as political as she was, I don't think a night ever went by where she wouldn't be found lying in bed at 11:00 pm, her little portable television just next to her, tuned in to any one of the 4 local stations for her nightly fix of gossip and politics.

I can almost imagine her face. Probably spooning a mouthful of jello between her lips as the news caster came back on after the commercial break to talk about a little local political excitement that had taken place just a bit earlier that very evening. That declaration would have certainly grabbed her attention. I don't think she would have spit out the Jello when she saw her family name boldly printed at the bottom of her TV screen, but she sure as hell just might have when she realized that it was her family named, situated on the screen just below my bare thong clad ass, with the hands of Willie Brown's wife firmly gipping each of my butt cheeks!

Looking back I can say I've never been happier than to have lived in a time free of cell phones and instant contact. It wasn't until a full day after the show that she managed to get ahold of me, and really all she could manage to say was "when can you come to the house because we need to talk".

There's really only one thing left to explain about my grandmother, and quite frankly her whole side of the family. Regardless of just about any other factor, cash is king. If there was a solid profit to be turned from it, whatever "it" may be, more than likely she'd find a way to justify the means to make it. I had actually heard her say once with my own ears that she really didn't like "the blacks" (she actually said the blacks, I shit you not), but that she'd do business with them if there was good money in it.

I watched the expression on her face change from the horrified look of a woman whose great and honorable family name has just been tarnished for all time to come, to a face of resignation and grudging acceptance, as soon as I told her how much money I was making. The instant she found out I was pulling down some serious coin for dropping my drawers, she was if not fine with it, not the least bit opposed. Like I said, cash was king.

I guess looking back I probably should have thought about it a bit more before I became a male stripper in my own home town (a fact that dawned on me many times during my career). I probably should have come up with a stage name and alternate background instead of using my real one. Perhaps letting my family know before they found out in such an incredibly far fetched and public way would have been a wise choice as well, but I did none of those things because hey, I was 21 years old, as selfish as hell and at times about as sharp as a spoon.

A less than perfect month

The stripper life was good. It was actually really good. I'd hit a few snags along the way of course and a few of them could have been really fucking bad, but luck seems to have been an overriding factor in my life, either good or bad, and this time in my life was no different.

After well over 8 months of driving all over Northern California in the most derelict illegal car on the road without one single hitch, my poor little Fiat finally gave up the ghost. But fuck me, It did it in seriously spectacular fashion! It was just about four o'clock on a Thursday when it happened. I'd ended up with an afternoon show in West Sacramento, and was just on my way home to chill for a few hours before I headed back out for a relatively busy night of stripping when all hell broke loose...

Driving along as happy as can be in the fast lane, I was buzzing right along at about a 75 mile per hour clip just past the major exchange between I-5 and I-50. I'd just gotten through the looping part of the road and into where the two major roads merged together when without any warning I found myself fucking airborne! Well, there was a little warning I suppose, in the form of a blood curdling metal grinding and pounding sound that was a mix between that heavy machinery they use on construction sites that works like a huge jackhammer, and Freddy Kruger dragging his knife blade gloves across concrete.

About the time my mind decided to tap me on the shoulder and fill me in on the fact that there may be a problem, time, just like I'd heard it would, slowed way way down. As I hit what was clearly the apex of the magical jump the Fiat had decided to perform, I took a moment to look around and try and assess the situation. I was, or at least appeared from my vantage point to be in mid-air; a level of performance I was completely unaware my little car was capable of. I tried to think about wether or not I'd turned the wheel at all when it had happened as although I wasn't sure what would take place once I was back on solid ground, I was sure I'd prefer to keep going in the same direction. I even remember trying to work out what exactly might have happened to put me in this predicament, but then gravity won it's minor battle with my little Italian convertible and we hit the ground like a freight train that had jumped the tracks.

The instant the car made full contact with the ground I was going right. And not in a "blinkers on, can I get over please" kind of way, but a "FUCK YOU! MOVE OR DIE" kind of fashion. Of course my knee-jerk reaction was to crank my half steering wheel as far to the left as I could, but alas, to no avail... Still in slow motion, I recall looking in the direction I was turning, seeing the cars that I would most likely slam into either beside or just behind me; and then wondering why on Earth there might be what was clearly an automobile wheel, complete with what looked to be steering linkage attached to it, in mid-air, floating just off the right side of the car. It was a captivating site if I'm being honest, and I couldn't take my eyes off it.

I was completely transfixed as I watched the wheel which must have been a good ten feet off the ground when I first spotted it, drift almost daintily toward me, arching at the perfect angle and trajectory to allow it to land with a huge thud and a jolt quite comfortably in the passenger seat beside me; but not before asking the windshield if it wouldn't mind fucking off for a bit, which it did with great haste. As the glass from the windshield jumped forward and then flipped backward over my head like a playing card tossed away in one solid albeit cracked to fuck piece, I was busy watching what I believe was a Mercedes just barely make it past me as I careened completely out of control across 8 major lanes of traffic. With the guard rail looming at about a forty-five degree angle in front of me, I once again took a moment for myself to take stock.

The tire which was now riding shotgun with me had clearly gotten tired of running around so much up front and had decided to rest for a bit and ride inside instead, which seemed to me to be the likely cause of my aggressive right turn. The rail I was about to slam into I would hit at enough of an angle, I believed, that I wouldn't actually go through it and over the embankment to the road 40 feet below, but more than likely side swipe the shit out of it and with any luck only end up with only a few broken bones and perhaps the loss of an eye.

As I came to a grinding stop, the right side of the car having been ground down to shredded strips of metal by the fifty feet of guard rail it had only slightly dented, all I could think was "huh". Any of the other drivers who had been there to witness the events of the last thirty seconds of my life were all now long gone, on down the highway probably assuming they'd turn on the news later to find out about the dead guy on the highway, so nobody who was currently watching me walk around the car had any idea what had just transpired.

Turns out I'm pretty good at assessing a shitty situation on the fly. As I walked around the car to the right side to see just how fucking bad it was, my attention was first drawn to the lack of a right front drivers side tire, wheel, axil or linkage that I could make out from where it was mashed against and under the rail. Not being a mechanic, nor an accident scene investigator I'll never really know, but clearly some major part of the suspension or axil had just let go, and the wheel buckled under the car, not only ripping itself free, but launching both the car and me into the air. The wheel, now free from it's bonds, had been happily bouncing down the highway at great speed, and it was my insane lurch to the right which allowed it to hop back into the car and finish it's last drive as a passenger.

The fact that I didn't end up causing a 20 car pile-up is bizarre. The fact that I didn't end up dead, having slammed almost head on into a highway guard rail still traveling at probably fifty miles per hour while not wearing a seatbelt (because the car didn't have any) is equally wow. Even more of a surprise to me really was the fact that I was still with it enough mentally to make sure I took the screw driver I used to open the trunk out of the glove box so that I could pry the vin number off the dashboard and remove the license plates before I strolled on down the highway with boombox, costumes and order forms in hand.

As luck again would have it, the crash had taken place all of about a twenty minute walk from my grandmothers house, located in the still very quaint neighborhood of Land Park. Walking into the front door and yelling so she'd know who was coming in uninvited, I was quickly greeted by what was by all outward appearances, just
The sweetest old lady on the planet.

"Deeeeeeeaan…. What a surprise! What brings you here?" She was staring quite suspect at my boom box and what was obviously a police uniform over my shoulder, and I could tell, was already trying to figure out how my visit might negatively impact her (as my un-announced visits almost always did).

"Well I actually had some car trouble just down the road a ways, and had to walk here. And now that I think about it, I'm in a bit of a bind…"

Written on the list "Strange shit that's happened to me", what came next certainly wasn't at the very top of the list, but it was pretty fucking close. For the entire week that followed, starting at anywhere between 5pm and 7pm and going straight through until 11 or later, my grandmother, the wealthy Italian racist Republican herself drove me all over the Sacramento Valley in "Driving Miss Daisy" fashion while I ran in and out of houses and bars dropping my pants for money. She would sit waiting for me in her older model Chevy Caprice outside whatever venue I was in, engine running as if she were the getaway driver for a robbery waiting for her cohorts to emerge.

On one evening we damn well almost managed to get pulled over when a Sacramento PD cruiser with a pair of cops pulled up next to us at a light, and took at least two double takes at what they saw. In the front seat, a little old salt and pepper haired lady in a bright green polyester pant-suit holding "ten and two" on the steering wheel, blinker on signaling a left turn while clearly waiting anxiously for the light to change, and in the back seat a three quarter naked guy wearing a thong, a guarder around one arm, one boot and a police duty belt. Had they not been going straight instead of turning and I had not had a seatbelt on, I have no doubt we would have ended up telling a story they'd be laughing at for years.

Not only did she drive me around that entire week, but as the week came to a close and I'd made other arrangements, she even dropped me off and the finish of the last night at the apartment of a girl I'd been having all kinds of dirty sex with under the guise that I was going to see if I could borrow her spare car while I was dealing with mine. It had been one interesting week to say the least.

Waking up the next morning, I had to laugh out loud as I started up the Mitsubishi my booty call had agreed to loan me, for an indefinite period of time no less. Indefinite I had assumed would be at least a few weeks as I hadn't saved shit for money, and had no clue where I'd find another super cheap but running car, but as it turned out a few weeks was a bit of a lofty goal.

Four days later, as I sat in the Sacramento County Jail, I was pretty sure I wasn't any more likely to drive that Mitsubishi around than I was the Fiat. Had I only gotten pulled over for speeding or something, then jailed for having a suspended license, I would have actually been pretty happy. As it was, the situation was a fuck load less chipper.

I'd pulled in to the offices of Take-it-Off to pick up the shows I had coming up, and had done exactly what I and every other dancer just running in did, I double parked next to the building and ran in, knowing I'd be all of 5 minutes. I was just looking at the last of my order forms and turning for the door, when it was opened quite aggressively by the middle aged lady who owned the travel agency just across the hall.

"Whoever owns that damn car parked in the lot needs to get out there and move it NOW!" I'd say that she was just in the middle of what had to be a bit of a bad day, but it was a well known fact that she hated Take-it-Off, and assumed that every girl that worked there must be a hooker, and every guy a porn star. She decided that she'd had enough I guess, because as I walked down the hall to the parking lot, she stormed along behind me, squawking the whole time. "Fucking God damn strippers running around this place like its theirs... Jesus wept I can't believe they let this stuff go on... world is going straight to hell...little assholes like this little shit..." and that brought me to a stop. I'd just rounded the corner to the lot, and could quite clearly see there was more than enough room for her to get her car out, but she'd obviously decided that she would rather be a bitch that make due. After the "asshole" comment, I wasn't prepared to do a thing to help her out, and said with more than a little attitude "there's more than enough room there for you to get out, so ya know what? I'm not moving a fucking thing."

That had been the second mistake I made that day. The next one though was what capped it all off.

I watched her do it in complete shock. I saw the reverse lights come on, I saw her look in the rear view mirror of her soccer mom ride, then actually make eye contact with me in the side view mirror as she stomped on the accelerator and bashed right into the side of my loaned car. HOLY FUCK!

As she threw the car in drive and peeled out down the parking lot, I was screaming my ever loving head off at her. "GONNA CALL THE FUCKING COPS! YOU NEED TO STOP, YOU BITCH!" She didn't listen, and I stopped thinking. I sprinted through the courtyard that led to the only exit from the area, spotted her pulling out of the parking lot toward me, and did the only thing I could think of. I dove on the car. Then I quickly flew off the car when she mashed on the brakes and ended up skidding on my ass to a stop a good fifteen feet away.

Why she didn't drive away as soon as I was up from in front of her car and moving is beyond me. Why she sat there as I yelled that the cops would arrest her was a mystery, but why the cops put me in cuffs, half naked and in shock was quite clear. In order to keep her from leaving the scene of an intentional accident, as I thought I should, when she finally started the car rolling again I reached in to her car and took her glasses. Off her face. Because in my mind, how could she leave the scene of what I considered a crime if she couldn't see where she was going. That my friends, is the definition of "strong armed robbery". Oh. Fuck. Me.

When I was finally released about 18 hours later to my father I had to make what I still think must have been a pretty devastating walk of shame, as I shuffled out the front doors of the county jail smack in the middle of downtown Sacramento on a busy afternoon; barefoot and clad only in a pair of shorts. My father was less than thrilled as you can imagine, and nothing I could say was gonna make it any better, so I just kept my fucking mouth shut.

I lost about a week of work because of the incident, and a months worth of sleep, not to mention going deeper into debt to my family to help sort out my not so cheap legal issue. When I sat in the courtroom for what was to be my Felony arraignment the bailiff read a statement.

"If you hear your name called, you are to remain seated and

wait until we call you again to stand before the judge. If you do not hear your name, and you are sure today is the date of your arraignment, then your case has been sent to misdemeanor court, and you will be contacted by mail with the details of your case."

Fucking alphabetical order sucks ass! At least it does when your last name starts with an R. But when I hear the bailiff say "Smith" and hadn't heard my name, I breathed the biggest sigh of relief of my life! Misdemeanor I could live with.

The only funny part of the whole damn story to me? The "Booty Call" that had given me the car in the first place? As soon as she got a call from the tow company telling her she could come pick up her car, she called me. Did she call to scream and yell and demand money to have it fixed? no. Did she call to ask me if I was okay, but follow it up by saying she didn't want to see me anymore? Nope. She actually called to tell me that anytime I was ready I could swing back on by to pick up the Mitsubishi again and continue on!

And with that, back on the road I was (still very illegally), having survived one of the more fucked up, unusual and outlandish weeks of my life, and I'll be the first to say, that my friends is saying something!

Rave On

In the few weeks that followed the dramatic and near cataclysmic suicide of my beloved little Fiat, I had been working hard to save every last penny I could. I knew that the Mitsubishi wasn't going to be mine to use all that much longer, as my booty call had gone more from "booty" to "call", wondering when the fuck she was gonna get her car back. I'd managed to stall her enough to get a few weeks worth of time, but there was no doubt that asking for more would be out of the question.

Happily all my shows had been going quite well, and I'd even spent a few weeks in a row on the stage of the El Dorado saloon. The stage show had added to my requests for telegrams which was good, and the guys in the show had even apparently learned to tolerate me, which was great! But the thing I never would have expected by turning into a working stripper was the negative effect it would have on my social life. I simply no longer had any time for things like the Yucatan or my friends on the weekends.

Price on the other hand, had been taking things to a whole other level when it came to the party scene, and had been heading into San Francisco on a pretty regular basis; returning almost weekly with not only stories of the new "rave" scene that had become all the rage in the US, but of the most amazing substance ever. "Ecstasy", also know as "X" had all but taken over the city and Price had nothing but good things to say. I on the other hand didn't have a good feeling about it at all, and had yet to head down to the City by the Bay for a look. I had a handful of years before had an experience that had scared me off drugs in a major fucking way, and I was about as opposed to them as anyone could be.

Cut back to about 3 years before. It had been an all around epic night with a few friends. I'd had four or five previous experiences with LSD before then, and most of them were with the same crew, so I felt completely comfortable and at ease. I had been told that the trick with "acid" was a great frame of mind an the right people around you, and I suppose it must have been a pretty accurate statement since all my experiences had been beyond positive.

The details of the night escape me if I'm being honest, but when it was all said and done, it felt as if it had been something special. The power that can be contained in one tiny little square of paper is quite literally mind boggling, and as the drugs we clearly starting to wear off, my group made a decision. There's a time with acid, or with any drug I suppose, where you either want to continue on with the experience or are ready to call and end to the ride. After almost ten hours of "frying" (being high on LSD) we all came to the same conclusion. Party on!

The LSD we had taken the night before had been procured in about the most cliche way one can get the stuff. At a Grateful Dead concert. Well, not exactly at the concert, but in the parking lot of said concert, which was an experience all to itself. As we drove to the California Exposition Fair Grounds in the center of town where the weekend long concert was taking place, we formulated a plan for the day. We'd grab some more acid from one of the hundreds of "Dead Head's" camping out in the parking lot, a shit load of supplies for the adventure and then spend our time "day tripping" at the lake, which would be a very new experience for me.

Now without going into the physiological effects of lysergic acid diethyl-amide, which if I'm honest I doubt I could do anyway, I can try and give you the very basics of what it does. Acid does not, as commonly assumed by those who have never tried the stuff, make you hallucinate. When you're on acid, you aren't running around seeing a bunch of things that aren't there. You won't be walking down the street and suddenly have Jesus stroll up and ask you how your day is going is what I'm saying. What acid does is change you perception of what it is you're seeing, and open your mind to pure imagination, which can be incredibly powerful. It allows your eyes to play tricks with light and shadow, your ears to play tricks with sound, and your body to play tricks with sensation.

It also has the ability to change your awareness of your surroundings quite substantially, and can drastically heighten said sensations, so physically things can feel just as surreal as they may look. The drug in my experience always was much more visually striking in almost near darkness, and a very mild light or a candle would allow the drug to play with my eyes in a way that would make walls appear to move, plants to dance to the beat of the music playing, and would make colors and patterns come vibrantly alive, providing you with your own personal kaleidoscope if you chose to focus on the effect; as the longer you focused on something specific the more your brain could alter the way you perceived it. I always found that the more brightly lit my surroundings, the less likely my eyes were to play tricks on me, which was generally the effect we were going for, so day tripping as it was called had never really appealed to me.

Still being under the waining high from the previous evening though, I decided as did the other guys that it was a great idea; and as we pulled away from the Dead show, chewing up what had been a rather large piece of paper with a picture of Snoopy staring back up from it, we figured we were in for a great day. An hour later, as we finished gathering all of the supplies we assumed we would want and need for our excursion, we were still anxiously waiting for Snoopy to kick in. Another 30 minutes later, still with no effect that we could perceive, we all came to the same conclusion. Snoopy had been fucking bunk. Fake shit pawned off by some asshole that clearly saw us as easy marks.

Fuck it! We were ready for the damn day! Even though we were all getting pretty tired, and even though I suspect none of us were nearly as motivated as we had been, back to the Dead show we went.

"This is Blue Unicorn fellas…. Fresh dipped blotter straight from Berkeley. I promise you this isn't fake shit. You're gonna love this ride!" Two hits a piece handed over by a guy that looked like he'd been with The Dead since day one. At four bucks a dose, we figured why the hell not. Lets make sure this ride is what we had planned the first time around!

I remember the moment as if it were digitally imprinted on my brain. The instant, and I mean the very instant that the two hits of Blue Unicorn went down the back of my throat, Snoopy jumped up and kicked my right in the side of the head! Then when I was down, that little fucker dragged his balls across my face for good measure just to make damn sure I knew he was the real deal. It was at that moment that I fucked up. In a major way. And here in lies one of the major hazards of LSD.

As soon as the stuff we thought was fake kicked in, I flipped a switch. A little mental twist that would determine the next 16 hours of my life. Instead of thinking as my friends did that this was going to be absolutely fucking amazing, all I could think was "Oh shit…. This is gonna get really bad!" And in that instant I was done.

Not even ten minutes later, I say ten minutes as if I actually have a clue, but the truth is, one's perception of time on LSD is nonexistent really. So, an indeterminate amount of time later, we were stopped next to a Carls Jr. fast food joint with me behind the wheel. Trying with all my might just to concentrate on the task of driving, I almost didn't notice and most certainly didn't acknowledge the building seemingly spitting bricks out of itself which would then simply side down the wall to the ground where they would disappear.

I didn't mention to my friends, who were all in their own little worlds by then that as I drove down the highway, not only had the steering wheel melted from my hands, and was, if I didn't look in any other directions simply gone from my view, but that it seemed the car was pushing along a rather large section of highway in front of it that we simply couldn't seem to get past.

I can't actually tell you how I managed to make it back to my apartment, but I hoped desperately at that point that being on familiar ground would help to soothe the metal melt-down I was sure was coming. I practically dove out of the car the instant I had it in park, and sprinted to the front steps of my building, where I sat down heavily to try and take stock. Physically everything seemed as though it were happening as if my sensations were trying to imitate an echo, which let me tell you is one fucked up sensation. Add to that the fact that it seemed as though I could hear everything happening within the entire city all at once, and I was dealing with some serious sensory overload. Just about the time I caught myself staring at my car as it slowly melted into the street, I'd had just about enough.

I needed sensory depravation, not more stimulation! I needed nothing in front of me that could fuck with my head. The park that was just about half a mile down the road seemed as though it would be the perfect idea for this, and I sprinted there at break neck speeds, hardly feeling a thing.

Lying on my back dead center in the middle of a soccer field, I actually thought for a few seconds that my idea just might pay off. Looking up at that clear blue cloudless California air, there was nothing in my field of vision that could possibly indicate how high I was. Until the first rainbow shot across the sky. And then a second, and third, and...

Now of course looking back I know exactly what was going on. The more I paid attention to just one thing, the more opportunity I gave my mind to try and alter and distort my perception of it. One of the consistent effects of acid on users is that it tends to make people focus, hyper focus you might say on an item, a face, a view. Even sober, if you stare long enough in one particular direction, your mind will begin to play tricks on you, but add the effects of LSD, especially as much as we had taken…. Stare intently for a decent chunk of time at a single point on a painting even sober, and before long it will start to alter, but now for me, anything more than a glance anywhere was having a dramatic effect. Over the course of the next hour or so, nothing I tried to calm myself down came even close to working. My friends long forgotten, I hung on to the rational part of my mind, still present but deeply buried, looking for answers. Then it came to me. John.

My friend John lived close. My friend John was a pro when it came to acid. My friend John would know exactly what to do. When he opened the door and saw the look in my eyes with pupils so blown out that you could have shined a spotlight in them and they wouldn't have dilated even a touch, covered in sweat from running all the way to him and clearly terrified, he knew exactly where I was an what to do.

According to John, it was just over 12 hours later when I started coming back to reality. He had put me on the floor in front of his television, popped a tape into his VCR, hit play, and calmed me almost instantly with of all things the cartoon Ren and Stimpy. Not the series mind you, not even a small collection of episodes, but the same episode played over and over and over again. I never knew. It turned out just as he knew, to be the exact distraction I needed.

It had tons of movement with never a still frame. It had color, it had energy, and it kept me from focusing on something I knew shouldn't be all fucked up, and instead forced me to simply and completely focus on the randomness of the cartoon, and just like that, I forgot to be terrified of just how high I was…

Two full days it took for all of the effects to wear off. Two fucking days! As you can imagine, by the time that substantial ordeal was finally over, I swore to never under any circumstances take another drug again.

So the first time Price came back from the city with his stories of X, I told him to fuck off. The second and third time, I listened, but still told him no damn way. The fifth time, when he had an absolutely stunning woman named Lori with him telling the same kinds of stories, I didn't say much of anything. By the time he'd been going to the city for more than a month, he had stopped telling me much about it at all, but was clearly captivated by his time there, and I started feeling very very left out.

I knew it long before the next time we hung out. I wanted to go. I was feeling pretty isolated with work taking up all of my time, and I wanted to see if I could managed to get ahold of a little of the joy that Price seemed to have found, and knew damn well that if he didn't invite me for his next trip into San Francisco, I was gonna ask to go. I hadn't yet admitted (to him or myself) that I also wanted to try what was by Price's description the most magical substance in the history of mankind, but as it is with such things, good friends know long before you do.

There was no real arm twisting involved. There was just Price and Lori, both telling me what an amazing time I was in for, even if I didn't want to try any ecstasy, but by the time we crossed into the city limits I knew damn well the pill Price told me he had for me "just in case" was gonna end up down my throat.

The party was crazy huge. They promoters had rented out an absolutely enormous warehouse in the Army district of the city, and there must have been three thousand people in the place. There was music literally oozing out of the walls, lights everywhere, people with glow sticks and outrageously colored outfits, artwork and graffiti on every wall and the most energy and happiest people I'd ever seen being pumped into one place. It was a fucking circus! Yet the very real specter of my horrible acid trip was still very strong in me, and when the time came, I could only bring myself to take half the pill Price had provided.

An hour later and I still didn't feel a thing. Both Price and Lori were clearly under the effects, as they were not only smiling ear to ear and overly affectionate with everyone around them, but they couldn't stand still! Dancing but staying close to me to wait for the drug to start working on me, I could tell that they were barely able to keep me in their thoughts. Still stone cold sober, I told them that I was gonna go try and find a bathroom to take a piss, and off I went through the crowd.

Fifteen minutes of standing in line for the porte-potty was just about as fun as you might think when waiting for a drug I was seriously regretting taking to kick in. As I worked my way back through the crush of the crowd, I was almost relieved that nothing had happened, and guessed it just wasn't for me. But as I stepped through the doorway into the room where I'd left Price and Lori…

The second half of the pill was in my mouth as quickly as I could get to it! I almost sprinted into the room to try and find my friends, and the moment they saw my face, both of them screamed and jumped for joy! Then they dove at me knowing instantly that I'd "joined" them, buried me in hugs, and Lori with a few kisses, and just like that, like Alice I had chosen to take the red pill and dove on down the rabbit hole to change the course of my life once again.

Role Reversal

About the time the Brunette's top came off, I was sure this wasn't going to be just another strip show for me; but I'm getting a bit ahead of myself.

An absolutely manic night was thankfully coming to an end. Usually the maximum number of shows I could pull off in one night was eleven, but this time I'd been stacked with twelve, and I was next to late for every damn one of them. None of the shows had been terribly noteworthy, but that was a really fucking good thing, as any little glitch would have screwed my entire night. The traffic to and from all the shows, and their distance apart was most certainly apparent thought, because I criss-crossed around Sacramento so many fucking times that if you drew out my route on a map it would have looked like Charolette's fucking web.

As I headed out toward American River Drive for my final show, all I wanted was for it to be quick and easy. I was beat tired, I had next to no energy left in me, and had no damn desire to entertain anyone. The end of a busy night would usually see me feeling a little like this, but on this particular night, show number twelve was the last thing in the world I wanted.

As I took time on the drive to get a better look at the final order form a few things stood out. Or should I say the lack of a few things stood out. There was no specific contact name for who I was suppose to meet before the show, and no occasion listed, which wasn't really a problem as the address was a house and not a bar or restaurant, but it was strange regardless. The costume listed was "any" as well which was also a bit unusual although not unheard of, but I didn't put any real thought into it and just grabbed the flight suit as it was by far the easiest to deal with.

Walking up to the door I instantly noticed a few things that were just a bit, well, off. Only one car in the driveway and none in the street. No music coming from inside the house and as I listened more intently, no noise at all for that matter with only dim lighting coming from inside. Not exactly the scene you'd expect for any occasion that would require the services of a male stripper!

When the door was answered shortly after I knocked, an extremely attractive short little brunette with a pleasant smile and very casual demeanor quite clearly dressed for an evening on the couch stood happily in front of me. "Hi! Oh you'll do… He's here girls! Why don't you come on in there Mr. Pilot guy." Then she took me by the hand to lead me inside.

No screams greeted me as I walked into the living room, no guest of honor seated in a chair in the center of the room, no party favors or streamers, balloons or punch bowl, no giggling pack of ladies crammed on the sofa to see the show; just the first little brunette who said her name was Grace, a very pretty blonde and another rather curvy dark haired girl both looking back at me. The blonde had been seated in front of the television, which was quickly turned off, leaving the room dimly lit and almost on the romantic side, which was just weird!

"So" I said, "who's the guest of honor I'll be performing for?" with a very practiced look of confidence that I most certainly didn't feel. I was already quite a bit off balance by now, as the element of surprise or at least the opportunity for me to be in the know and the one in charge was gone. "Well we all are!" said the blonde. "Yeah! We decided last minute yesterday that we were gonna have a girls night at home and wanted something new and well, that new is you! We even made sure it was your last show, so you wouldn't have to go to soon…"

Yup. They had me on my heels for sure. I was very clearly not in charge of the events currently unfolding, and in an attempt to get back in front of the situation, I tried asserting my control by grabbing a chair from the kitchen and placing it in the middle of the living room floor.

"No no no honey, that doesn't look comfortable at all! Why don't you just dance for all of us and we'll stay here on the couch, that way we don't have to move around all over to get a turn!"

Get a turn? A turn at what? I was completely and totally at a loss. Yeah, I know… Once again I believe it's time for me to remind the readers that I am not always the quickest on the uptake of a given situation, and this was most certainly one of those occasions. As they all lined themselves up on the sofa right next to each other, I really had nothing left to say or do except hit the play button on my boom box and get down to it.

Of course the major problem for me was not only that I didn't have an act for this kind of thing, but that I had no clue how to handle girls like this. None of the funny gags and quirky routines I had come up with to embarrass my customers and keep me in charge was working on these three, because none of them seemed the least bit uncomfortable with what was happening. After a few minutes of bumping and grinding, an even a shot at using the handcuff's, little Grace who had so kindly greeted me at the door did not seem particularly impressed with the way the show was going, and decided that taking off her top might help the situation along just a little.

"See! Just take that stuff off! It's easy!" The sight of her not insubstantial tits now being aggressively bounced around on the sofa was the first thing that got the other two ladies to sit up and take real notice, and they hooted with approval as she pinched her nipples and then smacked my ass, hard! This shit appeared to be on its way to getting way out of control, or should I say just way the fuck out of my control! With her friends help, the trio finished the unzipping job with my jumpsuit, and I found I was not too gracefully having to take my boots off with my pants around my ankles.

As I was hobbling back just a step or two in an attempt to get my boots and jumpsuit off, Grace's friends had decided that she was on to something good, and had relieved themselves of their tops as well. Looking back at the three of them, topless, giggling and reaching for me, the reaction I'd been working hard to control for almost a year now won the battle.

"Oh look! Here we fuckin' go! Now this looks like it's gonna get fun…" Said the blonde as she reached for my quickly stiffening cock with a lot more will to get to me than I had to try and get away…

Even as things started to progress at speed, I was having a really difficult time getting my head around the situation. You see In my mind, I was still very much that ridiculous guy who just sat and sweated all over some poor girl for her birthday. I was still the guy who'd had a crazy crush on one of his co-workers who wouldn't give him the time of day in any romantic fashion, and so decided that telling her and all his co-workers that he use to be a stripper hoping that might impress her. I really just couldn't believe that these girls were doing anything more than teasing and playing around and simply getting ready to make one huge fool out of me. But then the most amazing thing dawned on me. Even if that was exactly there plan, and even if they did tease me and end up making me feel like an ass, was there a single guy on the planet that wouldn't happily fall into the same trap? I'd be a much bigger fool not to take the risk. Fuck it. If I was gonna be a fool, this was absolutely the kind I wanted to be!

So, cock in hand, I let the blonde pull me the two or so feet that separated us back to her, and as she tightened her grip on me, I reached up to grab a handful of one of the three sets of titties that were responsible for my now substantial hard-on. Right up until I had hers as well as Grace's boobs in my hands at the same time I was waiting to hear them start laughing and push me away, but as I stood there being aggressively groped now by all three women and playing with all six tits, I came to grips with the fact that this shit was actually going down!

Things started to get pretty damn out of hand from there on out. The blonde decided that as long as the music was playing, someone should damn well be dancing, and chose to jump up and put on a show herself. She shoved me to the couch with as much force as she could muster, and the next thing I knew, I was sandwiched in-between Grace and her friend while Blondie started a sexy stripper style dance that was shit tons better than I could manage! The little shorts that had been snugly wrapped around her hips were now on the floor around just one ankle, and she was spread legged and grinding in front of me, leaving not one thing to my imagination.

The next thing I knew, bare naked and crawling toward me I could see that the she was done playing around. As it turned out, so was Grace. Breaking my eye contact with the naked stalker working her way towards me, Grace grabbed my face and pulled me in for one hell of a first kiss! And about the same time the kiss started to get crazy intense, I found that hers wasn't the only mouth I had to contend with! My faithful purple thong had been discarded, and in-between kisses I could see had been replaced quite skillfully with the back of the blondes throat.

I'd never had a threesome before. And I sure as hell had never had a foursome! What was the etiquette in a situation like this? Was it rude for me to grab the second brunette's (no, I don't know hers or the blondes name, and never did) ass with Grace's tongue down my throat and my balls in the blondes mouth? Was I going to broach the subject of condoms? And how exactly did that work? I mean, did I swap for a new condom for each girl? Should I leave the condom question up to them? If I ended up going down on one of them, was it then rude to kiss another one on the mouth afterward? So many fucking questions! They actually started to fade pretty quickly about the time I'd been pushed onto to my back with Brunette #2 going down on me, and the blonde straddling my face. Seemed there weren't a whole lot of rules being observed really...

And then, a bit later, as for me time had ceased to have any meaning, a sensation that was most certainly not a mouth slid down over me, and as a very pleasant groan could be heard, both the blonde still seated firmly on my face and I glanced over to find, that Grace had gone ahead hopped onboard, and was grinding away with me as deep in her as she could get me, faced the other direction so that she could make out with Brunette #2. A sight that will thankfully remain burned into my brain hopefully even long after I'm dead.

It was a porn. No doubt about it. It was exactly like every porn that had a guy and multiple girls in it that I'd ever seen, and I started behaving exactly as if thats what it was because I didn't have a single original thought at that moment. Somewhere in the back of my mind, I was re-running every dirty movie I'd ever seen where the pizza delivery guy gets dragged into the sorority house and attacked by a squad of hot cheerleaders. Pulling hair, bouncing from girl to girl, watching them going at it, them watching me go at it with one or two of the three... It was, well lets face it, it was FUCKING AWESOME!

It was two incredible rounds of craziness before I was gathering my clothing. As I was just about to cum for the first time, I remember thinking that although this was gonna feel great, I was gonna be bummed for this, the most epic sexual episode of my entire existence to come to a close. Still, when I announced that I was about to explode (etiquette? Don't cum in, on or near a girl without first clearing it) while taking the blonde from behind and kissing, or shall I say practically inhaling one of them while groping the other, all three of them in unison spun around to present all six titties for me to, well, mark. It was as if all three had very recently been watching the same fucking porn's I had, and as I almost uncontrollably turned all three of their chests into my own personal Jackson Pollock painting (google his work if you don't know) I thought that even though it was now clearly over (all over their tits that is), that had been the most spectacular experience of my life. And then the blonde dove in and started going down on Grace, and to my infinite joy, I realized "the show must go on!"

It was close to two o'clock in the morning when I finally walked out the door. As Grace was being serviced by what was clearly her very good friend, I gave the same attention to Brunette #2, then to the blonde, then to Grace, then to… You get the point. On and on it went until they'd made sure I was more than ready for round two, and I did my best to make sure I stayed in the game for a long time! About the time they pulled out the lube because we'd been at it so much, I was feeling pretty damn good about my stamina! And my reward? As I announced that I couldn't hold back anymore, Brunette #2 slid me out of her, and lovely little Grace dove face first on my cock as I came, even harder this time into her mouth than I had all over the three of them.

I walked out of the house so dizzy from the experience that I flat out forget to collect the money for the show. Which, looking back was a good thing! I'd had to come out of pocket for the cost of the telegram, but it meant that I'd fucked around for free, making me just another slut, instead of the hooker I'd have been if they paid me!

It was by far the first time for me that I'd ever seen what I was doing for a living as even remotely sexual in nature, as I'd worked so very hard to turn it in to nothing but a joke. From the first, I'd made all my shows about the laughs, and even though those laughs were earned by joking around in a sexual manner, they weren't sexy. At least they sure as hell didn't seem that way to me! But now… well shit, now that had all changed for sure. If borderline out of control sex with three

different women at once didn't adjust my self image just a
touch, well nothing fucking would!

Boy in the Hood

She was a dark blue late model Chevy Astrovan, and she was absolutely amazing! It had been converted over by the previous owner from a cargo van into the coolest little sleeper I'd ever seen. She was the type of mini-van that you would see delivery companies and plumbers buzzing around town in, and could not have been any more perfect for my needs.

Not only had the clearly talented previous owner installed an almost queen sized bed in the back, but under it was a full compliment of drawers and storage space, and even a closet area complete with a hanger rack that could accommodate all of my uniforms. I absolutely had to have it, and was literally willing to kill people to take her home. Happily nothing quite so dramatic was required.

I had put away about three grand specifically for a set of wheels, and was staring down the barrel of having to return the Mitsubishi in another day or so, so I swallowed a bit of pride and took all that info to Grandma, and promptly begged. To my shock, it actually didn't take all that much begging as soon as she knew I was gonna be out of work if I didn't have a decent car , and in all honesty I was only asking her for a couple thousand dollars which was jack shit to her.

Plus, I had an even more entertaining reason for desperately wanting that van. San Francisco! As I'd driven away from the City that first time with Price and Lori I had only been able to think about the next big rave we'd go back to. I along with them and about two thousand of my newest closest friends had danced our asses off for the entire night, drinking water, laughing and having an incredible time. The drug that I had been so flat out scared of had turned out to be what I can only describe as energetic joy in a pill, and I could not wait to try more! As it turned out, I only had to wait until the very next weekend, and then the weekend after that, and...

As career planning goes, I couldn't have done better if I'd actually known what I was doing. As a working stripper, on the weekends my last show usually happened at about 11 o'clock at night. As a "raver" as they (and I) had taken to referring to themselves, 11 at night was about the time it might cross your mind to get up off the couch and start getting ready for the fun to come, so it was almost seamless! Finish last show, drive to city, PLAY! The van was tailor made for it all with its bed in the back to either rest in-between shows when possible or crash in the city, storage for all my costumes and clothing for the party nights...

As soon as I'd taken possession of it I was on my way to Price's to show him the new party bus, and he saw all the same possibilities I did. Within a week I had a monster stereo system installed with the help of an old friend who knew all about that stuff, and ended up with what was basically one huge rolling speaker ready to carry way too many people to and from the City for some serious entertainment. It was perfect. But, it was also an amazing party bus I needed to pay off with a quickness. I had promised Gran that the first two thousand I made would go straight back to her, and for a change, I actually planned on not flaking on her. To that end, I'd told Rick to load me up with as much as he possibly could if it was possible, and he did his best to oblige.

I'd not had too many daytime shows come up with Take-it-Off which had been good. For some reason, it always just seemed better working as a stripper under the cover of night. Even though I'd be bouncing from brightly lit house, to romantic restaurant to smoky bar, none of it seemed as strange once the sun had gone down. This week though had seen a few different daytime gigs with the extra work Rick had been giving me, and I was in no position to bitch. It was one of those daytime shows that turned out to be one of the worst I'd ever had to deal with.

Occasionally Take-it-Off would book parties that required more than one dancer. Up until now I'd not had to perform in any of them though, and this one was not only a team effort so to speak, it was with one of Take-it-Off's female dancers no less. Could be interesting for sure! We'd planned to meet before the show in the parking lot of a local coffee shop so that we could figure out how we wanted to do it, and must have looked really strange indeed, both of us almost but not quite looking like cops.

"So I'm guessing we just each kinda do our thing? The music doesn't really matter, right? Maybe put the chairs back to back, and you can dance on one side while I'm on the other?"

It was only booked as a fifteen minute show each anyway, so not a lot really had to be put into it. Even if it was a bit sloppy, the crowd was gonna have two naked people dancing around their living room, so I doubted we'd hear much bitching. As I hopped in the van with my "cop" partner following close behind It was 3:15, and I guessed we'd arrive just a few minutes early, just before 4:00. Left turn here, right turn there... I was paying more attention to the map than I was the neighborhood, and literally didn't realize that our show was to take place smack in the middle of the roughest Hispanic area in Sacramento. And both of us dressed as cops.

"Birthday" was the occasion listed on each of the forms. Apparently we were hired to dance for twin brother and sister who were both turning 21, and the family had decided a couple of cop strippers would be a great way to do it. As I turned the last corner and spotted what was quite clearly our destination, I was a lot less happy than I wanted to be, and could only imagine what my "partner" must be thinking behind me.

The entire block was packed with people and custom cars. "Low Riders" to be specific, and around those low riders were more crisp white t-shirts, oversized Dickie's (pants) and flannel shirts buttoned only at the collar than I had ever seen off a movie screen. I'd like to think I had avoided, both consciously and unconsciously the racist mentality that my Grandmother had so carefully cultivated over her life, but I wasn't immune to stereotypes by any stretch, and as I put the van in park on the corner near the house, the last thing in the world I wanted to do was get out of the car dressed in my uniform. This was a recipe for disaster. It wasn't a Latin family I was performing for, this was clearly a gang. Fuck.

I tried almost to creep out of the van, hoping I'd have a chance to speak to my counterpart before anything happened, and I could see by the look in her eyes that she was just as intimidated as I was. By all appearances he was every bit Cholo (Hispanic Gangster), and if he had looked our way all of 60 seconds later, I'm pretty sure neither of us would have been there. The smell of pot in the air was almost as thick as the fear that was oozing from my partner, and the moment I saw the look in her eyes I knew she wanted out of there fast! If he hadn't yelled "YO!" and come running over to us in his crisply creased baggy's and white Jordan's I honestly believe both of us would have bailed without a second thought.

He didn't seem like a bad guy one on one if truth be told, and had a sincere smile on his face as he spoke, but between the substantial tattoo's on him and the way he set the scene inside it was not appealing at all. The brother and sister were gonna be in separate rooms that were side by side, that way all the guys could watch the girl dance, and all the girls could watch me. He told us that the BBQ had been going on for a few hours now, and that it was getting a little crazy as it had turned into more of a block party than anything else. They had a DJ playing music for them inside, and he'd have him put on some dance music for us when we got in there, which didn't sound sinister at all, but it meant that we as the entertainers weren't dictating the way the show was gonna go right from the start.

Clearly we were never going to be in control of this party like we usually were, but now, it didn't seem we were even in control of our own shows, and that felt to me like a really bad omen. The problem was, we were already in too deep. To try and back out now was to risk really pissing this guy and a whole lot more off, and as I realized that all eyes on the street were on us now and I doubted I'd be able to manage to get both of us in our cars and out of here if they didn't want us to leave.

My partners eyes were the most pleading I'd ever seen. It was liking watching a self aware lamb being knowingly led to the slaughter, and I was starting to wonder if she was gonna break into tears at some point. As we were led into the house it was clearly the first time anyone ever dressed as a cop had been invited inside, and not one person didn't watch every step we took. Some seemed amused, some a bit confused, and others, well from others I could sense downright hostility. It seemed that not everyone knew a couple of strippers dressed as cops were gonna show up that day, and the sight of two uniforms in the crowd had them instantly on high alert. All I could think was "please get this fucking show started so they know I'm not a cop!"

Things almost seemed like they might go the way we wanted when the music stopped and the DJ announced that the birthday girl and boy were about to get a big surprise. As the birthday pair were tossed into their chairs in adjoining rooms the people were actually paying attention to the "entertainment", and I was able not only to start my show without hassle but also able to keep a good eye on my partner through the large double doors that separated us. As the music rolled from the stack of speakers, both rooms filled almost to a crush, and the body heat mixed with the almost overpowering stench of weed and tobacco smoke had me spinning just a bit as I started my "routine". Still, all seemed alright.

A lot of what I did as a telegram dancer required my speaking and being able to interact with the crowd, but it was apparent in less that a minute that there was no chance that was gonna work with this show as it was simply too fucking noisy. The guys in the next room watching my partner starting her show were yelling so loudly, and getting so out of control so quickly that I had to pantomime all my jokes and gags, none of which did any of the girls give one good fuck about.

As I skipped over a lot of what I normally did, and just started dropping clothing and reverting to bump and grind ass slapping. I couldn't even really dance not only due to the size of the crowd jammed into the room, but the literally dozens of beer bottles and cans scattered all across the floor. I also tried to keep and eye on how my partner was doing in the next room. I'd manage to get flashes here and there through all the white T's and flannel to see her face, clearly still scared shitless and wanting things over as quickly as possible, but too intimidated to not perform. Up until now, not a single guy had been paying the least bit attention to what was happening with me and the ladies, and it meant that I could get away with checking up on her without getting confrontational with any of the men.

Unfortunately it didn't last. Her scream was most certainly not a happy one, and it stopped me in my tracks immediately. As I stood up from the lap of the birthday girl I'd been grinding on, I could see my partner slapping back hands from a guy in the crowd who'd decided to grab a handful of tits once her bra had come off. It was her snapping point for sure, and she was clearly ready to bolt, borderline terror in her eyes! One of the other guys in the crowd realized how freaked out she was as well and he didn't seem to like it any more than I did, because he was face to face with the handsy one, yelling at him to give the girl a fucking break and let her do her show. Things were only gonna go one direction.

I had only managed to take off my duty belt and uniform shirt so far, so as I heard more than saw the brawl start to break out in the next room, I didn't have all that much to try and collect. The ladies I'd been dancing for didn't seem to notice the commotion nearly as much as I did, and as I got up and started grabbing my things, I didn't bother to think that I just might be throwing myself into my own little shit storm. As soon as they realized I was grabbing my shit and trying to get to my partner, these girls were pissed! They went from happily yelling to just yelling really fucking quick, and it didn't take more than a few moments for some of the guys to notice. Someone was pissing off their women. Oh my holy fucking hell…

How does one go about politely pushing his way half dressed through a bunch of pissed off Hispanic women shoving him around into a room full of pissed off Hispanic Cholo's who have just about hit their boiling point without getting killed? Well the answer is, there really isn't any good way to do it! Half of the men in the room had forgotten all about the stripper and were much more focused on the brawl that was about to get started just a few feet away. The two guys were locked to each other, face to face with handfuls of clothing in their fists, just moments away from throwing the first punch, and that distraction was the only thing that let me shove my way through the crowd to grab my partner by the wrist and pull.

At first she pulled back from me like her life depended on it until she saw it was me, and then practically dove at me topless and barefoot in her cop pants, being grabbed by a dozen hands as I pulled her from the room; through a few very loud protests from the men who were trying to get ahold of any piece of her they could. As good fortune would have it, at the instant the tide was about to turn against me for taking their prize away from them, all hell broke loose between the two guys who'd faced off, and fists had started flying. Had those two not started to brawl at that very moment, I have no doubt that every man in that place would have turned against me for pulling their dancer away from them, and I would have been beaten by every fist close enough to reach. As it was, racing through the room I had just a minute before been performing in, I and my partner were subjected to at least half a dozen slaps and shoves from the women, and one damn good shot to the back of my head as they too turned aggressive as hell. Tripping over bottles and cans as we went, things were not looking good.

Had it not been for what was now a full on mob of guys in the far room watching what sounded like a prize fight, and had it not been for the crowd just one room over pushing in to see what the fuck was going on, we never would have made it out of there without bleeding. As we ducked and pushed our way out the front door and raced toward my car, we had more than a few of the substantial crowd outside looking at and moving toward the house, the noise inside, and us, but no longer clad in the police uniforms we'd entered in, we didn't cause quite the same reaction. We clearly didn't look like much of a threat to anyone but we certainly didn't belong, being a cute little topless white girl and a still kind of skinny white guy in a brightly colored vest, and more than one yell was aimed in our direction as we passed by.

I unlocked the driver side door of the van as quickly as I could and shoved her in. Diving across the seat and into the back with a scream, she did as I told her as I yelled "GET IN!" and climbed in behind her as fast as possible. The moment I heard the "click" of the door locks engage, two very pissed of guys were at the side of my van, slapping their hands on the glass and asking what the fuck was going on. Starting the car without answering them did nothing to calm their growing agitation, and as I put the van in drive and hit the gas, I could clearly hear the handles of the doors being tested, and then fists and shoes punching and kicking the sliding door as I pulled past and onto the street.

I was completely prepared to run anyone who was in front of the van over, but thankfully as we got to the thickest part of the crowd on the street, they stayed clear, apparently not knowing that we were a substantial part of why shit was getting so out of control. As I rounded the first corner we came do, desperately praying that it wasn't a cul-de-sac we'd be cornered in, I honestly thought I heard a gun shot, although looking back that shot could have very easily been my imagination.

My partner, who up until then I didn't know was named Erica, was lying on the bed in the back of the van having a full on nervous breakdown. She was crying as hard as anyone I've ever seen, and I tried to do what I could to comfort her as I drove, but there was no way in hell I was gonna stop that van until we were long gone from there.

Ten minutes later I had a stream of mascara running down my shirt as still topless Erica, curled up fetal in my lap, finally managed to get the tears under control and regain a bit of composure. Her car, which had been left at the house was a real problem for her, as there was no way in hell either of us were going back into that neighborhood to collect it, but I offered to give her a ride wherever she wanted and suggested she had someone go grab it for her the next day, perhaps escorted by the "actual" police.

When I dropped her off at her apartment now clothed in one of my t-shirts, she gave me a huge hug and a kiss, thanked me for getting her out of that place and then disappeared inside. Both of us still completely overwhelmed with just how crazy it had been, and how much worse it could have gotten. It was the last show Erica ever performed, and I sure as hell couldn't blame her. Even as a guy that shit was intense and scary, and I couldn't have begun to imagine how much more intimidating it must have been for her.

What a crazy fucking career.

90's Hippie Remix

Methylenedioxymethamphetamine. As it turns out is a really fucking long way to spell WOW.

Methylenedioxymethamphetamine (MDMA), more commonly known as Ecstasy
or "X" is a psychoactive drug used primarily as a recreational chemical. Desired
effects include increased empathy, euphoria and heightened sensations. When
taken orally, effects begin somewhere between 30 to 60 minutes after ingestion,   with its effects lasting between 3 to 6 hours.

MDMA, first made in 1912, began to be used to improve psychotherapy
beginning in the 1970's. It became a highly popular street drug in the 1980's.
MDMA is commonly associated with dance parties or Raves. Somewhere
between 19 and 29 million people between the ages of 15 and 64 have used
Ecstacy.

-Wiki

There's no doubt that I was certainly one of those 19 to 29 million, and in fact, when it was all said and done, I'd be willing to say that I'd probably taken quite a few peoples shares. It's 27 years later now, and I can say without a shadow of a doubt that I don't regret one single dose. Not one. Now that's not to say that I didn't have a few shit nights where X was part of the mixture, but it was most certainly never the cause of the shit night. Here's a collection of a few of my more memorable experiences with that, and a few other substances that I encountered and experimented with over the course of what I romantically call my "Rave Days". In no particular order as to be honest the order has long escaped me, here's a few of my greatest hits.

One.

It was perhaps my fifth time to the city with Price. I was still crazy new to the scene, and to be honest so was he, but he still knew the lay of the land a bit better than I did. The scene had quite quickly begun to effect my life well outside the city, most obviously in the way that I dressed, as well as the way I behaved. My clothing had finally taken a step away from the style that I'd had almost since high school; shifting from the skin tight Levi 501's that had been popular for so long to the baggy Martha Francois Girbaud's that had taken over the rave culture. I'd gone from tight t-shirts to loose fitting hoodies, and no jewelry at all to a silver ring on three different fingers and a hoop earring in my ear, and had basically taken the very "relaxed" fashion of the scene to heart.

It (raves) had a similar effect on my day to day demeanor as well, as I'd found quite unintentionally that I had begun to drift away from the overly confrontational "angry guy" that had become a hallmark of my personality, and started to simply let the little shit slide. A huge change for me I assure you! I had also begun to gain a massive amount of confidence, not in any specific situation really, but just in myself in general, having started to finally decide that who I was wasn't so bad after all.

It was a warehouse party again, which was mostly where the bigger parties took place. As the scene took over the city, owners of all the huge warehouses down in the Army district were making a killing renting out spaces that had literally been empty for years. It meant that there was almost no limit to the size some of the parties would grow to, and that could sometimes mean more than three-thousand people!

This on the other hand was a much smaller "after" party that was taking place in a much more intimate space. We, along with pretty much everyone else in attendance had been at it the entire night before but as was usually the case once you were in the scene, one party was almost never enough. It was only the second time that we'd kept on going after the first big party was over, and again only the second time that I had gone for round two with the X. Man oh man was hit number two a rock-n-roller, and as it kicked in to full throttle, I was completely off my ass. So much so, that I'd fallen victim to what any self respecting raver had at least once in his or her career. It hit me so damn hard I threw up.

But, like any self respecting raver, I took the advice I was given by Price that very first night. "If you think you're gonna puke, do yourself a favor, swallow that shit back down!" Which of course was exactly what I did. Totally fucking disgusting without a doubt, but at $20 a pill, and with as long as it sometimes took to kick in, you didn't want to waste that shit! Especially not the stuff strong enough to make you a bit sick at first.

I didn't even have the energy to dance because the ecstasy was kicking in so hard, and I found that every sensation in my body was screaming for my attention, so with eyes only half open, I allowed it all to wash over my like a wave. The bass from the speakers was flowing right through me, the lights seemed to push and pull me along with their beams and I, well I didn't have a care in the world. As I allowed my gaze to criss cross the room satisfied to simply observe and soak in all that was happening, I saw her.

I saw her, and she saw me. Same look in her eyes, same clear satisfaction with the world and her place in it, and clearly the same thoughts flowing through her head, because she was walking toward me just as I was closing the distance to her.

Not a word was exchanged. No handshake, no happy hug that had become the standard raver greeting, even when meeting perfect strangers. She stood in front of me less than a foot away, a wave of hair flowing down across one eye as she looked up at me, and just like that, thought became action and I brushed the hair from her face, cupped her cheek in my hand and pulled her in for what was the single most monumental first kiss of a lifetime.

Lost in a kiss doesn't even begin to come close to describing it. It was all-encompassing... Eye's closed and locked, the light from the party flashing like echoes against my eyelids quickly turned into a kaleidoscope that was beyond three dimensional. Sounds became almost as physical as this incredible girl in my arms, and the kiss... Well I'm quite sure I'm not nearly a good enough writer to put into words just how amazing it became. There was no end to me and beginning to her. There was at least for a while no me really. Time became irrelevant, location was forgotten and everything that wasn't that kiss no longer existed. I have no idea how long we were there...

I can tell you firsthand it's true. People on drugs, more specifically on the same drugs are drawn to each other. They know just at a glance when they are looking at someone in the same mental space as someone else, and in this case, likes attract. I knew even without thinking that she was seeing the world through exactly the same eyes as me. An amazing thing really, when you consider that its as much your imagination driving you as the drug itself.

A lifetime later and we pulled back from that kiss. A minute or an hour of all knowing eye contact and we both stepped back, turned, and walked away. I never knew her name, never harder voice and never saw her again.

Two.

The first outdoor rave I ever attended was in Livermore California, at a fairground and sprint car dirt racetrack. I had driven the Chevy down on my own after a late night of shows, and was going meet Price as soon as I arrived. He'd given me a general idea of where in the party he was going to be, which posed no real problem as we'd become professionals at locating each other even in the largest of crowds.

I knew without a doubt two things. I knew Price would have scored some Ecstasy for me, and I knew that we were both going to want more, so I was on the lookout for any familiar faces as I searched for my partner in crime. As luck would have it, I'd only been in the mash of people for all of about ten minutes before I crossed paths with one of our most entertaining "rave" friends.

Dee was about as flamboyant as they came. Working as a female impersonator at the famous San Francisco Finocchio's, Dee could always be counted on for a few things. A good laugh, a crazy outfit, and ecstasy. As soon as he saw me he launched at me with a massive hug and a big kiss on the cheek! "DEAN!! BABY!!" He was off his ass! Dee was by and large usually one of the ones with the most solid grip on reality, as he was usually holding, but on this occasion he had clearly gone big.

He didn't even wait for me to ask, but simply started groping through all his pockets with a huge smile on his face, saying that he knew exactly what it was I needed, cause I clearly looked too god damn serious!

"Hold this..." Whoa was the only thought that crossed my mind. Dee had handed me a zip lock sandwich bag three quarters full with a slightly off white powder that was the exact same color as the powder you would find nestled happily in the gel caps named "Black Liquorish" that were the gold standard of X at the time. When all else failed, if you had a few caps of Black Liquorish in your pocket you were in for a good night.

"Here, take this too... Just tell me how many you fill and I'll catch you in a few", and with that, Dee sauntered off into the crowd to continue dancing his ass off.

The second bag Dee had handed me was another sandwich bag, this time filled with empty gel caps. As I stood there looking at the two bags in my hand, which in total must have been 500 doses worth at the very least, I quite suddenly came to grips with the fact that I was standing in the middle of a thousand people or more! I instantly hid my surprise packages, tried to clear the shock from my head, and started my search for Price in earnest. But not of course before I licked one finger and dipped it into the bag of terribly bitter chemicals, then popping it straight into my mouth.

"Price! Oh fuck man! You're never gonna believe this shit!" Clearly not paying attention to me, he started to tell me almost apologetically that he had yet to find any party favors for us, as all the usual suspects had not yet surfaced near him. As I dragged him to the side and told him who I had bumped into and what he'd given me, his eyes drifted down to the bag in each of my hands, and the same look of utter disbelief that must have been on my face now crossed his.

After filling a pretty decent number of caps, and dipping our fingers into the bag more than a few times a piece, we set off to find Dee and return the rest, as the last thing in the world either of us wanted to be doing was strolling around a drug infested rave with enough product to go down for distribution!

Bag returned, an unremembered amount of money handed to Dee, and a giggle between the two of us, we headed into the fray now pretty ridiculously fucking high ourselves. That night, like most of the big parties went by in a bit of a blur, being mostly water bottles and dancing, but two more memorable things happened.

First off, The lasers that had been set up as part of the light show had been streaming back and forth not only across the crowd, but across the scrub brush covered ground that surrounded the area, and actually managed to set alight a small fire on the side of one of the nearest hills. The music cut out instantly, and it's sudden absence when high as we were was felt like a blow to the gut. As the DJ took to the microphone to warn people of the danger of the fire and the impending end to the festivities, hundreds of intrepid ravers, myself included, ran the four or five hundred yards between the party and the fire, and stomped and water-bottled that fire to death. Fuck if we were gonna let something as paltry as fire screw up our party!

Second, The party was over, the last song was spinning from the DJ, and the sun was coming up. We had been partying our asses off all night long in the fairgrounds, and on the dirt racetrack for hours and hours, and dancing and stomping as we had been, we had kicked up a steady cloud of dust all night long that had gone unseen in the darkness. As the sun finally broached the foothills that surrounded us, everyone started to notice the same thing. Each and every one of us had been dusted with the fine tan particles that made up the topsoil of the area. There wasn't a single person that wasn't covered, and especially in our still very high states of mind, the lack of color, no black, no white, was not lost on us. It was our own rebirth of the 60's hippy movement embodied in the fact that at least for the briefest of moments, we were all exactly the same.

Three.

"You said what, and I said who!" I tried. I really REALLY fucking tried, but it simply was not working! Again it was an after party. This time, in a local early morning hot spot called

DV-8 (get it? Deviate?? HA! Still makes me laugh…). Price and I as always arrived to the club together in the Astrovan, and headed inside to continue on with what had been another pretty big night. I'd headed upstairs to sit and chill by the window for a while as I waited for hit number 2, or was in number 3 kick in? At any rate, looking in a bit of a daze out the window at the real world, lost in random thoughts, a tap to my shoulder caught my attention, and an outstretched hand with what was clearly a joint in it was offered to me.

Now I've never been much on pot. It just wasn't my kind of drug if I'm being honest, but still going from my previous doses that night, I didn't put a lot of thought into it as I took what was a pretty hefty pull and then passed the joint on its merry way. Five minutes later, it felt like a freight truck made of pure ecstasy slammed into me doing about a hundred miles per, and my first thought was "Oh fuck! Price!" The weed had acted as an incredible booster to the Ecstasy, and holy shit was it kicking in!

Down the stairs I went, although going down was a monumental effort, as it now appeared in my substantially altered state to look a bit like down climbing Mt. Everest. As I finally made it back down to the ground floor, having put to use the not insubstantial help of the railing and even a few people, I went about the almost impossible mission in my new mental state of finding Price, which I somehow managed to do in all of about 30 seconds.

I didn't say a word. I grabbed him by the arm, looked him dead in the eyes, and began leading him back up the stairs. I didn't say a word when I sat him down in the very spot I had just been. I'd backed up about ten feet and was leaning against the balcony railing when Price tried to stand up but stopped dead when I vigorously motioned for him to stay put! The joint, or perhaps just a joint was making its way toward Price, and as it was offered to him, he looked at me as if to say "this?" All I could do was nod.

After he'd passed it on, Price once again began to stand, and I once again aggressively motioned for him to stay. Then I waited. I leaned (I think I was leaning, although I could have been standing on my head for all I knew) against that railing and didn't take my eyes off of him until… BAM! Prices eyes lit up like someone had just shot him in the ass with a happy taser. We both started laughing so damn hard that we were both practically doubled over in hysterics!

We'd somehow managed to make it down to the dance floor in an idiotic attempt to go out and groove a little bit, and although we hit the floor, I don't think we danced a step. Somewhere in-between finding our way back down the stairs and onto the floor, I forgot how to speak english. Every time he tried to get anything across to me, it sounded like Greek…

"You said what, and I said who!!" Had to have been 20 minutes at least. There we stood, head to head and smack in the middle of the dance floor, the same words being said over and over and over and… "Okay" he'd say with an incredible amount of patience "one more time…. You said what… and I, said, WHO."

Four.

It was the 25th anniversary of the world famous "Peoples Park" in Berkeley. In 1969, Peoples Park officially went from a derelict lot to the epicenter of the Sixties movement in Northern California. Everything from massive parties to huge protests had taken place in that park with the likes of the Beetles, Jim Morrison and the Doors, Bob Dylan and many more spending time within its confines. Twenty five years later, Price, myself and about a thousand of our closest friends were there to celebrate it.

As was the standard, we had been going big the night before, and by the time we were stretched out and enjoying the sunshine on the grass, we had been going strong for a good dozen hours. As we relaxed and waited for the next round to do its thing, I don't think either Price or I had a single complaint with the world.

We sat and watched the crowd ebb and flow to the tunes being spun somewhere on the other side of the park. Naked guy was going strong in his Birkenstocks and backpack, little tater-tot bouncing to the beat. Hippies and Ravers everywhere doing their thing and enjoying the day in their own way, and us just watching it all happen.

Lying on the grass, leaning back on my elbows looking out across it all with my glasses sagged down on my nose, I almost didn't notice the hand that came into my field of vision with a joint in it, clearly just hovering there until I reached up to take it. As I accepted the offered joint from the unknown hand and took a healthy toke, I looked up over my left shoulder to a sight I never would have expected.

Dressed in blue shorts, a blue shirt, duty belt and a badge, what was clearly a uniformed Berkeley cop smiling ear to gold hoop earring clad ear waited just long enough to see the recognition in my eyes before he strolled along his merry way, knowing damn well he'd just blown my mind.

Five.
That time I ended up lying on my back on top of a pool table, doing what was clearly a great impression of a back-stroke. When Price found me and asked just what in the fucking hell I was doing, I answered quite matter of factly that clearly I was a fish. The dust that you can always see under the lights that hang over pool tables looked to me like air bubbles floating up underwater, and I found it infinitely entertaining at the time to imagine myself a fish, swimming around without a care in the world. Of course I knew I wasn't a fish, but that did nothing to diminish the raw entertainment I felt by pretending!

Six.

It was a full moon rave, and It took place in a bird sanctuary in San Jose California. Price, I and an entire van load of people had made the trek from a party in San Francisco and had managed to navigate our way as far as the parking lot of the party but opted to stay in the van instead, chilling on the bed and watching the scene happen through our picture frame onto the world in the shape of an Astrovan door.

One of the ravers that had managed to ride to the party with us was a San Francisco stripper and part time drug dealer name Evangeline. Not only did Evangeline have the most massive set of tits I'd ever seen nature provide, but she also had a massive crush on me, and a rather large quantity of a designer drug called "Illusion" that was making the rounds at the time.

I didn't even have to ask before the first tab was dissolving on my tongue, but did make sure to ask if she had enough for Price to play as well. Ten minutes later, when she asked how I was feeling and I shrugged my shoulders in response, a second tab went on both my and Prices tongue. By tab number 3, Price had decided he was all set. By tab number 5, the look of shock on Prices face as he watched it disappear down my throat told me that I should probably be all set as well! So of course I took a 6th.

As the sun came up over the sanctuary with birds flying and water glistening, I was way too damn busy to notice the scenery, as I was happily paying attention to the fact that the gravel in the parking lot where the van had been parked was hopping of it's own volition up and down to the beat of the music. Fuck me, I was really really really fucking high! Luckily, I was also really really really fucking happy, as the stuff we had taken was a mix between Ecstasy and LSD, so I was hallucinating my ass off, but I was really quite pleased about it.

And then, without warning and completely against my wishes, I was having a conversation with a police officer. "Is this your vehicle Sir?" Oh shit, he's talking to me! "Ahh, yes officer, this is my, ahh, Astrovan." "Well, the party is over, so I need for you and any of your passengers to get in the vehicle now and go." In a moment of clarity I decided I simply had to ask him point blank "You want ME to get into this van, and drive it. Away. Now?"

My pupils were completely blown. They had to have been solid black even though I was looking the cop in the face with the sun coming up behind him. There was simply no way this guy didn't know that I was high as FUCK! But what was I to do? I was clearly damned if I did and damned if I didn't, so, fuck it.

I was pretty positive that the second I turned over the engine, this cop was gonna reach in shut it down and toss me in cuffs, but to my and everyone else surprise, the next thing we knew, we were motoring on down the road completely against our wishes, navigating our way back to San Francisco by psychedelic Zen means…

"Ding Ding Ding" was the sound of the bells as the train track gates dropped, warning of the oncoming train, and prompting me, even in my drastically altered state to put the van in park and wait it out. The music was cranking, the half dozen really fucked up people in the back of the van were having a blast, and Price and I sitting up front were as happy as could be.

Now both of us by now were very aware that the drugs we were constantly partaking in were great at altering our perception of time, but there was no doubt from either of us that we'd been waiting a long damn time, and even though the gates were still down and the bell was still ringing we had yet to see any sign of a train. And then, without ever having seen one, the gates went up and the bells stopped ringing. Price and I looked at each other as if to say "did we just fucking miss an entire train?" and I put the van in drive, wondering if I was just that fucking high.

"BAAAAAAAAAAHHHHHHHHRRRRRRRaaaaaaarrr". The van was in drive and I'd just let my foot off the brake. My right foot had that instant started to apply pressure to the accelerator when the train came barreling through. The gate was up, the bells were still quiet, and both Price and I were completely sober. Instantly. Although the high most certainly came back, as Price and I watched the cars of the train clickity clack in front of us, I had never been more clear… Not one person in the back of the van had noticed a thing, and when the end of that day came around and I thought back on the events, still a bit altered, I had to wonder if it had happened at all.

Seven.

That time I ended up in hot pants, fish net stockings and shirtless on stage, wearing a mask and wrapped in bright red twine.

Eight.

Miss "Make a monster noise" who would, upon greeting us each and every time, make some random monster noise, whether it be a growl, a bark, some kind of squeaky screechy shrill or some other bizarre sound of her own design and then refuse to converse with us in the least until we had done the same.

No Guts, No Glory

By my second year with Take-it-Off, there had been a most definite changing of the guard at the El Dorado Saloon. Gone now were the days of the Spandex, cuffs and collars, and the next generation of "entertainer" had most certainly taken over. I'd been on stage every Thursday for quite some time now, mostly because of my dancing, which had morphed into a funky high energy "rave" style, due completely to my ongoing experiences in the city and I'd managed to solidify the anchor position in the show and was always the last act to hit the stage. I had also managed somehow to become the MC for the troupe as well, which not only kept me busy through the entire night but meant that I was constantly in front of the crowd keeping the energy up and getting them to laugh and enjoy, but mostly to wonder when I was gonna take off my fucking pants!

The other young guys, Donny, Vince and Eric each had their own style as well, and between the four of us and one hold out from the "good ol' days", we had managed to put together a pretty damn good stage show. No more "Greased Lightning" routines. Now we came out to Nine Inch Nails "I wanna fuck you like an animal" and put on a blistering sexually charged stage humping routine that never failed to crank the humidity in the club up to a good ninety percent!

No more horrible "YMCA" shit, but instead a dance routine choreographed by Price himself which had us dancing a slightly outdated but still fun hip-hop routine to Janet Jacksons "Rhythm Nation". Each of the guys had in turn found a way to either spice up the old classic costumes, or ditch them all together in favor of something a lot more indicative of their personalities.

The crowd had, in response to all the changes not only swelled in size, but had its own changing of the guard as well as news that the El Do was no longer the boring show a lot of them had come to expect and skip but one they wanted to check out because it was always changing and always exciting. Thursday nights had become something that I and all the other guys had come to look forward to each week because we'd managed to turn it into one hell of a fun time, not just for the crowd, but for the entertainers as well.

As was becoming the standard, the show had gone perfectly, and as I hit the stage running, the crowd was huge, happy and really fucking loud. My dancing at the time was as high energy as It had ever been, and as I went off to one of the songs I'd fallen in love with in the city I was feeling great! Feeling great, right up until I found myself curled up in the fetal position on stage, less than half dressed, glistening with a bit of baby oil and in more pain than I had ever been in.

During one of the more acrobatic dance moves that I was learning, I had managed to quite literally bust a gut while I was twisting and turning around. I had no idea what I'd done to myself, but as I lie there in agony, I knew it wasn't good!

An Inguinal Hernia is a protrusion of the abdominal-cavity contents through the
Inguinal canal. Symptoms are present in about 66% of affected people. This
may include pain, sometimes severe and discomfort especially when coughing   or exercising. A bulging area will commonly occur. This bulging is caused as the
abdominal-cavity contents (intestines) push through the damaged muscle tissue.
The main concern with this is strangulation of the protruding intestines, where
blood supply can be blocked, and lead to much more serious medical issues.

- Wiki

In short, I'd ripped a hole in the muscles all of about two inches above my balls, and as I danced, everything behind it was trying to push its way through the hole. I cannot even begin to describe just how much it sucked! After a good five minutes of rolling around on the floor of the stage in absolute agony I was finally able to let the guys help me off and into the dressing room. An hour later, with lots of help and multiple refusals for an ambulance, I was back inside my van and slowly on the way to the hospital.

By the next morning, the surgery was scheduled and booked for Thursday, six days later. The only way to deal with a hernia such as mine was either to wear this horrible looking belt/jock strap contraption around your lower waist with a hole cut in the middle so your cock and balls could hang through, then acting to keep all the important stuff inside (not exactly good for my work) or to let a surgeon cut you open, push everything into the position it was suppose to be and stitch the muscle back up.

The last thing I remember as I went under the anesthesia was telling the Doc not to fuck up anything important down there as I was my career he had in his hands! As a quick side-note, let me just say that it being my first surgery, I was wholly unprepared for just how fucking cool being put under is. What a rush! Even though it did only last about 30 seconds before I was out…

When I woke, it hardly felt as if time had passed. I felt no pain what-so-ever, and in fact, didn't have a care in the world! As I started to get my wits about me and realized I was in the recovery area they had told me about, I just smiled, and slowly surveyed my surroundings. Bed, another bed, curtains, some beepy thing across the way, I.V. stand next to me, tube in my arm, crisp white sheets tight across my body, huge red circle across my mid section… Wait.

It took a lot of effort to assess the situation. As I lie there looking at what was clearly a big red stain smack in the middle of my sheets, somewhere in the back of my mind flashed the words "blood" and "bad". Still, in my current chemically altered mental state I didn't really think that the situation called for alarm, no matter what might be wrong, so in just the most mellow way ever, I waved happily at a nurse that chanced to look my direction and very casually point at what I assumed was not a normal part of my post-op recovery.

One nurse was standing at the head of the bed talking quite cheerfully to me about the weather? Her cat? I really had no idea to be honest. A second nurse who was obviously a bit agitated was stripping the sheets and thin blanket from the bed and quite deftly wiping blood from across my stomach, balls and what not, while yet a third nurse was doing something with my I.V. that I couldn't quite fathom, right up until the world started spinning again in the most pleasant way. They never did explain what had happened...

Back home and on my couch. Water within reach, piss bottle within reach, remote control within reach, Vicodin within reach. All was right with the world, except... You know that bit about not leaving a post-op patient alone for the first 24 hours? Yeah, well apparently they forgot to give that information to my father, because as soon as he had me situated he was out the door!

Now lets talk about Vicodin. Although by this point I had plenty of experience with the so called street "Party" drugs, I had never taken a prescription opioid before, and damn... This shit was STRONG! For those that have been living in a cave for the past 20 years, heres a tiny bit of info on the stuff:

Hydrocodone/Paracetamol, also known and marketed by the trade name Vicodin
is a combination of a powerful opioid pain medication, Hydrocodone with

acetaminophen. It is used as a prescription drug to treat sever pain. Side
effects can be: Lightheadedness, dizziness, euphoria, sedation, nausea and
vomiting, headaches, poor reasoning skills and lack of coordinated motor skills.

What the warning label on the bottle they give you doesn't say, is that Vicodin is basically nothing more than a very highly refined and specialized heroin. So there I sat on my couch, a stapled fresh four inch hole in my gut, stoned off my ass on legal smack prescribed and dispensed to me in a huge bottle of chalky white pills courtesy of my surgeon.

The pain I felt as I sat there not five hours post-op was all but a distant memory. The bottle of pills had quite clearly said something about how much to take, and how often I should take it, and I remember my father saying something about it as well but I had apparently chosen to disregard all of it and took a pill whenever the fuck I felt like it, which I seemed to feel like quite a lot.

They aren't kidding when they say that shit dulls your reasoning, of that I am quite sure now because about an hour before I knew the El Dorado show was going to begin, I decided that there was simply no good reason why I should miss it! Sure, there was no way I was going to be able to dance, but I could sure as shit sit on the side of the stage and MC the hell out of the thing!

It was a little difficult climbing into the van I'll admit, but it wasn't pain that was slowing me down, it was just this strange tingly weak feeling. Driving to the show wasn't just easy, it was fucking fun! I had my tunes cranked up and the van almost bouncing down the road just from the immense amount of bass my speakers could put out, and by the time I pulled up to the show, I was in a fantastic mood having been singing along at the top of my lungs the whole way!

They were shocked to see me no doubt, but they were also happy as hell, because none of the guys had any idea what to do as an MC, and had been arguing over who was going to be stuck with the job since they showed up. As the music kicked in an the first routine got underway, I was seated quite comfortably and happily by the side of the stage, DJ voice in full effect as I announced each of the dancers in turn. One of the guys had even grabbed a beer pitcher from behind the bar and put a sign in front of it that read "Pity tips for Dean".

About half way through the show I was starting to get just a touch uncomfortable, but shrugged it off, as I had yet to feel even a stitch of pain since I woke up from the surgery. But then about the time the big routine was almost over and the last two dancers were getting ready to go on, I was actually starting to hurt, and reached over to grab a couple of pills from the bottle that I had left right within reach, if I had only been sitting on my couch at home. FUCK!

By the time the show finally finished, a few things were foremost in my mind. First, the pity jar that had been put out for me had more cash in it than any of the guys had made that night, which was kick ass! Second, I was in a whole lot of pain as the last effects of the Vicodin I had taken now hours before was fading fast and third, I still had to get myself home.

Standing up from the chair beside the stage was an exercise in pure agony. I didn't stop to talk to anyone once I'd managed to start moving, but simply grabbed the entire pitcher full of cash and hobbled straight out the door. It took almost everything I had to make it into the drivers seat of the van and as I turned the key, covered in a fine layer of cold sweat, my entire body was telling me that I was a complete idiot because I had gone through a major surgery THAT VERY MORNING!

Even the act of moving my right foot from gas to brake pedal was excruciating, and as I parked my car in my apartments lot

I knew I couldn't move anymore. So I sat. Windows down, van off, not moving. Trying in fact not to even take a deep breath. I needed help in a major way but had no idea how to get it! I didn't have a cell phone, and at at eleven o'clock at night the parking lot wasn't exactly bustling with activity, so, I sat. And sat. Two different times I decided that I absolutely had to do something, but each time I tried to move anything other than my head or arms a bolt of pain would shoot up through me that was so strong I thought I just might pass out.

As the sun came up the next morning I was in dire straights, and couldn't imagine just how much worse things may get when finally, a spot of good luck! The newspaper boy, cycling around on his morning route was just coming out of the walkway leading toward my apartment and past my van. I yelled, or should I say I attempted to yell as loud as I could for him as he rolled past the van, and was pretty sure I'd failed, when moments later he re-appeared along the side of my Chevy, asking timidly if I'd called for him.

It took a bit of convincing to say the least, but the kid could clearly see I was in some major pain, and decided against the whole "don't talk to strangers, especially ones that yell to you from inside a VAN, and especially don't go into their apartment alone rule" and grabbed the bottle of Vicodin from exactly were I'd left it 11 hours before.

I tossed three of the foul bitter pills into my mouth dry and chewed those little fuckers up like they were Pez candies. With no water to help wash them down, and dehydrated from not drinking anything for more than 7 hours I sat in the Chevy, twitching from the horrible taste in my mouth and the random stabs of pain in my gut for almost another hour before I could finally move.

The fuzzy feeling of the Vicodin had started to take effect within all about about fifteen minutes after I'd chewed them up, but I had been in such complete and utter agony, that I waited until I was flat out stoned and almost completely numb from head to toe before I tried to move a muscle.

I learned two very valuable lessons that night that have served me well ever since. First, I'm a complete fucking idiot. And second, I firmly believe in the new world adage "Better living through chemicals".

Shifting Gears

Clearly, group sex was the answer.

For three years now I'd been working as a professional stripper. It had been a hell of a job all and all, and I don't think I had any real complaints about it in me. Between the job and the rave scene, time had literally just flown by, and even then I found myself looking back with more than just a little amazement. But I suppose like it is with all things, it was most certainly starting to get if not old then at least certainly a touch stale.

Generally I'd work four days a week, and only three of them terribly busy, but when I was busy, I was really fucking busy. An average "work" night of shows for me would begin at anywhere between four or five in the evening, and end at close to midnight. Eleven shows a night was the average, and trust me, it was exhausting. There was no time during the course of any of those nights to do a damn thing other than go go go. Eating? Didn't happen. Drinks usually consisted of whatever the parties might have given me, or the occasional can of soda I'd grab if I had time to stop into a gas station.

Couple all of that with the fact that I'd made "raving" my full-time job for over two years now, and you'd start to understand just how damn tired I was getting. The rave scene had most certainly taken a turn, and unfortunately not for the better. After what had been a life changing community filled with amazing music, people, mind altering and mind expanding drugs and just a general lust for life, it was quickly turning toward the darker side and it wasn't something I had much of a taste for. Friends, or should I say "rave friends" had begun turning to drugs that were way outside anything I found attractive, and nothing I saw or heard from them worked to change my mind.

Coke, Crack, Crank, Meth…. They were the primary reasons rave's were now seeing something they never had before. Fighting, theft, dis-trust and a general uneasy feeling in town that started leaving me empty inside instead of full. When I had started the whole ride with Price and the gang, ravers weren't just going big at the parties, they were also taking really good care of themselves outside of them. I swear you've never seen so many muscular, slim heathy people in your life! And why? Well its simple really, the drugs we enjoyed worked a hell of a lot better on a trim healthy body! I'm willing to bet though that you've never seen a healthy looking Meth Head.

When it came to work the story wasn't all that different, and I wasn't the only one that was starting to feel a bit dissatisfied, and more and more the conversation at the El Dorado was about striking out on our own. Making our own rules, and doing things our own way instead of putting more money in the bank for Take-it-Off. We had made the "new" El Dorado show more popular than it had ever been, and gave zero credit to the company for it's success. Each of us had begun to wonder if the telegram side of the business might not do better if we were taking care of that as well.

Tensions had begun to grow between the dancers and the management of Take-it-Off steadily over the last year or so for a number of reasons. Although the dancers who worked full-time at it were pulling down a fair bit of money, there hadn't been an increase in our per show pay even though the company was charging more for services. We were being booked with shows closer together in time, but further apart in distance which occasionally caused dancers to entirely miss shows, which per the company the dancer was required to pay for, and Rick himself was just being a bit of a cock.

Although Rick had been approached by a number of the dancers on quite a few different occasions he clearly didn't want to hear anything about it and went from simply dismissing the ideas we came to him with, to actively telling entertainers that if they didn't like the way he was doing things they were quite welcome to quit. Not exactly a good way to keep a bunch of young and mostly irresponsible people in line. As any parent will tell you, most times if you tell a kid to do something its the first damn thing they work to avoid.

It was Vince, one of the now senior dancers that had the idea to have a little sneaky company meeting and talk about the possibility of doing things on our own. It was also Vince who thought talking to a few of our female counterparts in the company would be a great idea as well. There was no doubt that the men of Take-it-Off did huge business for the company, but compared to what the women brought in we were small change! No way could we even think about striking out on our own if we didn't have at least a few of the girls along with us. With that, we set up a group meeting between the four of us guys, and five of the T.I.O. girls at my place the following week to shoot the shit and see if we thought we could make it happen.

When Vince showed up early at my place with some beer to put into the fridge and the idea to order a pizza I thought it was a good plan. When he suggested we hang out by the pool as well I thought it was a pretty good idea too. When he pulled out a baggie with what was clearly a good dozen hits of "X" I knew that very little talk of business was going to get done!

"Just do me a favor Vince. Please keep that shit put away until we at least have a chance to talk a little about all this, okay?"

"Totally Dude, I get it! I figured you'd be into it with all the time you spent doing the party thing, and most of the girls coming tonight have never tried it, so they were super stoked... Actually I don't think most of us have! Should be fun!"

And with that little bit of news, my expectations for the night changed drastically. Four guys and five girls in my little one bedroom apartment. All of them would soon be "rolling" their asses off, and for most of the girls, and at least two of the guys, it was their first experience with Ecstasy. I was pretty sure the night could now be counted on to get just a little weird.

Twenty minutes. I think thats about how long conversation about work lasted. Now don't get me wrong. I wasn't exactly this super responsible organizer type that wanted to really push for change and rally everyone around a common cause, but I honestly did want to at least hear what other people thought about trying to strike out on our own.

The general consensus from the few that were actively engaged in the conversation was that sure, we could easily put together a stage show no problem, and sure, we could continue to do telegrams with the crew sitting around my living room, but we'd need to come up with a business name first and of course advertise, but clearly since there was a bag full of Ecstasy sitting on my coffee table which Vince had prominently displayed almost immediately, the meeting about logistics could wait for another occasion.

Vince had snatched the bag up off the table and circled the room quickly, tossing a dose into everyones open mouths before anyone had a chance to say a thing. When he finally got to me, he politely placed one in the palm of my hand, and gave me a look that clearly said "C'mon man, fuck it… This is gonna be FUN!"

From then on, I ended up being a lot more in control and in charge than I wanted, but it was never going to be any other way. Considering the majority of the gang had never tried the stuff, I had no doubt they were gonna be a bit out of it, but easy to control. I also knew instantly from the taste of the pill as it hit my tongue that Vince had managed to get ahold of some seriously good stuff, and although I was sure I would enjoy it, I knew it wasn't going to throw me over the edge like it was some of this crew!

Door locked, twice. Music on, but not too loud. A few sour candies and treats and a shit ton of water grabbed quickly from the mini-mart on the corner that I knew the newbie's were gonna love, and then it was just a waiting game. I was fielding a ton of questions from the girls about what to expect, as they had all known my reputation for being in the City every weekend, and as I filled them in on what was most likely to come, I was keeping a sharp eye out for the telltale smile that would eventually creep across each and every face in the room.

One of the girls that had never done the stuff before happened to answer her phone to find her mother on the other end of the line. The music was turned down a bit so she could hear, and I watched her movements and mannerisms as if I were viewing a movie I'd seen a hundred times before. As the drugs washed over her almost in an instant, it slammed into her so forcefully that it caused her to practically moan "Oh my FUCKING GOD! Mom I gotta go!" and drop the phone on the floor.

I watched that reaction repeat itself 8 more times over the course of the next few minutes, and even though I was getting hit quite hard myself, I'd spent so long now in this exact state that I was still basically in complete control. The real plus to having partied as much as I had was that I could still enjoy the amazing feeling the drug could give me (although never like the early days) but still play it as if I were stone cold sober and cool as hell. From then on, and for at least the next hour, I got to play tour guide…

The sour candies had come in quite handy and had me laughing my ass off as the sight someone rolling while trying to desperately cope with something terribly sour, clearly unsure if they were enjoying it but just as unsure if they wanted to spit it out had me almost in hysterics! Faces twisted in sour agony with no desire to make it stop was just some funny shit! Then I got them all well and deep into a few songs here and there that were my favorites in the moments when dancing was the last thing on ones mind. But, inevitably, one of the girls discovered how good it felt to run her hands through one of the other girls hair. Then how good it felt to have her hand massaged, and then...

Let me be the first to say that I'm not exactly a huge fan of the whole group sex thing. I suppose depending on who you are a threesome could be considered group sex, and if I'm being honest, even that can be a bit of a pain, but I'm also a guy, and if there's two girls and I involved, I suppose I can muddle through. But this, well this was just... Messy. It's not that there were a bunch of other guys in the mix either. After as long as I'd lived in Northern California, and especially after all the party time I'd spent in San Francisco, I had exercised any homophobic demons I might have had long before. Not that I had any desire to cross swords with anyone, but I was far from worried about it.

I honestly think from the time the first hand was being rubbed, to the time the first naked body was being slobbered and slid all over was all of about 10 minutes! This group was wasting no damn time. Like I said though, "Messy" seemed to be the best word to describe it all. They were all so clearly fucked out of their minds that any pleasant coordination you might want and or expect from someone trying to get you off was seriously lacking. I actually had to stop one of the girls from giving me a hand job (at least I assume that's what she was trying to do) because it was so bad and so out of whack that I would have derived more pleasure from shoving my dick into a bag of frozen peas.

One huge upside to my experience with the drug in question was my bodies ability not only to fight off any negative effects like clenching your jaw, or rolling your eyes involuntarily around your skull, but in retaining the ability to do the one thing all the other guys were currently having a really hard (not hard) time with!

I stayed pretty damn busy once the girls caught on to the situation, let me tell you! Watching poor Vince and the boys do what looked a lot like trying to shove a length of toothpaste back into the tube was part painful and part hilarious if I'm telling the truth, and it wasn't just the girls who took notice of the fact that I wasn't having the same issues. By the time each of the fellas had tried, and tried again, and the girls had each tried and tried again to help them with their dilemma and all given up, all the boys ended up spending a whole lot of time eating pussy while I got fucked. Still messy as hell I'll tell ya, but I was clearly winning on that particular night!

Not that I hadn't fallen victim to the worst catch-22 ever, because I most certainly had. Ecstasy had the incredible ability to turn a guy into the most sexually charged, sensual creature walking the face of the earth, and at the same time, give him a limp dick that would make him jealous of a wet noodle! Fucking brutal stuff let me tell you. I will tell you one benefit you could get out of a situation like that though... A deep desire to please the living hell out of whoever you were with, and let me tell you, spend enough time crazy horny but completely unable to fuck, and the one thing you'll walk away with is the ability to eat pussy, and a real desire to do it!

The one major downside to the drug for me was the complete inability to "finish" as long as the chemical was still coursing through my veins. As long as there was still even a lingering hint of the effects of Ecstasy in me, the possibility of an orgasm was non-existent. That A. Made me a bit on the ornery side, and B. Made the girls think I was super human, because I had to call quits on the whole group sex thing as soon as the lube ran out, and the guys couldn't move their jaws anymore.

All and all, I wouldn't exactly call the so called "Business Meeting" much of a success, but I certainly couldn't complain about the topics we'd covered! In the end, the only business we ever got going was the business from that night, and I knew without a doubt that my professional stripping days were nearing their end.

The Wheels on the Bus go Round and Round...

"Fuck it Rick, I quit". And that was that. I'd had just a horrible fucking week, and I was done. Done with it all.

It was about six months after our failed attempt to band together a group of strippers to start our own successful business. All we'd managed to accomplish was quite a few stains on my carpet from spilled drinks and pizza, and a bunch of bodily fluids, none of which led to or caused by an orgasm.

I'd actually not only started dating the most adorable little Latin girl who worked as a leasing agent in the apartment complex I lived in, but had been convinced by her that doing the same job she did there would be a great source of extra income for me and I'll be damned if I hadn't taken a gig renting out apartments. Even if she hadn't suggested that I try something different, I was really in need of a change, and one way or another it was going to happen.

The biggest benefit to the job was the fact that as soon as I took it, I lived rent free! The single largest bonus to the leasing companies employees was the fact that we all lived courtesy of the agency, which in a heartbeat saved me a good thousand a month. Not too damn bad at all... It was one of the factors that played a pretty decent part in telling Rick I'd had enough. The other part? My complete exit from the rave scene.

It had all just gotten to be way too much and even Price and I were having a difficult time keeping our friendship together. He had continued steadily with the San Francisco scene, and I, well I had all but stopped playing. It was the first time that he and I hadn't been on the same page about things in a very long time, and it had me more than a little off balance. We had been the SF dynamic Duo! Everyone that knew us knew us as

Price and Dean, and that just wasn't the case anymore. The real catalyst to my walking away from it all was bumping into one of my "rave friends" outside San Francisco. His name was Mike, and Mike had gotten started with it all around the same time as Price and I. The reason bumping into him pushed me out of the scene so forcefully was the fact that I hadn't even recognized him when he walked up to me on the street begging for change.

It shocked the living shit out of me. He looked like he'd aged ten years since the last time I'd seen him, and after he finally recognized me, he gave me the low-down on what he'd been doing. As it turned out, it was a shit load of crank. Twenty pounds lighter, twitching and scratching as if he had an anthill running up and down his back and clearly half out of his mind, all I could think of was how damn lucky I was that it hadn't been me. I gave Mike all the cash I had on me at the time, then turned and walked away not only from him, but from the scene as well. I never looked back.

About a month into renting apartments and getting quite a kick out of a paycheck that didn't have to be shoved down my pants, I decided enough was enough, and it was then that I walked away from Take-it-Off, and hung up my thong too. What was left of the appeal in being a stripper had faded like the joy I'd taken in raving, and with the shine off both my favorite pennies, it was time.

It turned out that having an actual schedule, a job that didn't require my always being lively and happy and not having to race around town all night long was really quite pleasant! What wasn't pleasant was the pretty drastic cut in pay I'd subjected myself to, but I'd managed to save up enough that at least for the time being I wasn't feeling it too badly.

The Astrovan that had served me so well over so many miles was finally starting to struggle mechanically, and not wanting to spend the money to keep her going since I no longer spent any time carting a bunch of high people around, I opted to trade her in to a local motorcycle shop on an even swap for a CBR-600F2. I'd been on and off motorcycles quite a bit in my life and since I wasn't going to be banging around town having to manage costume changes and a boom box, a break-even swap for a pretty little cafe-racer was great!

Drastic life changes were nothing new to me, and I went from the crazy lifestyle I'd been leading for three years now, to a relatively sedate one seeing just one girl, doing just one job, and being what was now widely considered an upstanding member of polite society. I fell into it like a duck to water, and was pretty damn good at the job if I do say so myself; but...

As the holidays rolled around, I'd decided to drive one state over to visit my sister and brother-in-law for Christmas mostly because my mother was going to be flying in from Seattle and had basically told me I had no choice in the matter. Hell of a fucking drive on a crotch-rocket let me tell you, but it turned out it was totally worth it. I'd never been to Las Vegas before and even though I was going to see the family, I was really curious to see what that town had to offer as well. I mean who hadn't heard the stories about Las Vegas?

I stood on Las Vegas Blvd at 11:30 at night on Christmas Eve, watching a full sized pirate ship sinking into the frothy water in front of The Treasure Island with bodies flying through the air, explosions going off from every direction and fire blasting so hot you could feel it from across the street. All the while surrounded about about 3,000 Japanese tourists, I knew without a shadow of a doubt that this was most certainly the town for me! It was simply too fucking insane for me to not call this place home!

I'd spent the following four days after Christmas filling out applications for every apartment complex and leasing company I could, and started the ride back to Sacramento determined to make the move. By the time I made it back to

Sac on the fifth day, I had a message on my machine asking me if I were available for an interview. By the seventh day I was playing sick with my job and back on the bike, motoring toward sin city on a mission. Back in Sac on day 9, and after a brief conversation via telephone with my new manager I'd put in my notice with my current employer and was busy planning my move! Las mother fuckin' Vegas here I come!

Like I said, major course deviations in my life just didn't seem to scare me, and as the last of my belongings went into the shipping container that would greet me in Las Vegas a week or so later, I didn't even blink. The only twinge I had through the whole thing was with the thought of leaving the wonderful girl I'd been dating in Sacramento, but the fact was she had a lot going on in her life as well, and I was too young and too selfish to even consider not leaving. (Looking back on it all, I'd almost be willing to say she was the one that got away…)

It was fucking awesome! Nobody aside from my family knew me. Not one person in Las Vegas was aware I use to be a stripper, a raver, or for that matter even gave a damn. I was hired right out the gate as the Assistant Manager for an apartment complex managed by a company named Pacific Properties, and even though I didn't have the qualifications for the job (and personally didn't think I could hack it), my new manager Ericka had pushed for me to be offered the position as she thought I'd be perfect for the job and would learn what I needed. I intended to make sure she was right, even though I thought she was crazy for making me management!

The first four weeks in Las Vegas were pretty good all and all. I'd left behind a lot of shit for a completely clean slate, and a clean slate is exactly what I got. It was also, if I'm being completely honest, a bit boring. I had as you can imagine, gotten my fill of the whole club scene, so the idea of hitting the hot spots in Vegas really didn't even cross my mind. Work, and learning all that I needed in order to not be a complete ass clown at the job was certainly a challenge and I was clearly making a fair amount of mistakes, but I was getting better every day and even starting to think I might actually be able to handle it.

I spent a good chunk of my off time in Las Vegas that first month simply strolling around The Strip, relaxing in a few of the nicer lounges in a few of the casinos, listening to live music, and generally just enjoying something completely new. I found that just walking around people watching completely sober and anonymous was really pretty nice, and didn't even feel the need to go out to meet anyone. Not dating was not an issue at all after having spent the last few years in full on party mode and the complete lack of them was honestly a relief.

What wasn't a relief was the feeling that hit me after I'd received my first paycheck and covered all my Vegas bills. Unlike the job I'd had back in Sacramento, the apartment I was provided in Vegas was only at a fifty-percent discount, not free. That, coupled with pretty high electrical and gas bills, and an outrageous cable costs, and I was in dire straights right out the gate! Not good at all!

I honestly had managed to save up a bit of money while still in Sacramento, but the truth of the matter was that the move itself, and the fact that I was complete shit with finances took care of the little nest egg I had in quite short order. By month two I was completely broke, and looking for ideas. The idea of another job to supplement my income really sucked though, and I guessed that any job I could manage on a part time basis was gonna have to be at least a three or four night a week thing, and I could picture exactly how things would go with that recipe. I'd be miserable and burnt out in a month or less!

The Olympic Garden. I'd actually managed to make it for all of about four months before I started walking back down that road. "One god damn lie" was all I could think as I walked through the door of the only club in Las Vegas that had a male review at the time. Wednesday was their open audition night, and I was sitting down having a quick chat with what was clearly someones grandma. Gloria was her name, and she was the sweetest looking lady you'd ever seen. Pants suit, grey hair in a short bob style cut with very tasteful jewelry, she sat across the table from me asking about my previous stage experience.

"Well… We have nine guys performing with us now, and to be blunt, I'm not really sure that a tenth is necessary. I'll tell you what though. Come back next week same day and I'll put you up first on stage and take a look. If I like what I see then maybe we can use you as a substitute now and then."

I really didn't want to do the stripper thing again, but with the money that I wasn't making ensuring a life with little enjoyment in a town I'd moved to so that I could enjoy, I figured that it was at least worth a shot. If I managed to get the gig, it would only be three nights a week. There wouldn't be any driving all over town, no eleven costume changes a night, no special requests, none of that shit. Even if the money wasn't spectacular, it would bridge the gap between fucking broke and fucking living, and as the week went by, I dusted off a couple of costumes, came up with a play list of tunes, and prepared for yet another fucking stripper audition.

The one and only O.G.

The Olympic garden was one of, if not the most recognizable strip clubs in all of Las Vegas. The self proclaimed "Only strip show on The Strip", it was most certainly easy to spot. Sitting just kitty-corner from the Stratosphere Hotel and Casino, the massive two story bright white building, with its pink trim, ornate iron work and a massive "OG" neon sign was pretty damn hard to miss. It had earned itself quite a reputation over the years for a number of reasons.

First off, it was upon its opening, physically the largest strip club in Las Vegas. It was not only an enormous building with two levels, a main room downstairs with five separate stages for the girls, a VIP room with its own private stage and four different bars, it had an upstairs with a huge main stage as well as its own bar and a completely separate entrance. The upstairs even sported a glass walled shower where entertainers could be paid extra to go get wet for customers willing to pay. The OG also boasted that it had the capacity to hold close to fifteen hundred people at once, which was an enormous number of people to cram into a strip club. Rumor had it that the OG had been started by a Greek mafia family, and if rumors were correct, they were damn good at what they did.

About the time my audition was coming around, the OG had been at it for many years, and on any given night there would be anywhere from two to four hundred female dancers inside, catering to the visual desires of three or four times as many men. The money that came through that place was almost beyond belief, and somewhere along the lines someone decided that adding some swinging dick into the mix for a bit of extra income was worth a shot.

The "Men of The Olympic Garden" had only been around for just over a year when I tried out, and the nine guys that worked there were managing to bring down some pretty decent coin. The review itself took place in what was originally suppose to be the "Champagne Room" for VIP guests. It had been converted over for the guys, with its one small stage, and had seating for about 100 women if they were crammed in. It also had the smallest god damn dressing room I'd ever seen.

Early as always, I ended up having to wait to meet Gloria out in the front room, and although I was doing my best not to look like a customer, I couldn't help but watch all the mostly naked women strolling by, each looking at me as if to asses wether or not I should be approached as a potential paycheck. Just about the time a rather overly silicone enhanced blonde started to saunter my way, Gloria appeared from a back room, took one look at me and barked to the girl "Back off Vette, he's one of mine." A curt smile from "Vette" to Gloria, a slightly nastier version to me and she was off into the dimly lit club to find some work.

Gloria, for her matronly appearance turned out to be anything but. She laid it out pretty straight for me from the start.

"Look, The boys that have been working with me here have all been here for a while now, and they work well together. We audition people now and then, but it's been a while, and nobody has yet to really stand out, so you're gonna have to do your best to have any chance." I could clearly see while she was talking to me that she was trying to scope out my demeanor and my build, and didn't seem all too displeased so far. "You'll go up first, so there won't be much in the way of a crowd as this show runs from eight till two in the morning, so our customers know they can show up later if they want, but I'm gonna grab some of our girls to come in and watch so they can tell me what they think".

So far it seemed pretty straight forward, and wasn't much of anything I hadn't expected.

"Only a few rules for you… One, Keep your cock in your shorts. Always. We aren't running that kind of show, and aren't looking to piss off vice. Two, Keep the girls you're dancing for under control. They can get pretty grabby, a whole lot more than men, and I don't want to see anyones hands where they shouldn't be, and three, Those hands, they include yours! No getting grabby with the customers! You're here for work. If you want to get laid, go to a fucking nightclub. Be sexy, but don't cross the line." She didn't bother to expand on exactly where that line may be…

I'd expected when I got into the back room and the other guys started to arrive, that I'd be in for a fair amount of attitude, being that I would expect to be seen as an interloper in their eyes, but in all honesty, I got handshakes from most of them, and even a conversation or two and a "good luck" before It was time for me to go up. I assumed that either they were alright with the idea of new dancers coming in, or they just didn't think I had a chance. Either way, fuck it!

As I hit the stage to my now signature "DA DA DA, Get ready for this" Song, there were only about 30 women in the club, but I'd worked doing telegrams for such small crowds for so long, that it didn't really bother me. That, and the fact that the only women I really had to try and impress was Gloria gave me the inspiration I needed to make sure I danced my ever loving ass off!

I'd almost climbed down off the stage once I'd stripped down to a brand new (Las Vegas purchased, and let me tell you they had an amazing selection!) thong, but was waved back onstage by Gloria, and quickly discovered that the padded rail that ran around the octagon shaped stage was there for a reason. Affectionately named "The Meat Rack" in this club, the money came to me, I didn't go to the money, and if I'm being honest it was too damn easy. Cash either shoved into my thong, or down the front of their blouses or even between their teeth for me to retrieve, I didn't even have to walk anywhere to get the cash but instead just slide back and forth to whoever had the money.

As the third song I was given came to and end and I gathered my costume, hoped down the stairs and was heading toward the dressing room when I was immediately approached by a very pretty little brunette who batted her eyes at me, and asked teasingly for a "Table Dance". I really had no idea what she was talking about, but as I looked over at Gloria, she nodded to me as if to say, "get to it!" And I was led to the nearest booth by my, customer?

Still just clad in my thong, the second entertainer for the night was already up on stage with his music playing, so the girl motioned for me to sit down next to her.

"So I'm Ella. I work here too!" She yelled over the sound of a slightly too loud "Thunder Struck" by AC/DC... It seemed even in Vegas some of the guys were desperately outdated. "So this is your first time dancing here? When I told her that yeah, I'd just moved up from California and was looking for some extra work, she hooted, and told me how cool she thought it was that she was gonna take my OG virginity!

She quite quickly explained that a "table dance" for me was exactly the same as it was for the girls in the other end of the club. When I'd been waiting for Gloria not even an hour before, I had the chance to see from a distance the girls dancing for men scattered around the club, and although I didn't see how I was gonna have the chance to be nearly as sexy as the brief glimpses I'd taken, I figured I could sure as hell give it a shot.

I guess I must have been the only guy of legal age out there who had never been to a strip club before. I suppose about the time that the urge to head to such a place would have hit me, I was already not only working as a professional stripper myself, but was way too wrapped up in the San Francisco scene to give a fuck about a titty bar.

As the next song kicked in and I stood up to face little miss smiles and cleavage, I'll admit I had to concentrate a bit to avoid any unintentional reactions as she grabbed my hips and pulled me toward her a bit, but seeing that gloria was not too far over my shoulder kept anything from getting too out of hand. It seemed my dick had learned its lesson, at least this time!

Then, only thirty seconds into the song, little Ella gave me a piece of advice that would end up serving me well for my entire stripping career. "Look, lemme give you a tip if I can. When you're doing a table dance for a girl, or even for a whole fuckin' table you want to dance for 'em like you hope the song just goes on forever." I'd all but stopped dancing, and was practically kneeling down in front of her so that I could hear what she had to say.

"Make those fucking girls think you're having as much fun dancing for them as they are having you there, cause the idea isn't to just grab twenty-bucks off a chick, the idea is to empty her fucking wallet. Make 'em tell you to keep going if you can... And hey, table dancing is a contact sport, remember that!"

Kneeling there in front of her, listening intently and not breaking eye contact so that I could read her lips while I strained to hear over the music, I realized how right on the nose the advice she'd just given me was. I also realized one other thing. Down on her level, basically squatting between her legs and making solid eye contact I couldn't imagine a better way to dance for a woman than right there, face to face. That, and of course a whole lot more contact!

For once, sliding up and down a woman's leg seemed to be exactly what was required, and as I did my bump and grind for her quite intentionally dragging my thong up her thigh and back, I certainly seemed to be getting the reaction I wanted. As I shoved in a bit of room onto the seat in front of her, jamming my ass between her legs and taking her hands and placing them on what had actually turned into a man's chest over the last few years, I let her hands wander around my upper body while I pushed back against her and made sure she felt the pressure from me. Just about the time I was really grinding on in and getting into a groove, the song I'd been "dancing" to came to and end, and I got a happy little squeal and a hug from her. Then, to my great surprise, I got a twenty-dollar bill.

"Its for the dance silly! You didn't think you had to do this shit for free did you? Jeeze! A table dance is twenty bucks a song. That's where all the real money is…". And with that, a quick kiss on the cheek and a squeeze of my ass, she was out the door and off to get naked herself.

I could see as she passed by Gloria they exchanged a few brief words, and I decided that the table dance must have been set up by Gloria to see how I'd handle it. As I headed back to get dressed, Gloria told me to get back into my street clothes, then come and have a word with her before I left. I guess I wasn't really sure what I'd been expecting, but I'd certainly hoped after that table dance that I'd at least be able to work a bit of that night, if for nothing else, just to toss a few extra bucks in my pocket. Didn't work out that way unfortunately.

"So not too bad on the stage, although you NEVER leave the stage empty! If the girls want to tip you, they'll do it there. Ella said you did a decent job with the table dance too, and I saw some of it as well. Looked alright to me, but you need to make damn sure you're in control! I saw her pulling at you in the beginning, so remember not to let them get carried away."

Everything she was saying sounded a lot like I'd gotten the gig, but I couldn't figure out why I was back in my street clothes and being shown the door. As it turned out, Gloria thought I could do a decent job for the club, but according to her, she really just didn't have an open slot for me. The best she could do is have me come back on Friday and Saturday nights prior to the show, and see if all the guys showed up on time. She said pretty flatly that if I were there on time with outfits and a routine and any one of them were late, I'd get a crack at working. She had a zero tolerance for running late, and at least for the time being, that was the only way I'd see that stage again.

After three fucking weeks of showing up early at the Olympic Garden only to be turned away, I was pretty sure word had gotten around through the guys working there that if they fucked up or were late, there was a pretty eager guy willing to step in. At least up until then, every damn one of them had made sure that I didn't get that chance. But then week number four rolled around, and I got my shot.

My New Normal

The first six months at the OG were quite a learning experience to say the least. I'd managed to keep the fact that I was dancing weekends from anyone at my property management company, and even thought I didn't think there was any real conflict of interest I didn't feel like taking the chance. It may have been Vegas, but you just never knew how people would react, and I didn't want to risk the secure income I had with the apartments.

After the first full night I was able to work, courtesy of a flat tire on another dancers car, I was offered a Thursday through Saturday slot full time. I'd come to OG every night while trying to get in with three different costumes, three sets of music, and a few different gimmicks to stand out, and when I had the chance to work the entire night it turned out the variety I showed had impressed Gloria. As the last of the ladies walked out the door that evening, she grabbed me by the arm, pulled me to the side and told me that she was pretty sure they had room for ten guys in her show.

It didn't take too long to realized just what a shot she had given me. On the very first night that I worked the OG, I strolled out the door having made well over five-hundred in cash, and according to the other guys, it had been a slow night. Awesome!

Now no doubt some of the money I made had to do with the fact that I was the new guy, as I was to find out quite quickly that OG had a hell of a lot of very regular customers, but I was also pretty sure that some of it was just that I'd put on a good show and I was more than happy about it. The way the show and the whole evening was run was a different story though, and it was something that was going to take a hell of a lot of getting use to.

Back at the El Dorado Saloon, unless you were performing in a "group" routine, you had the stage and the crowd to yourself. Your songs, and your time in the crowd was all yours to make as much money as you could; but in the OG, the only thing that belonged to you alone was your time on the stage. When you were on the floor, you were competing head to head with every other dancer in the club, walking around from table to table trying to entice the ladies to hire you for a coveted table dance, and the twenty bucks that one short little song could bring.

It wasn't exactly what I would call a cut-throat environment really, as there were usually ten women to every entertainer, but you still had to get yourself out there and be a hell of a lot more of a salesman than I was use to, and to be honest I couldn't decide if I liked it or not. But the way the show ran wasn't the only thing I wasn't use to…

Because the telegram business in California had me running around as much as it did, I'd have the chance to flirt with some of the women I met while working, but was usually in such a rush from show to show, that I was lucky if I even had the time to get a phone number.

Here, I not only was expected to flirt not just with individual girls but with entire tables, and would sometimes literally have hours to chat with them, which led to a dynamic I wasn't use to. It most certainly could have led to a "kid in a candy store" type situation for sure, but luckily for me, having the job at the apartment complex kept me from really taking advantage. That, and right from the word go, as soon as I decided to play a little it bit me in the ass!

On each of the nights that I'd worked, I'd been offered or given a room key by at least one of the customers. I'd always been pretty good about declining, and would simply tell them the truth, which was that I had a job that started at 8 in the morning that I couldn't miss. Most of the ladies that had been bold enough to suggest a little fun after the show were most certainly not my type as well, so it made it pretty easy to politely say "No thanks". But then this one night…

She was just adorable. Blonde hair, and at least what appeared to be green eyes in all the flashing disco lights, I'd been hired to dance for her by her friend. After what was always the first minute of embarrassment during a table dance, she was starting to enjoy herself, and dammit so was I. One dance led to another, which led to another, which eventually led to her leaving me her room key after telling me that she had a place all to herself as her friend had her own room, and that she'd love it if I stopped by for a visit; and it seemed just to put at touch more emphasis on "visit", she reached out and gave my knob a little tug. This was one visit I had no desire to say no to, and as she left the club at about eleven that night I had already decided I'd be taking her up on the offer if it killed me.

During the remainder of that night I'd had one other room key given to me by a rather, shall we say, big boned lady from the Midwest who said something along the lines of what an amazing time I was gonna be in for that night. She'd hired me for a number of table dances herself, and on the final one had wrapped her room key in the hundred-dollar bill she gave and shoved it down my thong, not really giving me the opportunity to refuse it.

The mistake was completely mine. The show was over, I'd gathered all my things, headed out the door, and hopped on the back of my bike, on my way to the MGM to meet up with green eyes, and what I was sure was going to be a hell of a good reason to be tired the next day at work. As I was walking down the hall and digging into my pocket I ended up fishing out two room keys instead of one, and realized I flat out had no idea which key belonged to green eyes! One for the MGM and one for the Mirage. I guess I'd conveniently forgotten that I'd been given two keys that night, and now I found myself standing in a stereotypical Vegas hotel hallway in the MGM, tacky carpet and all, wondering if this was the right one. Oh fuck me!

So the way Vegas works is this. You can't actually get to a guests room either without the guest, or the guests key. So if you gave someone a key to your room, you also basically gave them a pass to the entire hotel portion of the casino that would otherwise be off limits. If I couldn't manage to remember if green eyes was in the MGM or the Mirage, then I was gonna simply have to take a gamble, which I supposed was kind of exactly what Las Vegas was about.

I really didn't want to fuck this one up. Behind door number one was a beautiful little thing that I was sure had nothing but wonderfully bad intentions in mind for me, and behind door number two? Well, there were still a lot of bad intentions to be sure, but they were bad intentions that reminded me of that scene in Return of the Jedi where Jabba the Hutt licks Princess Leah's face while she's in that sexy little gold bikini thing. Fucking yuck! There was no way in hell I wanted to play a "Princess" to her "Jabba'!

It couldn't be the MGM. There was no way that my gorgeous little doll would stay in a tacky place like that, so I hopped back on my bike, rode the two miles over to the Mirage and strolled past security with the flash of the room key that told them I belonged there even if they looked at me funny; but as I looked around the hall I now found myself walking down, I had to admit it was just as fucking tacky as the MGM. FUCK! I was literally wracking my brains and pacing around trying to remember which damn key Green eyes had given me, and clearly I'd stood there too long, because the next thing I knew I had security from the hotel up my ass wanting to know why I was wandering up and down the seventeenth floor without going inside a room.

They absolutely insisted they escort me. They stood and waited as I put the little plastic key in the electronic lock, and as the door chirped and the little lights turned green, I was secretly praying as I smiled at them as if to say "see? Now fuck off...". But they didn't fuck off. They waited until my fate was basically sealed.

As I stood there face to face with big boned Midwest, I was literally speechless. "Is this gentleman with you Miss?" Smooth as can be, she smiled at the security officer, grabbed my hand and pulled me toward her with a "Of course he is" said almost with a purr. Visibly a bit bummed they weren't going to get to fuck with me the officers backed slowly away from the door and walked on down the hall, looking more than once over their shoulders to see if they could find any reason to stay. Midwest didn't bother watching them go, and closed and latched the door with me standing there basically frozen in place.

I waited speechless for as long as I could, but about the time she leaned in to try an bite my neck and grab at my crotch I was done! All I could think to do was hand her the room key I'd just opened the door with and tell her in a terribly strained voice that I thought she'd dropped her key accidentally and I wanted to make sure I returned it to her so it didn't cost her money... I basically ran away before the terribly excited, then terribly confused look on her face had the chance to turn to terrible anger! I was so fucking horrified at the mistake I'd made that I almost decided to just go home and try and forget the whole damn thing; but then the "visit" squeeze I had received popped back into my head, and I was back on my bike and headed down The Strip once again!

This time when I knocked I instantly knew I'd made the right choice by trying again! She wasn't wearing a damn thing, clearly still slightly wet from the shower she must have just climbed out of. She grabbed my by the shirt, pulled me into the room and had me up against the wall without a word.... It was a full fifteen minutes before I even made it completely into the room as after an intense make-out as a "hello", she'd dropped to her knees and made damn sure that all the teasing I'd put here through in the club was returned ten fold. I may have been exhausted the entire next day, but I'm pretty sure the smile I'd had as I pulled back onto the strip just after sunrise never left my face. My first "Vegas Stripper encounter" was almost a tragedy that happily ended as anything but.

The money at the club was getting steadily better for me as I was learning how to play the game, and I had even managed to end up with a few regular customers that could be counted on to come see me every week or two. It was great! I was both making money and having a bit of fun as well, and I wasn't having to kill myself to do it!

I also discovered that I had a major advantage not only over the other guys that I worked with at the club, but even over the customers themselves. You see prior to my "rave" days I'd never been a drinker. Alcohol had just never really held any appeal to me, and seeing how stupid drunk people would generally act was certainly not a high selling point for the stuff. After I'd started hard in the San Francisco scene, alcohol was most certainly not appealing, as all the drugs I had access to were a hell of a lot more entertaining than booze.

By the time I'd left the scene, I was so far behind in the drinking game, that I just decided not to try it at all. I could honestly say that I'd only been legitimately drunk once in my life up till then and hadn't liked it one bit, so I lived a completely dry life in Sin City. I'd never performed a single show with a drop of booze in me unlike most of the guys I worked with, and the ladies that came to see us were usually tanked thirty minutes after they arrived, so I was able to soberly assess the situation every night and outmaneuver them all. When stone cold sober, making money and flirting with the tipsy ladies turned out to be pretty damn easy truthfully. It also meant that I never had to go to work at the apartment complex with a hangover, and never risked doing something stupid that I might not remember. Not to mention, being a high energy dancer while drunk would have led to blood and tears at some point!

I'd ended up being once again billed as "Dean, Dean the dancing machine", as I was still the rave style hip-hop dancer I'd been at the ElDo. The way that I danced had even led to a routine with myself and one of the black dancers on staff named "Magic". He and I would get up and perform a pretty easy choreographed routine together and then to keep the crowd engaged, would have a mock dance off where the ladies would scream and yell for their favorite, the winner of which would be announced by the MC. Both of us would end up making a fair amount of cash off the stage for sure, and even though Magic was in my opinion a better dancer than I was the simple fact that a "white boy" was keeping up with him meant that I usually won.

I even ended up spending a little time each night on the microphone as well. Once the MC for the show, a guy named Brice found out that I use to announce back in California, he had me bring him out for each of the three or four sets he'd do each evening. I'd end up losing out on time on the floor while I did it, but the MC would be tipped out by all the dancers at the end of the night for his work, and he'd toss some of it my way each time for helping him.

All and all, shit was flowing along fantastically really. Unfortunately, although Las Vegas is one of the most visited cities in the world, it's also one of the smallest, and I really had no reason to be surprised when for a special occasion a big group of girls from my property management company decided that the OG was the perfect place to go. I had managed simply by keeping my fucking mouth shut to completely separate my day job from my night job, but on this occasion of course my manager Ericka just so happened to be one of the girls in the group.

She and I had been working in the same small office of our Pacific Properties complex for six months now, and all and all it had been going pretty well but we hadn't exactly become close friends. Cordial co-workers was more accurate really. She had a family and a pretty new baby at home, and wasn't the most social of people from what I'd seen, so I'll admit I was a bit surprised to see her in the group that night at the OG. None of the other girls with her were ones that I worked with regularly, but I'd seen at least a few of them in the monthly management meetings we were required to go to, so as soon as one of them spotted me it was a done deal. Fuck.

Of course the next thing I knew, they'd bough me for a table dance. For Ericka. Fuck fuck FUCK. Suffice it to say that it wasn't a particularly pleasant experience for either of us, and as the dance finished she and I both swore to each other that as long as one didn't say anything, neither would the other. There was no doubt that the other ladies in the group were gonna talk about it eventually146146 but hey, if my manager was gonna try and keep a lid on the fact that I'd basically been naked in her lap in public, then I was pretty sure I didn't have too much to worry about!

My new normal had found itself a pretty decent balance point, and I was not only managing to bank a fair amount of cash every week, but I was holding up my responsibilities with the property management company as well, and somewhere along the lines I decided that moving to Las Vegas had been a damn good choice.

Sitting in the hospital though, I had to wonder if I had done something personally to Karma. I'd been riding along, minding my own business on the way to a date down on the strip. Dressed in a sweater vest and a pair of blue jeans for the whopping five mile ride, I had left early as usual and was in no particular rush.

When the little old lady pulled her Lincoln out of the gas station parking lot in front of me without looking, I had two choices. Lock up the brakes and more than likely slam into the side of her car, or lay the bike down before I got to her, and hope. I could feel the heat building up through my jeans as I hit the pavement doing about forty-five miles per hour, and as I shifted to try and avoid sanding off half of an ass cheek, I caught a heel on the pavement and was sent tumbling for the remainder of the crash, at some point slamming my wrist on the ground and shattering it in about seventeen different places. When the ambulance driver showed up and initially told me I'd probably just sprained it in my fall, the sight of my fingertips touching my elbow as I held up my arm changed his mind pretty quickly.

My medical insurance with the property management firm had literally kicked in just the week before, which turned out to be the best luck I could have possibly asked for, because by the time the surgery was over and done with and the final bill was tallied the little old lady in her Lincoln had ended up costing a little over forty grand in hospital bills! Although the bike was good and scratched up, it still ran like a champ though and at least I still had that going for me. That, and the fact that the surgeon who repaired my wrist handed out Vicodin like it was aspirin. Unfortunately, I feared that my salad days in Las Vegas may have already come to an end, even just as they were getting started…

Sin City Special Needs

Unlike the warm, fuzzy and happy feeling I'd come out of my first surgery with, this was as polar opposite as it possibly could have been. At first there was no pain, or at least nothing that I could conceive of as such, but there was a whole lot of confusion and disorientation going on.

The nurses were completely opposite to and unlike the gentle and soft spoken ones who had changed the bloody sheets off my bed the first time I'd gone under the knife because these nurses just kept fucking with me! All I wanted to do was to keep my eyes closed and make whatever fucked up version of the world that was trying to climb into my head go jump off a fucking bridge. I wanted no part of whatever was out there waiting for me, but the god damn nurses that kept coming to my bedside just wouldn't let me be and I finally snapped and yelled "DO YOU NEED THE FUCKING BED THAT BAD?" Which was exactly when reality stepped completely into the room, told me to shut the fuck up and pay attention and ensured that I stopped enjoying life even a little bit.

I'd been in surgery for just over six hours to repair my left wrist, and it had turned out to be quite a job. I'd managed to break bones a total of seventeen times when I'd decided to slam it into the pavement I was sliding across, and the job of putting it back together had involved three screws, a pin that ran completely through my arm, and four bolts that were placed two in my forearm and two in my hand on which the external fixator (which would be holding my wrist in one place for the next six months) was to be attached. This surgery had also required a substantially larger amount of anesthesia than for the hernia surgery which had taken all of forty-five minutes, and my body was not at all happy with the after effects.

Now looking back I realize that the nurses were simply doing their jobs by trying to get me up and moving as quickly as they did, but at the time I thought each and every one of them was satan's spawn, and I believe the word "cunt" may have escaped my mouth a few times while they did it. When I was lying down things were not good. When I stood up… Oh fuck me sideways.

My arm was as you would expect, bound up in a ton of gauze that made it look like it had been wrapped in bright white cotton candy, but when for the first time I allowed it to hang down at my side, I was pretty sure that they had attached some type of device designed to shove red hot spikes through my wrist at the perfect pace to match my heartbeat, and I almost dropped to my knees in searing pain. At the very same time, the nausea that was a side-effect to so many hours worth of anesthesia kicked in without warning, and I started projectile vomiting all over the little changing room they'd put me in to get dressed.

Each time my body would heave in an attempt to get whatever the fuck was making me sick out of it, the strain of it would cause my left arm to feel as if it were trying to rip itself free and hide in a safe space, and I ended up on my knees in the corner of the room holding my left arm as high above my head as I could, having discovered that keeping it well above my heart was the only place that didn't make me want to cut it off. Anything lower, and with every beat of my heart a bolt of lightening would shoot through the entire left side of my body, and it didn't take even me all that long to figure out not to drop it down again.

When I finally managed to pull that little chain for "assistance" you see in every hospital bathroom and a nurse came in, what they found was me moaning incoherently, covered in puke in the corner and holding my arm up in the air as if I were trying to ask my grade school teacher a question.

I think I must have greyed out just a bit, because my next clear recollection was climbing into the car of the girl I'd been dating at the time and driving to the pharmacy to pick up drugs as fast as humanly possible because the hospital hadn't seen fit give me anything else for the pain before they had me out the front door all of an hour or so after being wheeled out of surgery. The level of pain that I was in as I waited for the first handful of Vicodin to kick in made my post-op night in the van look like a distant happy memory, and when I was finally back in my own bed an hour later, even high as a kite off the narcotic pain killers I was still in agony.

The entire next week was really just a blur of pain and drugs, and they took turns being in control of my every waking moment. If I wasn't thinking about the next pill I could take to make the pain back off, I was thinking about how much longer it might be before my arm would start screaming at me again which would make me think about the next pill I could take... Vicious circle to say the least!

By the time I could finally manage to lower my arm down by my side, and think straight, or at least as straight as the drugs would let me, I was ten days post-op. Having followed the instructions on the paperwork they'd given me at the hospital, I had after the first week unwrapped my arm, and gone about cleaning the areas where they'd bolted shit into my arm, and it looked to me as if someone had taken what looked a lot like a skinny gun sight and jammed it into my flesh. If nothing else it was a hell of a conversation starter! I must admit though, it was oddly satisfying to see the four not insubstantial pieces of metal shoved into my arm. Very strange...

For the next few weeks, life was nothing but constant re-adjustments and learning. I was back in the office, albeit at a slightly reduced schedule for the apartments which was needed, because quite frankly the paperwork alone was causing me crazy grief. The problem was that I'm left handed by nature, and very very left handed when it comes to anything requiring fine dexterity, so learning how to write right handed meant that anything I had to fill out or sign in the way of company paperwork may as well have been in crayon as it looked that childish. Couple that with the fact that I was legally high as a kite all day, every day, and you can imagine the quality of my book work!

As a not so funny little side note, I happen consider masturbation an activity requiring a pretty high level of dexterity. Although tugging away with my right hand most certainly made it feel as though someone else were doing it, it was obviously someone who had no fucking clue how to give a handjob! I also discovered through what just ended up being sad attempt at jerking off that one of the major drawbacks to taking high levels of Vicodin was not only a drop in sensitivity physically, but also a complete and total inability to fucking orgasm.

After my first hernia surgery I never found out that my pain killers would do this, because go figure, after having someone cut into your lower abdomen and stitch a bunch of muscle back together you weren't likely to need a tug. Unfortunately this time for me, not only did the "urge" come back around within a few weeks, but it seemed that the Vicodin itself was making me pretty damn horny as well.

Lying on my living room couch, glistening with sweat and basically covered from hips to knees with Jergens Lotion, I was out of breath, out of patience, and out of porn. The VHS tape of dirty movies that had been with me as an "In case of emergency, push PLAY" for years had been run from end to end, twice, and more than an hour of furiously and aggressively yanking about had come and gone when I finally fucking gave up. I let out a frustrated groan imitating sounding as if I'd managed to do the job, spit on my stomach and attempted at least a fake sense of satisfaction. I am, as far as I know, the only person ever to fake an orgasm while masturbating.

After week four, having by then long given up on writing like an adult, or getting a nut, I managed to make my way back to the OG out of sheer boredom. Turned out to be one of the better choices I'd made since the crash, because Brice, the MC and DJ for the show had been desperate to find someone who could not only fill in for him in the DJ booth, but be able to announce the acts on stage. He'd had a number of different things going on in his life outside the club, and was having to both arrive late and leave early, making being the voice and music of the show problematic.

"So heres how it goes" he explained. "You'll do all the normal intros bringing the guys up on stage for the night, and they'll usually tip you out forty or fifty bucks a piece as you know. What you may not know is that you also get a cut of the money we take for the girls we put up on stage. It can end up being a pretty good take each night, let me tell you…"

The male review had a gimmick that kept the crowd pretty entertained during the shows, which was important when each of the guys had already been on stage once or twice and the show started to get stale. For a price, the ladies could pay to have on of their girls placed on stage in a chair, where a very public and embarrassing table dance would take place right up under the spotlights. Every single time a group booked a girl on stage, twenty dollars went into the dancers thong, and another twenty would go straight into my pocket just for setting it up and announcing it. I was not even a little upset with that deal. I sat that first night, watching all that Brice did, and had decided that shy of the music changes, it really wasn't too much different that the El Dorado had been. No problem I thought. Easy.

Oh fucking hell was I wrong! The very next night was a Friday, and like all Fridays it was busy as could be. By the time the show got rolling and the room filled up, I had more requests from both customers and dancers than I knew what to do with! I was missing music changes, I was stuttering when I spoke because I was so far behind, I'd dropped the mic half a dozen times when I'd attempted to hold it in my left hand and I'd broken out in a cold sweat when I looked at my watch and realized I wasn't even two hours in!

About the time Gloria walked over almost casually, and asked me point blank "Are you sure you know what the fuck you're doing?" I half smiled and looked at her through sweat burned eyes, assured her that I would quite quickly pull my head out of my ass, and that things would be okay. As soon as her back was turned, I tossed two Vicodin down my throat, told everyone to back the fuck away from the DJ booth, took a very very deep breath. Then, I sorted myself out.

I'd managed to get one act at a time going, and that was a huge start. I also started getting all the special occasion girls up on the stage as well, and even though they were way late, the girls seemed to forget all about being pissed off as soon as their turn came around. I made my way through the rest of the night one song at a time. Then one special occasion at a time, and almost without realizing it, I'd rolled on through midnight, and was starting to see the light at the end of the tunnel. Understandably I didn't exactly get huge tips from the dancers who's sets I'd fucked up, but not one person stiffed me so apparently it wasn't quite as bad as it felt. When I counted out my money at the end of the night, I had actually made only about a hundred dollars less than I had for a usual Friday dancing, and although it had been a hell of a lot harder than dropping my pants it was still incredible money.

Gloria, who hadn't given a flying fuck about the special occasion girls, or even the fucked up songs as long as there was a naked guy on stage and some music playing, agreed to let me continue on with the position until Brice was ready to take over once again. I'd accepted, knowing full well that although it may take a bit of time, I'd most certainly fall into a groove with it as I had most things I put my mind to; and just like that, just because I'd stopped by because I was bored, injured and had no life, I was the new Olympic Garden Male Review DJ and MC.

To your Good Health

In time it seems, people can manage to get use to just about anything, and it turns out being the MC for a Vegas strip show, having bits of metal jammed into your body, and being high as fuck via prescription pills were most certainly no exceptions. The exquisite pain that I'd been in almost minute to minute for a month after my surgery had abated pretty quickly after that first thirty days, and if I'd been a responsible individual watching out for his health and well being I probably would have stopped taking the damn drugs, but fuck me they were just really nice, and the doc kept sliding those lovely little white squares of paper across his desk…. I stayed what I liked to describe as "fuzzy" through pretty much most of my waking hours, was just sweet as peaches to be around because of it, and life was just about as good as it could get while recovering from a shitty accident.

The show, which had been so completely daunting that very first full night had morphed almost quicker than I wanted into a very easy routine, and I was handing myself pretty flawlessly with each consecutive performance. Once I'd managed to get the hang of exactly how to not only announce the guys and run the booth, but to "handle" the customers as well, I was bringing in more money not stripping that the I'd made in the club while dancing. The average OG take-home for the night was anywhere between a cool grand and fifteen hundred for what I was doing, and it was all cash.

The Olympic Garden had either come up with, or adopted an absolutely genius way to get around all that horrible employer/ employee bullshit and it actually benefited everyone involved. Everyone that worked in the club, with the exception of the bar and wait staff weren't employees. They were customers. Every dancer, both male and female, every DJ, every bouncer was required to pay a cover charge each and every night, making them for all intents and purposes, just another customer. If they chose to form their own business as an independent contractor and claim and pay taxes on the money they made, well, that was up to them. As you can imagine, there weren't a lot of entrepreneur's running around the OG in a thong though…

Even work at the apartment complex was going amazingly. I was so damn happy and helpful to everyone during office hours, that even though I was consistently fucking up paperwork, both management and the residents loved me because I was just so damn sweet all the time! But then, as it is with all good things, it eventually had to come to an end.

"So. We'll be taking the hardware out in another 10 days like we talked about. Everything is looking great according to the images we took, and it looks like you're just about healed up! I'm sure you're gonna be thrilled to have this thing out of your arm, right?"

The Doctor was most certainly correct, I was going to be very happy when I could actually put on a shirt without either causing myself great pain, and or tearing clothing or bleeding because I'd been careless and snagged the hardware on a shirt. What I wasn't going to be happy with was the fact that during that doctors office, I received the last of the prescriptions of my beloved Vicodin which by now I was if not completely hooked on, I was most certainly leaning on for some serious support. Not good. When I asked him about the removal of the "hardware", he said that it was a painless procedure and that I shouldn't even give it a second thought. I didn't believe a word he said.

There was no fucking way in the world you were going to convince me that pulling a bunch of screws that had been drilled into the bones of my arm weren't going to hurt like hell when they were pulled out, and I made sure to save pretty large amount if Vicodin specifically for the occasion. Damn good planning on my part. I also made sure to inform everyone I knew, and I mean EVERYONE, that in about a week I was going to go from the happiest guy they knew to the biggest prick, and most likely there wasn't a damn thing I could do about it. Hell, I'd seen Trainspotting! I was completely prepared to see dead babies crawling across the bedroom ceiling, sweating uncontrollably like a pedophile at a Barney concert and twitching sporadically for a week.

As the doctor attached what looked like the front of a drill with a "T" handle for hand cranking on the first bolt with the use of a "chuck key", I was really fucking happy that I'd taken as many pills as I had.

The very first twist almost brought me to my knees, and most certainly without wanting to I actually yelled. Once the initial turn was made, and whatever was holding it in place let go, then the rest of the removal wasn't too bad. But just knowing that I still had three more to go was making me nauseous. By the time he got to the last bolt located in my hand, I had tears streaming down my face from the pain, and I couldn't believe they had subjected me to this not only wide awake, but with no local of any kind. Fuck me it was bad... But, I did get one really damn good laugh out if it all though.

After the last piece had been removed and placed to the side, the doctor leaned over my arm to inspect the four not insubstantial holes left behind in to try and determine if they might need a stitch to help them close up. As he was bent over and inspecting, he told me to go ahead and make a fist and see how it felt. As I did, a most unexpected stream of blood shot rather forcefully out of each of the four holes, spraying four very clearly defined lines up and across my shocked doctors shirt, tie and face. I hadn't laughed that hard in months, and didn't even try to contain it. As the doctor marched around the room grabbing anything he could to wipe the blood from him, I almost told him he fucking deserved it.

Within another week, the holes in my arm were closed up and near to healed, and I half assumed that when Gloria realized I was probably pretty close to being back into dancing shape that I'd be on the floor and out of the booth, but to my surprise neither she nor Brice said a word. On the contrary, on a number of different occasions Brice even went out of his way to tell me how much he was enjoying just being a dancer. Seemed the booth may just belong to me full time! With the exception of the few small snags (and blood stains) I'd had recently, life was going pretty fucking well, and it was time to try and enjoy it some.

I'd been stuck for so long being limited with my physical activities that I was beyond ready for a little physical exertion, and although I'd been cautioned by the doctor to take it slow I was still very ready to get out and do something new.

It was with that idea in mind that I once again without warning, through a series of seemingly insubstantial choices would once again start to completely change the course of my life.

It was a place called Flyaway Indoor Skydiving. I had seen a television show about the place when I was much younger, and the memory somehow stuck. When I came across a "Grand Re-Opening" flyer being handed out on the strip the memory of that show from so long ago came flooding back, and I simply had to go check it out.

Dressed up in a massive baggy suit with vents cut into the arms and legs, I went into the wind chamber or "tunnel" with my instructor, laid down in the middle of the massive round room on a metal mesh net woven into the floor above an absolutely enormous propeller and waited. I waited until that damn propeller started spinning fast enough to lift me quite literally off the net and into the air!

Of course my instructor, a guy by the name of Rob had been doing most of the really hard work keeping me stable, but the sensation of flying around in that little room was just the most amazing thing I'd done in ages, and I was hooked! I didn't even take off the goofy ass suit when I ran across the street to the ATM machine to get more cash so I could do it again... By the time I was finished, I'd flown in the tunnel almost half a dozen times and was walking to my bike with the words "Your'e a natural man. You should totally go out and make a skydive."

I'd booked a jump less than a week later. I and my girlfriend (brief story to come) had both decided to make a jump, and from the moment we made the appointment it was literally all I could think about. I was completely terrified at the thought of it, and I loved it! She seemed as though she was looking forward to the experience as well, but wasn't nearly as over the top as I was, and after she asked me to stop bringing it up about a dozen times I started trying to bottle it in.

When the day finally came to drive up to Boulder City to make the jump I was pretty sure I couldn't manage to wait any longer. So of course, I had to wait a lot longer... As we pulled up to the Skydive Las Vegas facility in Boulder City the weather had decided to take a nasty turn, and as we went to check in we were told that all the jumps had been canceled for the day. Bummed was not even close to how I felt, but it got nothing but worse as I had to suffer through the longest bout of shit weather I could have ever imagined in Las Vegas! Three weeks of clouds, high winds and even rain was what I had to sit through, because every damn day that we were available to jump the weather went to complete shit.

By week four, I knew beyond a doubt that If I woke up to anything less than perfect blue skies and calm wind, someone was likely to die. If it had't been for the wind tunnel as a distraction not only from having to wait to jump, but from the not insubstantial withdrawal from my pain pills, I do believe I would have lost my mind.

In all honesty, the shitty part of running out of the pain pills that I'd been on daily for the last six months really only lasted a couple of days. I was an irritable asshole for sure, and I slept like shit, but by the end of a long weekend, I really wasn't giving them too much though. My impending skydive was too busy taking control of my imagination. I'm the type of person who needs to have something to look forward to, and as long as I do nothing else will ever get too bad for me to handle.

"Look I know you two have been trying to jump for quite a while now, and I really wish I was kidding, but our plane… Well I'm afraid our plane is down with a maintenance issue and we're gonna need to re-book you again." All I could do was laugh. Clearly I wasn't meant to skydive, and even though our names were put in the books for the following week I was sure it wasn't gonna happen.

Even sitting in the aircraft in-between my instructor Bruce's legs looking out the side window as we taxied down to the runway, I was sure something was going to keep us on the ground. As I was interviewed by Chris my camera-man about ten thousand feet off the ground I still figured we'd have to land with the plane for some reason, and I don't believe I actually accepted the fact that we were jumping until I looked outside the open door of the aircraft at Chris, cameras rolling as he was quite literally hanging by his hands from the tire of the plane. "That guy is out of his fucking mind!" Is exactly what I thought, right up until I realized that I was about to follow him out!

The next five seconds of my life made no sense at all. As Bruce rolled us out of the little Cessna and into free fall, I tried desperately to remember all the things he had told me to do, but if you'd asked me, at that moment I wouldn't have even been able to tell you my name. "Whats up? Whats down? What the fuuuuuck…"

And then, the entire world seemed to be laid out in front of me. There was no sensation of falling, no ground screaming up at me, no insanity like I'd expected. Just the feeling of floating that I'd had in the wind tunnel, an the most incredible view occasionally punctuated by some guy who'd randomly float into my field of vision and wave at me. To see the world from ten thousand feet above the ground, without having to look out a smudged up dirty window to see it was beyond anything I could have ever imagined. Time for me both stretched out to a crawl and flashed like lightening by me simultaneously, and it was lightyears beyond anything I had experienced before. For that briefest of time, I had no past nor future, I only had exactly the instant I was in, and in later recollection I realized that for the first and only time in my life I knew what living in the moment truly was. It was magical and for me it was instantly addictive.

After a few minutes under the open parachute with Bruce, a whole lot of excited foul language spewing from me, a beautiful stand-up landing in front of my waiting camera-man and I was beyond hooked. I would have gotten back in the plane that very second. As it was, as soon as all my gear was off and I'd retrieved my personal belongings, I went into the little office inside the hanger, laid my credit card down on the counter and said point blank "charge it till it fucking says declined".

When I asked my girlfriend how her jump had been, so personally excited that I could barely contain my borderline joy, instead of hearing her mirroring how wonderful it had been for her all she could manage to give me was the reply of "It was fun…" I should have known that very second she and I were doomed. How on earth could anyone call leaping from a plane two fucking miles above the ground "fun"?? Chucky Cheese was fun, Put-Put Golf was fun, hell sex was fun, but that shit! That shit was EPIC! I mean come the fuck on! This was not a fun kind of thing. You could hate it for sure, or like me be instantly and terrifyingly in love with it, but "fun" was about as unacceptable as you could get!

As I drove back home from that very first jump, having not only booked my second tandem but enrolled in the ground school to become a jumper myself, I knew beyond a doubt that I'd found something I hadn't even known I was looking for.

Opportunities Missed or Mistaken

For those that don't want to read a short story about a shit relationship that lasted way too long, skip to the next chapter now. For those that are curious, read until it gets boring, then skip to the next chapter. For those that read the entire chapter, I apologize now. I'm gonna talk about this once, and only once, I promise. And I'm gonna keep it really fucking short.

It lasted just over four years, and it was absolutely amazing. For the first six months. We'd met just a few months after I'd moved to Las Vegas, at a time in my life when I was looking to settle down, at least when it came to women. I had been working in the office of the apartment complex when she walked in to deal with a maintenance issue, and after writing up a work order for what she needed once she'd left, I remember thinking just how cute she was. ("But wait Dean" you say, "If the relationship lasted four years, won't you be skipping forward way further than we're at in the whole story?" Yes we will, but like I said, I'm only gonna cover this shit once!)

Within ten minutes of her being in the office, the phone rang, and what do you know, it was her. Her name was (changed to save the innocent, and the guilty), and she wanted to know if I'd like to go out some time. I should have followed company policy against dating residents, even though there was no policy against dating residents. I shouldn't have gone. I most certainly shouldn't have asked her out on a second date, we shouldn't have fucked around in the jacuzzi, and I'm guessing moving in together only a month or so after we started dating was just as bad an idea.

When I'd confided in her on date number two that I was moonlighting as a stripper at the OG, she didn't seem terribly pleased, but also didn't seem to think it was a deal breaker, so we continued on. The mistake we both made, which doomed us from that moment forward was this: She thought I was the suit and tie office man that was working in the strip club for a little extra money, where as I knew that I was one hundred percent the stripper, who was working in a suit and tie for cheap rent and a little normality. Somewhere along the line I guess I had simply decided to embrace it, instead of trying to convince myself that I was simply living the life I was while in search of an earnest entry into the "real world".

No way were those two minds ever gonna meet. We'd moved in together our of convenience because both of her roommates at the time were relocating out of Las Vegas, and I lived for half price in a large one bedroom, so it just made sense, no? NO! It didn't make any fucking sense.

Right about that time was the motorcycle accident (this would be the previously referred to girlfriend) which certainly put a strain on our new and blossoming relationship, for a number of reasons really. First off, who wants to have to play nurse to your basically brand new significant other? You want to have fun, go out, sleep in on rainy days, have lots of sex, etc, not fetch food, run errands, fluff pillows and listen to a 180 pound baby whine… You may also may remember the ridiculous bout of masturbation I'd put myself through not too long after the surgery? Well, if I couldn't manage to get myself off because of all the pain pills, imagine how difficult a time she was having! I'm guessing not being able to get your new man to cum might be a bit of a difficult thing for a twenty-something to handle, and I was right. We'd managed to turn sex into a chore almost right from the start.

By the time skydiving had rolled around (yes, she was Miss "It was fun") I was starting to have serious misgivings with my choice, but seeing as how we were already living together, I really wanted to try and make it work, so I stuck it out. So did she, but as I was to discover later on, she absolutely hated how much I'd fallen in love with skydiving, and treated the sport as if it were another woman. Not good.

As we got deeper into the relationship, the true dislike for my work at the club started to surface as well. By now she had figured out that I wasn't the office type man she had thought I was, and although she tired to deal with it, it was catching up with her very quickly. Raging jealousy was becoming part of our daily routine, and tainting anything we may have tried to do for fun.

By year three (fuck me, I know), I was done. I couldn't handle the daily massive fights we were having, the huge distance in mindsets, the complete and utter lack of sex (when I say complete lack, I mean that in the course of our entire relationship we had sex probably less than a dozen times) and the palpable despair that soaked both our lives. I had started purchasing new items for the house using just my money. I had opened up a separate bank account in just my name, and was clearly making sure that when it happened, it would be a simple break, if not painful and ugly. She knew It was coming. We hated each other even though we still said "I love you" every day. We hated each others friends. We just hated.

And then one night she showed up at the OG. Something she'd done all of two or three times since we'd first met. She came toward the end of a weekday show, and she was drunk off her ass. Drunk, but to my surprise, not only happy, but very fucking affectionate. Although a night like that should stick out somewhat in ones memory, this is one of which I can remember every single detail. She was voracious, forceful, and seemingly on a mission…

Not quite a month and a half later, when she walked in the front door of our apartment and told me in the most timid of voices "I'm late", I didn't even blink. I walked across the street to the local pharmacy, purchased two pregnancy tests for her to take and headed on home, already knowing inside what was to come. She couldn't even bring herself to go check the tests, and as I walked back into the living room, all I said to her was "well, we better make some phone calls." She burst into tears instantly.

I can say this next bit without a single doubt in my mind. The absolute best thing to happen in my life came out of the absolute worst relationship I've ever had. Born on June 4th, 1997, my beautiful daughter Bailey Jessica joined us for the party, and has been since that day a constant source of love, joy, pride and a huge pain in my ass! She has been, is and always will be my little "Punk", and I would happily go through a thousand bad relationships over and over if it meant that she was the result. She's grown up knowing both her parents love her to death (in my mind the most important thing ever), and that our shit relationship never had a single thing to do with, or a negative effect on either her or our love for her. But more about Bailey later…

Eight months after Bailey was born, we called it quits for good. The fact was, she and I were simply shitty people together. I was a horrible boyfriend to her, and she was an atrocious girlfriend to me, and we never should have been together in the first place. When we split, she ended up moving back to the Midwest where her family lived, taking Bailey, our dog, our car, and about eighty percent of all my worldly belongings with her, ensuring that for the rest of my days, I'd be a long distance dad, and take an absolutely obscene number of vacations to small town Ohio to see my kid.

So that's it. You may hear me refer to my "Ex" again, but it'll only be in passing. You'll most certainly hear me refer to my daughter, but it's hilarious. So, this was short and painful, as promised! Now, back to the idiocy that was my life!

The OG's Greatest Hits

In one big mashup and in no particular order, here's a collection of some of the best, worst and craziest shit I either saw, took part in, or avoided in my long tenure at The Olympic Garden. Be warned, some of these are not for the faint at heart!

One.

He just wasn't looking good at all and I remembered asking as he came to the booth to give me his music for the night if he felt up to working. Waving me off with a shrug, he told me that something he'd eaten just wasn't agreeing with him but that he'd have a shot or two, and would be feeling great in no time! I'd basically forgotten all about it and went on with getting the show started.

After working in the club for as long as I had, I was use to the usual yells and screams from the ladies that attended the show, and had learned to block it out for the most part, but this one was different. It was absolutely blood curdling, and honestly sounded as if someone were being viciously stabbed to death with a dull butter knife. Jumping down from the DJ booth and running over to the corner behind me that was the source of the noise, I was greeted with a visual that I don't believe will ever leave me.

Dragging himself from one of the semi circular booths that was used for the more "private" table dances, doubled over with both hands gripping his mid section, the first thing to grab my attention wasn't the sight of him, or his screaming customer, it was the smell. As soon as it hit me I had to fight back the urge to vomit, and as my eyes adjusted to the mood lighting of the booth, I could quite clearly see that the booth and the floor, as well as the hysterical woman sitting in it were all covered in a glossy massive amount of liquid shit. Whatever hadn't agreed with his stomach had decided that leaving in the middle of his table dance for her was the best idea, and according to him, had just come flying out of his ass and around his thong with no warning what-so-ever. Unfortunately for both him and his customer, he'd just happened to be straddling her with his ass toward her face when it did.

Two.

It seemed like just another group table dance to me. I'd been grabbed by a very attractive blonde and dragged across the room to deliver a table dance for their bachelorette. The bachelorette was a bit on the nervous side according to her though, so instead of pulling her out on her own to dance for her, they wanted me to just dance for the whole group. No big deal at all. We danced for whole tables of girls dozens of times a night, so I hopped right in as the next song was starting up, and did my thing. I of course took notice of the fact that the whole group were pretty damn attractive young ladies, and I certainly enjoyed the song right along with them. As was the norm, girl talk ensued throughout my dance, and I listened while I did my thing as they argued quite boldly over who they thought gave the best head, even citing very graphic reasons why they assumed they were superior. Not exactly shocking chat considering the local and nothing I hadn't heard in the club before, so I only paid it mild interest (this was one of those times in my life that I actually did take a moment to take stock of just how far I had come. The Spiderman bedsheets drapes from that first show seemed so very far away!).

As the song ended, I thanked them and went about collecting my money. Taking the advice I'd been given on that very first night, during that very first table dance, I made sure I appeared to be in no rush to leave. All of the sudden, the girl that had hired me for the table came up with what seemed to her to be the greatest idea since Einstein's E=MC2.

"So lets find out!" She said as she hopped up and down at the table. "We've got a judge right here don't we? Lets just settle this once and for all! Whatcha think girls?" "totally!" Said one of the other ladies. "We TOTALLY need to have a blowjob contest!"

To my surprise, the rest of the girls seemed to think she was clearly on to something as well and had decided, all without asking me that I would be the judge for their impromptu cock gobbling competition. The winner according to them, would be the one who was able to bring me to completion, and upon hearing this little detail I decided to weigh in on the situation.

"Whoa...wait now... You want me to let the five of you take turns giving me head, and whoever manages to make me cum is the winner?" They all looked at me like I'd just stated the most obvious thing ever, and all agreed that that was exactly what they wanted. Well fuck, how was a gentleman to refuse such a request?

"Well... does everyone here swallow?"

Serious fucking question let me tell you! I couldn't go judging this all important competition just to blow a load all over the booth, now could I! Not only would I have to clean it up, but in the black light of the club the evidence of what had been going on would be way too obvious!

Three songs of back and forth in the booth. I started on the left, and at a fair pace simply worked my way like a typewriter around the booth. Three songs of getting blown by five women in a contest of their own devising, and let me tell you these girls were not kidding around! Three songs of wondering quite actively if this could possibly be real life. As I moved from girl to girl, the techniques were getting more and more creative. Clearly none of them had thought the contest (or I) would last nearly this long and as each girl got her next turn she did her damnedest to make it was the last. Three songs of not only looking over my shoulder constantly to make sure that Gloria wasn't paying attention, but that none of the other guys were paying attention either, and BAM! We had a winner! Wouldn't you just know it, it was their lovely bachelorette who took home the prize. All I could think as I strolled back to the dressing room to clean up a bit was "Wow, what a lucky guy she's marrying…"

Three.

She'd been a regular customer of the most popular dancer in the club for quite some time. A rich kid born with a silver spoon in her mouth, she'd started working in the club as a stripper just to piss off mom and dad. Lex, her favorite for months had always been the guy that she went to for her table dances and conversation, but when I ended up out of the booth and back in rotation at the club, she decided to grab me for a dance or two. I made damn sure they were fucking good ones.

My signature move was right at the start of my dance. As the song would kick in, I'd kneel down in front of the girl, look her dead in the eyes as I placed a hand on each of her knees, then, bluejeans, shorts, skirt or whatever, I'd slowly spread their legs, and before they had a chance to protest, I'd push myself half way up, then dive forward slowly running my face from their knee to their belly, then with my hands still on each leg, I'd use them to push myself up while sliding my body against theirs until I was face to face and crotch to crotch. After just one dance, she wasn't Lex's regular anymore, she was mine.

Almost every Friday and Saturday for months she could be counted on. She'd stroll upstairs around ten or eleven at night, grab a booth and wait for me. None of the other guys would do more than give her a passing hello because she had clearly marked me as hers. As soon as I saw her I knew my night of work was done. Without fail, every evening I was with her, she'd reach into her purse, pull out the wad of cash she'd just made downstairs and hand every penny to me.

The best part about the arrangement was that she didn't want to monopolize my time at all. In fact, she use to go out of her way to try and help me get more work. How? By playing the part while I gave her what was from outward appearances about the most erotic dance ever. I'd be pulling hair, she'd be kicking a heel toward the sky, biting her lip, grinding in time to the music with me... It was a real show! And the end of each, standing up and facing away from her, I'd lift one of her legs high in the air between mine and smack her ass so loud it would echo off the walls. It never failed to get me a dozen dances from the surrounding groups. Both of us always had a blast showing off, and to an exhibitionist as big as she was, I have no doubt being borderline ravaged while a bunch of women sat and watched got her as wet as the Amazon.

Four.

It was just another two girls sitting in a booth toward the back of the club. The male review had moved upstairs to the dramatically larger venue, and now had the capacity to hold close to four hundred women at a time. On weekends, you wouldn't find an empty seat anywhere in the house, and the now twenty plus dancers that worked the OG were just as busy as the original ten had been. Of course the larger club meant that it was much harder for Gloria to keep an eye on everything that was going on, which meant a lot of shit went unseen. At least by her.

The two girls hadn't seemed to be up to anything in particular really. They'd each had a couple of drinks and a couple of dances, but otherwise didn't appear the least bit out of place. I'd only noticed them from the DJ booth because of where they were seated, and both being attractive women, they of course drew my eye now and then.

At first I couldn't figure out why I thought something was off with them. One of the more high energy acts had just hit the stage, and although they'd just gotten a dance from one of the boys, they seemed overly quite. In fact, as I looked closer I noticed that neither of them even had their eyes open. They certainly weren't asleep with all this noise and commotion going on all around them, but it was just a bit too dark for me to make out what was going on. I turned up the dial for the lighting in their booth ever so slightly to see if I could get a better look, and I'll be damned if I didn't!

The extra lighting put off just enough of a glow for me to see that sitting side by side and shoulder to shoulder, each of them had a hand between the other girls thighs and both were holding what clearly appeared to be vibrators of some type that were going to fucking town! I even grabbed one of the guys who had brought his music up to the booth to point it out, and he was seeing the exact same thing I was… Within minutes I had more than the usual number of dancers around the booth trying to get a view of the two hot chicks banging away in the corner, when I'll be damned if one of the two didn't slide off the booth and under the table, without even looking to see if she was seen, and buried her face in the other girls pussy with what was clearly reckless abandon.

By the time she came up for air, the girl still seated still seated in the booth was practically lying down, one heel up on the seat, head thrown back without a care and handfuls of her friends hair as she clearly had one hell of an orgasm. I think almost every guy working the club that night and at least half of the customers were watching as she climaxed, and as the pair finally snapped back to reality all the dancers surrounding my DJ booth started a huge round of applause!

Five.

I'd gotten into the habit of getting pretty physical while collecting my tips on stage. The more "manly" and aggressive

I was on the stage, the more table dances I'd be hired for once I was back on the floor.

I'd taken to dragging their hands across my chest and stomach as they popped bills into my thong, I'd pull hair and arch them backward across my knee as I dove face first between their tits to snatch the bills that had been placed there, I'd bend them forward over my knee, pull a dollar from the waistline of their pants with my teeth and then leave them with the "CRACK" of a good slap on the ass as I walked to the next customer. Most of them thought it was great, some didn't care for it much, and a few, well a few thought it was license for them to get pretty aggressive with me too.

On my second stage set of the night, one of my more regular customers had bellied up to the meat rack to tip me a bit. She had obviously been drinking a fair amount, as had most of the women by this time of the night, and things could usually be counted on to get a bit more playful to say the least. After pulling hair and smacking ass with my regular who sat back in her chair with a satisfied smile, I shifted over to the girl sitting right next to her to gather a few tips. Having seen how I was just a moment before, she, like many before her assumed that it was okay to play a bit rough with me as well and as she slipped a few bills under the hip of my thong she bent forward and first licked, and then bit down pretty damn hard on my ass, prompting me to yell "FUCK" and push her back away from me.

When security escorted the paramedics upstairs to help I had to admit that this was a first. The second that her teeth were sinking into the flesh of my left butt cheek, my regular decided that she didn't approve of this behavior at all. The moment I pushed the girl away from me in surprise and pain, she took a right hook to the face that Tyson would have been proud of! My regular threw three massive consecutive punches that landed square in the middle of this girls skull, and knocked her completely unconscious right there against the stage! Then, with the offending girl lying bleeding and out cold, half on, half off the meat rack my regular turned, kissed me on the cheek and strolled right the fuck out the door.

Six.

I never dated customers. At least not ones that I was making money off of. It was simple, see a paying customer outside the club and they won't pay anymore. On the other hand, the girls downstairs were quite a different story.

In the more than four years that I was with my ex, I earned a reputation with the female dancers of OG. I was always at the club early, I was nice, I would chat and I always had a smile, but I didn't flirt and I didn't fuck around. They all knew I had a girlfriend and that I wasn't going to cheat. What that meant was that after four years in that place, I was a complete mystery. To them, as long as I was in a relationship I was just another one of the girls. I was just a dancer, and was off limits of my own accord.

Not too long after my breakup word got around quite quickly that I was single again, and as you'd expect it didn't take long until I ended up hooking up with one of the girls downstairs. Her name was Beth, and It was fucking great! I hadn't had good sex in so damn long that I could hardly remember what it felt like, and that night after we were both done with our shifts we fucked around like it was the last chance we were ever gonna have! As we parted ways early the next morning after a night of seriously aerobic fucking, it was with a very casual hug and a kiss and an "I'll see you at the club tonight and maybe we can play again after!"

Sitting in the back booth in the quiet part of the club like I did every night before the guys opened, I was quietly reading a book when Beth, dressed in the standard stripper pumps and micro bikini came bouncing over to give me a big hug and a kiss!

"So, I was really hoping I was gonna be able to see you tonight and have another go with you, but I got this big gig now and I gotta go make that money! I feel really bad though cause I had so much fun last night and don't want to leave you all alone…". She snuggled up to me in a very stripper like fashion, with the practiced pout of a true professional, kissed me on the cheek and then pulled me from my seat.

As she dragged me through the club by my hand with a big smile on her face, she told me that she had a great idea.

"Thumper, this is Dean, the guy I told you about that I was fucking last night!" Thumper, blonde, adorable, petite, topless and wiggling around on all fours on a stage that only had one guy at it crawled on hands and knees over to me, gave me a sexy kiss on the cheek and said "Well its very nice to meet you Dean!"

"So I have to go do that gig tonight instead of going back to Dean's place, so you should totally go home with him after work and fuck! You'll have a great time, I promise!" I had to admit as I headed home that night with Thumper grabbing at my cock from the back of my motorcycle that the OG was amazing place to be on the rebound!

Seven.

It was a birthday girl stage dance with two of our guys tasked to embarrass the living shit out of her. Her friends had hired the two biggest manliest guys from our roster to take her up on stage, asking specifically to just tear her to pieces. As I announced her name and asked her to join the guys waiting for her at the end of the stage, one of the largest women I'd ever seen in the OG bounded on over with a huge smile on her face, clapping her hands together and practically salivating.

As they sat her down on the chair and the music kicked in, she was bouncing up and down to the beat of the music, clearly not the least bit embarrassed as both dancers ripped their tear away pants off and got busy shoving ass and nylon covered cock in her face. One of the guys was doing his best to straddle her legs and basically thump his junk into her chest as the other was squatted down behind the chair, reaching around to hold her arms back to comically restrain her for the other guy. With an audible "SNAP" that could be heard clearly even over the very loud music, the chair that she'd been seated in decided that it was seriously fed up with this kind of shit, and committed suicide right out from under her.

As the chair split quite literally in two, the weight of both her and the dancer, as well as his vigorous bashing against her chest launched the two of them backward with a huge crash, completely pinning the poor bastard behind them to the floor with the full weight of not only the very plus sized lady but the other dancer as well. The only thing that could be heard more clearly than the chair snapping was the scream from the now very unhappy guy lost under mounds of confused flesh.

When three of the dancers who hopped on stage were finally able to help the poor lady up off the floor, the dancer had pulled his back so badly that he had to be taken to the hospital to deal with severe strain to his lower back. Who ever thought a stripper would need Workman's Comp?

Eight.

She had been coming into the club once a week for almost six straight months. The Daughter of a San Diego Native American Indian Chief, I assumed that her money must have come from casino's, although considering I never asked I suppose assuming that certainly makes me guilty of stereotyping.

I never once danced for her. She and usually a group of three or four friends would come in early to grab there favorite table which happened to be situated next to the big public viewing shower room, have a few drinks and chat with the guys. Every time she showed up you'd soon after find me sitting with her, chatting for hours about literally anything and everything, or not saying anything at all. For this, I was never given less than two-thousand dollars each and every time. It was crazy! But really, who was I to say anything. I had a great time talking to her, and even though I wasn't at all attracted to her I really enjoyed it when she was there.

They never usually stayed too late, and while they were there it was understood that I would tip Brice extra to keep me off the stage so that I could keep her happy. I don't think I ever knew her to stay past ten o'clock, which left me most of the night to still make money. The other rather odd side effect to her visits was that all the other girls at the show would see me, clearly one of the dancers not only not dancing but not socializing with anyone else at all, so when I was finally out on the floor I could often count on being very busy for the next hour simply working for women who were just curious!

On one particular evening, she had got me talking about skydiving. By the time I was speaking to her about it, jumping was almost all that I could think about. It had completely taken over my personal life. I was busy regaling her with the epic stories of my then all of a hundred jumps, all of which she seemed to find incredibly interesting, and she kept prodding me for more and more info. When I told her that I was very much looking forward to being able to afford to put together a camera helmet and new "rig" so that I could start working in the sport, I made sure to emphasize "afford". I was really only hoping I'd get a slightly bigger tip from her that night, but what I did get still shocks the shit out of me to this day.

"So the what did you call it? A Rig? You have to buy that from this place in California, and the helmet you have to order, but the cameras and stuff you can buy here in town? Like at a normal camera store? Well hell… we can take care of the camera stuff easy! Do you have any plans tomorrow?"

I was completely torn. On the one hand, If I saw her outside the club, I'd be breaking my number one rule when it came to regulars. Never ever see them after hours! But on the other hand, she was offering to foot the bill for both the video and still camera and lens that I would need to start building the camera set up that I desperately wanted, so I decided to take a chance and told her that I had the day free.

"Great! So write down your address for me, and I'll have my driver come and pick you up. I won't be able to come cause I've got a bunch of stuff to do, but I'll tell him to take you wherever you need to go and he'll sort everything out. Okay?"

Oh holy crap! Not only was she gonna buy me the camera stuff but she wasn't even going to come along, meaning I really wasn't breaking my rule! I of course told her that there was just no way I would be able to accept her doing this for me knowing full well she'd tell me she was going to do it anyway because she wanted to, which is exactly what she did.

As she left that night, I fully assumed that I wouldn't see anything for our time together, but I'll be damned if she didn't hand me the same two grand she did every time we sat and chatted and I was almost giddy!

The next day, her driver, a very quiet but pleasant older man showed up at my door exactly on time. He drove me to the two different camera stores I told him to, walked in with me and stood back while I requested the exact equipment I had known I'd wanted for a month, then only came forward when the cashiers asked for payment. Both times he casually slid a credit card across the counter and signed as casually as if he were buying a new shirt. He even followed it up with a "will that be all, sir?"

As we pulled back up to my apartment and I thanked him for his time, I felt no judgement from him at all. As I opened the door, he placed his hand on my forearm, pulled out an envelope from his inside jacket pocket, and said "from Miss, with her compliments. Have a very nice day young man." And off he went. Brand new shiny still frame and video camera in hand and grinning ear to ear, I walked into my place wondering what in hell was in the envelope, and ripped it open as soon as I'd set everything down.

On a handwritten note, with the loveliest handwriting I had ever seen was written:

Dean, I hope that you were able to find all the camera equipment you need to get you started. Hopefully this will take care of what you need to get the rest of your gear so you can start jumping. I know how much you love it from how excited you get when you talk about skydiving.

Good luck!

Inside the envelope with the note, was enough money not only to buy the thousand dollar helmet I'd told her about, but my complete skydiving rig, as well as all the little bits and pieces I needed to jump my ass off. She'd just given me a gift to the tune of five-thousand dollars in cash, and I couldn't decide if I was happy, or a bit freaked out by it. As it turned out, the previous night was the last time I would ever see her, and to this day I have no idea where she disappeared to.

Nine.

As I started the table dance I knew every guy on the floor hated me! She was the hottest little thing I'd seen walk through the door in a very long time, and although her and her relatively attractive friend had been at the show since the mid way point, they hadn't gotten a dance from anyone.

I had by then taken a much different approach than most of the guys working. They would wait only as long as it took a new group of girls to hit their seats before they would literally attack them, trying to get dances out of them. I on the other hand, stayed well away from the feeding frenzy, and would only approach groups much later, after the other guys backed off. This time, it paid off in a big way!

As she asked me if I could come dance for her and her friend, she practically purred the words, and as I got started, she made sure to tell me to make it a good and sexy one. I did everything I could think of! Sliding up spread legs, hot breath on necks, gently but firmly pulling hair, allowing both their hands to wander quite a bit… It was fucking hot!

When she handed me a slip of paper with her room number on it, and a spare key, she told me that they would be waiting for me when I was done. "No rush" she said, "we won't be going anywhere". This was the first time I'd received this kind of an invitation, and although I was super excited, I was also nervous as fuck…

I could not get out of the club quickly enough! Throwing my shit in my bag all helter-skelter and not even bothering to arrange my money, I was out the door and on the road the instant we were released. It wasn't until I was turning off my bike and walking into the hotel that I realized I hadn't even bothered to shower before I came, and I was nasty with eight hours of baby oil and sweat (both mine and customers). When I knocked on the door and she let me in, both she and her friend were dressed in outfits that left very little to the imagination. As I walked in to the dimly lit room, I was given a hug and a kiss on the cheek by each of them, and was by then just a huge ball of nerves!

"I hope it's okay, but I really should take a shower… I'm just not fit to be around after tonight, so is it cool?" It might have been my imagination, but they almost seemed a touch put off by the request, yet told me that of course I could, and aimed me to the shower.

I had hoped a quick rinse would settle me a bit, but as I walked back into the room, only dressed now in one of the hotel towels, I went into total brain lock mode. For me, when I get truly nervous, I talk. A lot. And sitting there on the edge of the bed, with these two very capable and ready women stretched out before me what did I do? I fucking talked my way right out of the pussy.

An hour went by. I knew how badly I was fucking up, but the more I talked, the worse it got, and the more uncomfortable I thought going in for the action was going to be, so I just kept talking, and talking, and talking. When the hotel room door suddenly opened up, the only person who was terribly surprised was me. As some guy that looked to be in about his mid thirties walked in and saw the three of us, clearly in our own "spaces" with nothing physical at all on the horizon, he grabbed a few things off the counter, smiled at the girls, looked at me and said "Dude, you should have just started fucking them!" Seemed I was most certainly not their first attempt at a threesome, and this dude, who's name I never heard and didn't give a fuck about had figured out in an instant that I was a complete knob. "C'mon Ladies… Lets go hit the floor and play or something if you ain't gonna be playin' up here."

The next thing I knew the girls were dressed and heading out the door to meet their friends, leaving me in the hallway behind them, feeling like the biggest idiot in Vegas, which at that very moment, I probably was.

Ten.

As the police officer told me to shut off the music and get all the dancers in the back room, I had no idea what the fuck was going on, but I knew enough to do what I was told. As I entered the now packed dressing room, I like each of the other dancers was greeted with the sight of yet another police officer, and one of our own, a dancer who went by the name Mac standing there in his thong a pair of boots and a shiny set of handcuffs.

"Did any one of you witness what happened with him and the woman who called us? Anybody? Does the club have working cameras up here? Nobody saw him and the woman together in the booth?"

After all of about five minutes of group questions, all of which most of us didn't understand and had no answers for, we were told to get back out on the floor and continue the show. As it turned out, during what must have been a rather hot and heavy table dance, the girl Mac was dancing for had reached into his thong, pulled out his cock and started playing with him. Unfortunately for her, she did too good a job of it, because, like the idiot that Mac was, he assumed she was trying to get him off and promptly blew his load all over her chest and dress! You could have seen her from across the room once the black-lights hit her, and it appeared he hadn't been serviced in a while if the volume of spluge was any indication. She had been shocked to say the least, and when after giving her a handful of bar napkins he left the scene, she hopped on her phone and called the police. An unfortunate move for both him and her, as the police decided that clearly it was a consensual act between two adults, but because it had been in public was still completely illegal, and they both went to jail.

Eleven.

I knew exactly which girl it was. She was about as skanky as they came, and was all over me. I wasn't enjoying dancing for this one at all, but her money was as green as the rest, and the night wasn't exactly busy, so dance dance dance.

When I woke up the next morning, it wasn't to my alarm, or bright lights or dogs barking, it was to a ridiculous itching I couldn't seem to scratch away. At a glance everything seemed just fine, but still being half asleep I wasn't really focusing. After a shower with some vigorous scrubbing it seemed to get better, but then as soon as I was on the couch and not moving around it started up again. And it wasn't a normal itch. Not normal at all, because it didn't feel so much like an itch as a tickle. A tickle from something fucking moving!

Hours later, having washed all my clothes and sheets, pulled out the clippers and trimmed off every strand of body hair and used a special shampoo I'd been horrified to go buy from the local drug store, I had finally gotten rid of the last of the crabs! If I hadn't thought stripping was a dirty job before, I sure as fuck did then, and never went to work without a bottle of hand sanitizer again (which I can tell you from personal experience is safe for all areas of the body, although it does have a bit of kick to it when it hits your balls…)

Twelve.

Normally the male review was closed on Tuesdays, but on this particular one, we had been hired out for a private show. It had actually happened a few times before, the most notable of which was when the daughter of the Sultan of Brunei bought the place out for her and a handful of her friends, and all of us had to perform while surrounded by armed body guards. On this occasion though, we were told that it was a private party for a VIP of the club for a birthday celebration, and ten of the dancers were asked to work.

Being the DJ and MC at the time, I had no choice but to be there, but as it turned out, not being there would have been the real tragedy.

The VIP the birthday celebration was for was a long time OG of the OG, a female stripper of local fame that went by the name of Asher. Asher had been in the game for as long as the place had been in operation, and a few of the managers of the club decided she should have her own special night upstairs. Special is exactly what it turned out to be!

Gloria was nowhere to be found. Not a bouncer in sight. Just the dancers, a few cocktail waitresses and me. As Asher and a group of her girls walked upstairs everyone began singing happy birthday, throwing confetti and popping balloons all over the place, and after taking a quick round of shots from the bar, the ladies sat up at the meat rack to enjoy their own personal show.

Thirty minutes into it there was no doubt this shit was gonna get hectic. Word had gotten around downstairs that there was a no public allowed, strippers only show going on upstairs, and more and more girls started finding excuses to come upstairs to check it all out.

By the time Asher ended up in the ceremonial victims chair on the stage, there were more than fifty girls from downstairs in attendance, and everyone, guys included was hammered! As the music kicked in for her public table dance, the first person to take a piece of clothing off was Asher herself, and with a complete lack of adult supervision upstairs, the whole thing went pretty bonkers from there…

You would have though, looking out over the scene from the raised DJ booth that you were in some nudist colonies version of a rave, because with very few exceptions, there wasn't a clothed body in sight! There were naked girls on stage dancing away, completely naked guys giving table dances to stripped down ladies in the corner, girls dancing for girls in the booths, girls and guys in the shower room. There was more rampant out of control sex in that place that I could have ever imagined. People ended up getting fucked on the stage, in the booths, on the floor, behind the bar (Yes, the bartenders and waitresses got in on the act too) guys getting blown in the shower room, girls sitting on each others faces, or pinned up against the dark tinted windows that looked out over the strip…

I learned more than a few things that night I can tell you. One, its very difficult to run a DJ booth properly while getting blown by, well I'm not exactly sure by who or how many (as there had been a number of girls in the booth with me) cause it was pretty dark, and two, if you put a bunch of strippers in a room together with music and alcohol shit is gonna get weird, and weird in the best way imaginable!

Fuck me, what a career.

Jumping into yet Another Life

Skydiving had truly taken over. I had unwittingly launched into yet another completely different way of life, and living in what I liked to call "The Lunatic Fringe" was all I had known for a very very long time; so skydiving it seemed was the perfect fit to say the least! My student training went by almost without a hitch as I'd spent a ton of my free time flying around in the wind tunnel, and by the time I started jumping as a student I'd managed to make all the normal mistakes there and correct them in the much more safe and secure environment of a padded room.

Between jumping as much as I could, and spending an excessive amount of time at Flyaway, I had managed to become a pretty decent flyer in a very short period of time. The only thing that the tunnel couldn't help me learn was how to fly the parachute, but I was in no rush to fly anything fast or out of control so I took that part of the sport one happy jump at a time.

Once again, due to whatever good or bad luck seems to have followed me around I was given opportunities in skydiving that came much quicker than they should have, and because of it I was able to start work in the industry in a matter of months instead of the sometimes years some people can wait. I'd met the right people, I'd had the money to spend on the training, I'd been tenacious about my desire to jump and had made it known that I was there to skydive. It was amazing, It was scary, and It was my new life. As my career got started in skydiving, Just like it had been with my career as a stripper, in very short order I ended up with more than my fair share of stores to tell. so here again in no particular order, are just a few of the funniest and nastiest from my first couple of years in the sport of skydiving in Las Vegas:

One.

"Yeah, I'll take a San Antonio Sirloin, the 12 ounce, with mushrooms and onions, baked potato with butter… Oh and shrimp on the steak too please."

The dinner went down just as good as it did every time I ordered it. I'm not much on chain restaurants to be honest, but Lonestar does a pretty good job on a cut of meat, and I highly recommend it. Follow it up with a good night sleep and then cinnamon raisin bread, an *entire loaf* of cinnamon raisin bread on the way to the DZ, and you have my recipe for success.

It was really just between Weasel and I, but of course it was a contest that pretty much everyone could enjoy. At least that's the way we looked it at. Mr. Paul Wetzel, more affectionately known as Weasel, was the other champion in this competition, and had his own special recipe to try and officially take the title of "Stinky Ass Mother Fucker" at Skydive Las Vegas. The sad truth of the matter was, a fart contest really isn't much fun for anyone other than the competitors, but neither of us really cared much what anyone else thought.

The contest got under way at just shy of three thousand feet on load number one, and Weasel and I fell into a pretty good rhythm, trading shot for shot and gauging our success on the faces of the poor unfortunate souls onboard. For the most part, it was a dead draw and beginning to look as though it was going to be an all day affair. Kind of like a game of cricket that doesn't make much sense and just won't seem to end. Then a twist of fate on load 5… With rare timing and completely without intention, both Weasel and I let loose with our own personal version of the atom bomb.

I knew that fact to be true even before the noxious fumes had left our respective jumpsuits simply by the look on Weasels face, and he knew the same of me. I could feel the heat from my best effort slowly creeping out through my zipper, and like scientists on the Manhattan Project who built Fat Man and

Little Boy, I feared that I may actually set the air on fire with this one… We watched together, Weasel and I, as the faces of those onboard turned from amusement to horror and eyes were opened wide with sheer terror. The radius continued to widen and drift towards the Otter door as each group in turn came to the realization that they had become the unwitting victims of a truly heinous attack.

The only true casualty of the war to end all wars turned out to be a little Japanese man nervously seated next to his instructor at the door of the plane. As Weasel and I traced the line of destruction floating quietly down the Otter, this poor mans face seemed for some reason to grab my attention, and I knew it was going to be bad. It hit him all at once, and with a viciousness I could never have imagined. As the man made eye contact, his tandem instructor had just enough time to pull out the one gallon zip lock puke bag he had stashed in his jumpsuit and hand it to him before all hell broke loose. With a force that would have blown the bottom out of a lesser bag, the poor man filled it up with everything he had in his stomach, and probably some of his small intestines… It was one of the proudest moments in both Weasel's and my career. It was also the reason that the "No Farting" rule was instated at the old Skydive Las Vegas.

Two.

When I was first "approached" about becoming a tandem instructor I was completely and totally against the idea for about 1,000 reasons. Those reasons being every damn one that I had filmed up to that point. I'd seen the ones that had gone very right, and I'd seen the ones that had gone very wrong, and the only part of tandems that appealed to me at all was filming them. It was primarily for this reason that when the owner and operator of Skydive Las Vegas at the time told me that if I didn't agree to become a tandem instructor for him I could fuck off and go be a cameraman for someone else, I just about shit my pants.

The best of the best tandem gear at the time was miles behind any of the gear that I had jumped over a thousand times now, and the equipment alone terrified me. Jumping that gear, and flying the tandem parachutes we had was like trying to do bar dips with two hundred pounds strapped to you, and when you flared these damn things try and land softly, the only fucking thing that changed was your expression… These canopies sometimes opened so fast and so violently, especially in a desert environment, that the cameramen were known to hurt their necks trying to keep the tandem in frame. Yet the fact remained that I had absolutely no choice but to agree to go thru the training. I was completely vested in the sport by that time, rooted in Las Vegas, and completely fucked.

Simon was the one that did it to me. He was the one that got me successfully thru my tandem course, and in the process forced me to believe that I'd made some serious miscalculations with my life. It was he who showed me the sidespin video (really bad shit), he who drilled into me all the different ways that a student could fuck me (figuratively), and he who also redeemed himself by being the dumb ass to ride on the front for the required drougeless tandem which meant that in freefall he and I reached speeds in excess of 180 miles per hour! He drilled into me the importance of making sure I communicated to my student all the things they needed to do to help make the skydive a success, and then sat back and laughed his ass off as manifest assigned to me a Japanese student who spoke no English…

Three.

His name was Randy, and he was a complete fucking tool. He'd been brought to Skydive Las Vegas by his wife and two close buddies to make the tandem skydive that he'd been given as a 40th birthday gift. He was sporting a pair of Oakley Blade sunglasses a few inches above his 70's porn star moustache, a nice fat gold chain around his neck and a No Fear T-shirt about 2 sizes two small stretched across his chest. He tipped the scales at just over 220 lbs and I hated him instantly.

As He put on the Skydive Las Vegas required jumpsuit, Frap Hat, gloves, elbow pads and knee pads he did nothing but bluster in front of his wife and friends about how he not only felt no fear over the upcoming tandem, but how disappointed he was that he was required to do it strapped to another person. When I told him that I was glad he wasn't scared because I was terrified, he thought I was kidding and laughed like a total jackass, right along with his No Fear (*and no jump*) buddies.

As we rounded the corner to load the Otter for the jump, his behavior flipped as quick as a Catholic schoolgirl the first time the hit of Ecstasy kicks in… He went from the full of himself could care less asshole, to a scared little kid, and I thought I might even have to help him up the ladder to get in the plane.

As I told him it was time to sit on my lap to start getting ready, he was totally done in. He looked me in the eyes, and with more sincerity than I'd ever seen told me to "Please please, make me do this, no matter what!" As I began getting him all attached and ready to go, I seriously began to fear that good old Randy just might take a piss all over me, and had about decided that he was going to be my first student refusal as a tandem instructor. To my surprise, just a few minutes later I found myself in freefall with him.

As the canopy cracked open I could hear, with increasing volume, Randy screaming his ever-loving ass off. At first I didn't know if he had completely lost it, or if it has just been that good… Then I started to make out the words "FUCK YEAH", and "HOLY FUCKING SHIT", and what I still to this day swear was a bit of a sob, and realized that Randy had just quite literally had the time of his life.

With more skill (or luck) then I had yet displayed as a tandem instructor, I put Randy down to within twenty feet of his wife and friends, and disconnected him expecting the usual jog over to give the boys a high five BEFORE kissing the wife… Instead, in a flash, he turned to face me, jumped up and wrapped both his legs around my waist, dropped me to the ground like a sack of flower, and kissed me full on the mouth! I was so completely shocked by the radical turn of events that I just flailed around like a turtle turned over on his shell, wiping off my mouth and trying to figure out why my face itched… And just like that, I loved being a tandem instructor.

Why? It was because for the briefest of moments, Randy was truly just Randy. He wasn't the image of himself he'd painted over the years, he wasn't the Randy that his wife and his friends expected him to be, he wasn't anything but the product of an event that he never truly could have imagined before that day, and it was I who had the privilege of giving him the experience. He had in turn, without knowing it, shown me just as quickly and clearly the gift that I had been given. The ability to show people what living in the moment really is, and just how amazing, even for the briefest of times our lives can sometimes be. For that, I will never forget, and always thank that big prick for being exactly the way he was when he arrived, and the completely different person he briefly became before leaving.

Four.

Until that moment, I had no idea that a grown man could be so completely entertained with his own junk. It's yet another bizarre visual from skydiving that I fear I will never be able to rid myself of.

Patrick was one of close to a dozen jumpers to sign up for a naked group skydive for the filming of a British television show on American sexuality. I had been picked to fly primary camera for the dive, which is how I ended up with the image of him stuck in my brain for life. Patrick, having abandoned the formation to show off a touch of his own flair, was basically lounging about half way between a sit and back fly, legs spread as wide as a cheerleader on any given night, with an enormous smile spread across his face as he vigorously pointed to the semi bouncing frantically between his legs. Thankfully, because he was a Frenchman, I was spared having to watch his sack bouncing around as well, as it was so hairy that it more closely resembled a blonde bonsai bush caught in a wind storm than a scrote. The kicker on the Patrick image was the oversized bright yellow smiley face hat strapped to the top of his head, adding a very surreal touch to the whole show.

Amazingly, all of the other fellas on the dive remained respectfully on their bellies, sparing me seeing a group of naked men holding hands with cocks-a-flying in a well organized O2 circle jerk. Once down, the rest of the group all had the good graces to cover up after landing, leaving me to end my video filming 4 men wrapped in parachutes while a naked Frenchman now sans rig, skipped circles in the landing area around them, kicking up a ton of dust and singing what I think was the French national anthem.

Five.

She was pear shaped. She was whiny, she was as uncomfortable in the harness as a pear shaped whiny woman was going to be. She wasn't just bitching under canopy, she was borderline screaming about how uncomfortable the leg straps were, and no matter what I said or did, she wouldn't shut the hell up. All those little tricks you learn along the way to keep this kind of thing from happening I still had yet to learn, and so I was so completely thrown off what little game I had that I pretty much stopped paying attention to anything but her mouth, and the fact that it wouldn't fucking close.

I was hanging under a massive beast of a canopy with this miserable human being hanging in front of me, just wanting to get back to Earth as quickly as I could. I'd given up on even trying to talk to my passenger at this point, because she had slipped from English into some sort of high pitched screech, occasionally punctuated by a random grunt or two and it was seriously freaking me out. Unfortunately for her, it freaked me out so much so that I committed the horrible Cardinal sin on those old canopies. I forgot to pick up the flair toggles. The flair toggles were an extra set of lines that ran to the rear of the canopy, and were used to give a lot more power to slowing down on landing.

When I realized I'd forgotten them, I made the whole situation a whole lot worse by snatching for them low, instead of beginning my flair early. The result? I flared all the way to my toes, and the only thing that changed was knowing how fucked I was. The next change to occur was the shape of her ankle as she sat on it. Hard. I probably didn't actually hear it snap, but I sure as hell imagined I did later. The rest was all her. Fuck me could that woman scream!

Six.

I wasn't particularly interested in the night jump until I found out that the "cute girls" were planning on doing a naked 6 way. Not surprisingly, the manifest started to fill up pretty quickly, even after the girls announced that everyone would have to go naked to get on it. It was to be my first naked skydive. Considering my previous profession, I wasn't terribly bothered by it, and since it was a night jump, I knew there wouldn't be any pesky video out there trying to bother me down the road. The way it all fell, I ended up in a good spot in the plane just behind the naked six way, but I also ended up solo, and last out.
As it turned out, the plane ride wasn't as interesting as it could have been. Between the darkness and sitting on the benches, the only view to be had was the occasional nipple slipping out

above or below a chest strap, and a decent six way butt shot as the girls exited. I gave the girls a reasonable amount of time and stepped out onto my back so I could watch the plane fly away.

I'll admit, the feeling of naked free fall is not an unpleasant one, and I caught myself giggling a few times on the way down. As pull time came, I found myself wondering how much damage a hard opening could do, but thankfully my canopy was feeling kind and the opening was plenty soft.

Alright. Canopy checks out. Slider stowed. Breaks released. Now head towards the DZ which isn't there. Wait?! Okay, relax. Probably just turned a bit on opening. So the DZ should be... Nope. Looking left... Looking right... Wait, if that's the supermarket, then the landing area should be... FUCK!

Nothing but darkness everywhere, and a landing area that had to be a good 2 miles away on a no wind night. The only place I could spot with certainty was the store, which also happened to be the only place bright enough to give me any view of the ground. At 9pm on a Saturday evening, I set up for my base to final over the parking lot of a moderately busy 24 hour supermarket. The only place in the lot with enough space to land was the drive directly in front of the entrance doors, and of course ended up being exactly where I landed.

My canopy didn't even have the good graces to land on, or in front of me, and instead decided to daintily fall behind, leaving me standing in front of a dozen or so very surprised people staring at me, clad in a pair of Nike's, some worn out football gloves and a harness. With really nothing else I could possibly do, I turned to the growing crowd and said the first thing that came to mind. "Anybody got a cell phone I can use?"

Seven.

They'd had to review my video of his exit from the Otter to try and determine what had happened. He'd been a traveling jumper that had made his way to Boulder City to get a few jumps in with his friend before hitting the strip for the long weekend. Both he and his buddy had been in a rush when they arrived, and had finished their paperwork just after the ten minute call for the next load was made.

Nobody in Las Vegas knew the guy, and nobody was paying attention as he was running around trying to get his gear in order. When he loaded the plane last as he and his friend were the only fun jumpers on the load and would exit first, it was me he ended up sitting next to. After the ritual handshake most jumpers exchange just before exit, they were on their way!

Just another jump was all I saw as the two exited in front of me, and I went about climbing outside the airplane to film my tandem. It wasn't until I had landed from my uneventful jump that I found out something had gone terribly wrong, and I, like every other Vegas regular only wanted to know who it was! It's a terrible thing to say I suppose, but there wasn't one person on the dropzone that wasn't relieved to find out that it was one of the visitors that had gone in ("Going in" is a skydiving term for hitting the ground without an open parachute, or more generally just dying on a jump, regardless of why).

As the search parties fanned out to try and locate the jumper, we all knew we were looking for a body, not a survivor, but it didn't change the fact that he needed to be found. Shorty after we had started the search, one of the groups near me on the right gave out a yell announcing to everyone that they had found something, and I reflexively ran over to, shit I don't know, help?

As I popped up over the little dune separating me and the group that had found him, I easily spotted the reserve parachute which had partially blown out of the container when he hit the ground. I remember following the lines down to a rather large desert bush that was mostly concealing the body from my view, and then remember seeing his helmet lying in the sand about thirty feet away from him and thinking how hard he must have hit the ground to launch it so far from his body; then I realized that to my horror, the helmet wasn't empty.

Eight.

God damn FUCKING PRE-MADONNA! I'd seen him flip out on people before, practically on a daily basis, but this was the first time Mikey had ever gone off on me. He was known for being a complete asshole by the entire sport of skydiving, but most of us that worked for the guy figured it went a hell of a lot deeper than that.

In the two years that I'd been shooting video at Skydive Las Vegas, I had seen this colossal prick go through over two-hundred different staff members, and I had yet to see one that was fired for a good reason. Because of how volatile he was, I did my best to stay away from him with anything but good news and hard work. That day had just turned out to be my day.

By the time he finished screaming at me in the middle of a hanger full of jumpers and customers, he'd called me a fucking pre-madonna half a dozen times, and skydivers being the sensitive lot that they are not only remembered he'd yelled the name, but they'd quickly taken to calling me by it whenever they had the chance.

A few months later, at a big goodbye party that was being thrown at a local restaurant It once again came up in conversation. Most of the guys that I worked with at SDLV were pretty big drinkers. Lots of beer and lots of shots. At least half of them in attendance were heavy Guinness drinking Brits, and not one of them didn't shoot me the most fucked up look you can imagine when I ordered a Coke to drink instead of something with more bite.

I'm sure I'd told all of them at some point that I didn't drink alcohol, but they all acted as if it were news to them, and told me point fucking blank that if I didn't have a drink voluntarily, they'd help me change my mind…

"Ahhh, I guess I'll have a, I don't know, like a white wine or something?"

Holy fucking hell you should have heard the noise erupt from the table! You would have thought I'd just bounced into the room wearing a pink tutu and halter top! "Fucking pussy" this, and "Complete Puff" that… Then one of the staff, a big brawly ex Royal Marine named Dale decided that between the whole stripper thing and the white wine, a much better name for me than pre-madonna would just flat out be "Princess". I've had that fucking nickname for 23 years now. What a cunt.

Nine.

As I hit the record button, I started as rehearsed with a tight shot of an eighteen inch semi-realistic appearing black dildo. As I panned the camera back to show the full scene, the viewer was able to see that the dildo was being held firmly in the gloved left hand of Simon, who stood fully geared on the ramp of Skydive Las Vegas.

"This video is being filmed to show wether or not a skydiver in freefall is able to properly track away from another jumper while holding this". The dildo was then raised toward the camera so that anyone not already focused in on the fact that he held a rather large phallic item could now draw their attention toward it. Without any further fanfare, Simon turned from the camera and started walking toward the C-206 behind him.

The plane ride to altitude was as quiet as Cessna rides usually are, and as we turned toward jump run, Simon and I leaned in to once again go over the dive. The plan was simple. Exit, face off for a few seconds then continue to film without changing perspective or angle while Simon first tracked away from me for about ten seconds, then tracked back. Exit we did, face off we did, back and forth Simon went, then at break off he tracked and pitched, I filmed, I pitched, we landed.

Once the video was dumped down on tape and a few copies made, that was that. It should have been a fucking joke. I can imagine all of the different reasons why we might have made such a video and pretty much all of them would have been funny as hell. Simon Wade, white as white, tracking around the skies over Boulder City, Nevada holding a massive black cock in his hand. This was unfortunately the only situation in which there was simply no humor at all, and as we knew then, it was also very important video for the entire sport of skydiving.

It's a fight that hasn't happened too many times in the sport, but it has happened, and it's a fight that skydiving can never afford to lose. The legal battle over the validity of the waiver that each and every one of us has signed. The footage that I had shot, along with the testimony of many jumpers and non jumpers alike was being used to fight a lawsuit over the death of someone most people had never heard of.

Vic was a Perris camera flyer, known by many, and as far as I could ever tell, loved by all. Vic and his partner Troy Hartman leapt to what by skydiving standards was huge mainstream fame when they won the X-Games gold in 1997 in what was by far the most publicized and watched form of our sport at the time, Skysurfing. By the time Vic hit 33, he'd managed not only to rank at the top in the world flying camera, but had brought home the gold in numerous competitions with and without Troy. He'd even filmed Super Bowl commercials, and been given an Emmy for his skill.

Then the unthinkable happened. On Mother's Day in May of 1998, Vic was killed during a skydive after a body to body canopy collision with another friend of mine. It not only shocked and horrified everyone in Las Vegas where the jump had taken place, it devastated all in Perris Valley, and indeed the entire skydiving world and all who knew him. None more of course than his family, who not only had to deal with the fact that they had lost a loved one, but had lost him under what seemed to be such ridiculous circumstances.

Without going into too much of the jump, the plan had been for Vic to film a birthday four-way between friends over Skydive Las Vegas which would unbeknownst to the birthday boy, include the rubber dildo. The plan had been to build a round, pull out and pass around the dildo while thumping the birthday boy with it, all of which would be captured on a film which everyone would no doubt laugh their asses off while watching later on. The jump had gone pretty much to plan until break-off, where Vic was suppose to dump in place as the rest tracked off. The next thing anyone knew, Vic had a main malfunction and spun into the jumper below him who'd been holding the dildo. He hit with such force that Vic's helmet and shoes were thrown off from the force violent impact. When the sun set that day, Vic was gone, the jumper he hit in critical condition, and the skydiving world just a little less bright.

I don't think a single person didn't hurt for Vic's family and friends, and when the lawsuit was filed and finally went to court a few years later, it wasn't difficult to understand why. They were destroyed over the loss as we all would be, confused by the events themselves, and pissed off by rumors and guesses over what really happened. Even though every jumper cringed when they found out about the lawsuit, they understood what the family was feeling, but they just couldn't win. If they won...

The worst part about the lawsuit for most of us in Las Vegas was that we pretty much all absolutely hated Mikey, the owner of Skydive Las Vegas. Had it been under any other circumstances, we all would have wished he'd end up eviscerated and spread out across The Strip to be picked apart by small furry animals. As far as I know, nobody else in the sport had ever been as universally hated as him, but we simply had no choice but to stand behind him in regard to the case. Why? Well it's a sick, fucked up and very simple answer. If the waiver we sign in skydiving is ever beaten in court, our sport as we know it would be done.

When the case was over, it was decided by the court that the waiver was enforceable, and that Vic held the responsibility for the accident when for a reason we'll never know he chose to track above the jumper he hit. It decided that it was his decisions that led to the collision, and the court released Skydive Las Vegas and the jumper he hit from all liability.

The win didn't make anyone feel any better. For the jumpers, it drew out the process of grief and caused an uneasy tension; and for Vic's family it was a financial burden which could only have amplified their pain. Even though the right decision was made, nobody won.

Ten.

"So… We're friends now, right?" "Yeah, for sure man. Why?" "Well, cause I've gotta ask a question. I don't know if you remember when I came out with my girlfriend and made my first skydive, but I have to know because of something she told me… Did you have a boner when you took her on her jump?" Will looked at me as if I'd asked him the stupidest question ever posed to anyone in the history of mankind, and replied in a very matter of fact manner. "Of course I did. I jam a boner in EVERYONE'S back!"

Eleven.

I had been jumping my ass off all day long. It was hot, it was dusty, it was hours from sunset, and I hadn't been feeling well from the first load. Usually, when I and the camera flyers were jumping together, I was the total ham. I'd have a blast with both student and them both on and off video, but today was far from the usual. As my camera-man hung from the strut and watched me and my student work our way out the door, I knew damn well I looked simply miserable. Even so, in freefall I tried to remain total control, and give my student a great ride.

Then came the signal of "five five" and the pull. Back then we were jumping tandem canopies that opened up in shall we say a less than forgiving way sometimes, and the only thing I could say when our canopy came out was "FUCK!!" My neck actually hurt from the speed my head was thrown forward, and if it hadn't been for the soft helmet on my students head I probably would have broken my nose! It was a complete train wreck.

As ! came in for a landing, I actually slid in, and sat the tandem down. I was pretty sure by the look on his face that my camera-man thought I may have hurt myself on the opening, and as soon as he had finished filming the post jump interview with the student, he went to make sure that he was alright. I only had one thing to say:

"I shit myself."

NoG

Almost 8 years. For the majority of that time I had spent most every weekend dancing or running the show at the Olympic Garden, and for the most part it had been one hell of a run. It had cost me a couple of relationships and more lost nights of sleep than I could possibly count, but all and all it had been an incredible and bizarre period in my already strange life! But as with all good things…. When I started there, I was dancer number 10. It stayed that way for quite some time, and looking back, even though we were in the small room with the tiny stage, they were the salad days.

When the show moved upstairs and started growing up, I was still in a great place, as I was once again the MC for the show, and in that club, being the MC was pretty much the best gig in the room. But as time and tide will do, shit shifted around and I ended up back on the floor as a full-time dancer. By the time my boots hit the stage again, we had gone from 10 dancers to 20 plus, and every night meant a hell of a lot more hustle than I liked. It had become too damn cut throat, and it just wasn't my style. The new guys that had been brought on were cocky, overbearing, and rude not only to the customers, but to their fellow dancers, and I had a hard time enjoying much of anything about the OG anymore. The customers as well weren't like they had been, I'd imagine in response to the way guys were hassling them now, so any approach to a table usually meant being greeted with more than a little hostility.

I'd been looking for a reason to leave for some time, but simple economics kept me from looking too hard. The more I had to hustle for money though, the more I hated it and the less I made. Even when I'd become a full-time skydiver and was jumping actively for Skydive Las Vegas I'd still hung on to my "thong-life". Although it was my entrance into the full-time world of jumping that finally convinced me that my life as a stripper was all but over.

Being at the OG until close to four in the morning, and then driving straight to Boulder City to sleep on the couch because I had to be ready for first load at eight was beating the living hell out of me, and if I were cornered into making a choice between the two lives, there really wouldn't be too much to think about. I couldn't count the number of times that I'd all but fallen asleep while climbing to altitude in the plane, and I'd be in such shit shape by the end of a full day of jumping that the idea of having to be back in the club a few hours later was just horrifying.

As it was though, my exit from the Olympic Garden didn't come because of skydiving, it came from one of the other dancers. David had been working with me for close to four years now at the OG, and knew me to be first and foremost a dancer. He was one of the originals at the club like me, and I don't know if he knew I wasn't happy working there anymore or not, but when the manager of his day job asked him if he knew of any dancers looking for work he thankfully thought of me. One phone introduction later and I had an interview.

Jed was his name, and he had been managing the stage of the Hard Rock Hotel and Casino since it opened in March of 1995 and had it running like a machine almost since day one. Having been on the roadie side of the entertainment business for his entire adult life, managing just one stage and handling all the different acts that came through was right up his alley. What wasn't up his alley was what the hotel had asked him to set up in their concert space when it wasn't in use.

It was named "The Joint" most of the time, but on the new nights the hotel wanted to set up "The Orbit Lounge" would be its name, Although it was most certainly anything but loungy. With the capacity for over two-thousand people, it was an enormous space, and the management of the hotel had decided that letting it sit empty while waiting for acts like Sheryl Crow and Carlos Santana to grace the stage was just a fucking waste.

The next thing you knew, Every Friday and Saturday night starting at eight o'clock, the venue would kick off as a night club that would run until two in the morning, offering the best in the dance must of the time, six different bars and at least an attempt at a lounge area. When the project was tossed into Jed's lap to deal with, he really couldn't have cared less about the small logistics of it all which is probably why I got the job.

My so called interview was about a five minute walk through the back halls of the Hard Rock, and by the time we had maneuvered our way through its passages to end up back stage I was told that the gig of Go-Go dancer for The Orbit Lounge in the Hard Rock Casino was mine if I wanted it. 8 till 2 no matter what, and it paid four hundred bucks a night. No more hustling, no more getting slapped or bit or spanked, no more having to dive face first into the sweat glistening cleavage of a four-hundred pound woman after one fucking dollar bill… Just get on stage and dance. That was it. Sold!

I had the chance to briefly meet the rest of the "dancers" for a quick meeting to fill out a bit of paperwork, and as it turned out there were only six of us. Five girls and me. Thank you David! The grand opening and the first night that I danced in Vegas anywhere but on the stage of the Olympic Garden. I actually called in sick to the male review, not wanting to burn any bridges before I was sure I wanted the new gig. I made sure I was covered at the OG that night, but by the time 2am rolled around there was no doubt in my mind that my life as a professional stripper had finally come to a close. I quit the very next day.

All the new Hard Rock dancers shared the same dressing room, but what a fucking room it was! The venue had three separate entertainers rooms for the big name acts that came through, but never used more than two at a time, so one of the little slices of rocker luxury was given to us to use. For every thirty minutes we were on stage we got a fifteen minute break, which meant enjoying the drinks and snacks that were kept constantly stocked in the fridge, watching the closed circuit television with all sorts of movies on it, or just shooting the shit with my usually half to three quarter naked co workers! As far as jobs went, for $3,200 buck a month this was a pretty fucking good one.

Besides all of the obvious reasons, the other huge benefit to dancing there instead of the OG was finishing a full two hours earlier than I could at the strip club. It made a world of difference not only in my mental state on the weekends, but in my performance as a skydiver as well; the perfect fit.

Over the course of the next two years I not only came into my own in skydiving, having become (against my will) a tandem instructor as well as a pretty accomplished camera flyer, I managed to get quite comfortable in life without a thong. The Hard Rock was more than enough public exposure for me, and the exhibitionist in me was quite satisfied. It was also a fantastic new dating venue for me as being up on stage gave me a rather distinct advantage over the guys in the crowd, and I was able to get more dates through hand gestures and facial expressions than I ever would have on the floor, which for me was very important.

It was an unfortunate discovery I made shortly after quitting stripping. In the "real world" I quite literally had no idea how to handle myself around women. I'd been a stripper since I was 21 years old, and just hadn't had to learn all the lessons the other guys did as they headed from bar to club and back. Stripping for a living meant never having to pursue a woman. It meant never having to wonder if you were liked. Never wondering If you were moving too fast. In the real world I didn't know a damn thing. The flat fact was, if you put me inside a bar or a club with a room full of people and told me that I had to basically "cold call" a women I was attracted to and try and make a pass at her, I would have not the first idea how to go about it.

Now if I were at the Hard Rock on stage, piece of cake. If I were at the Dropzone and jumping, easy. But in normal people land? Fucking useless. You see I was lucky in one respect, and that was that I had learned an important lesson a long time before. Looks have not one god damn thing to do with your ability to get a girl. You could be the best built, most chiseled man on the planet. Perfect hair, perfect body, perfect everything, but if you didn't have "game", you didn't have a thing. Truth be told, I really didn't have a thing. But... I pretty much always did my best to avoid the real world like the fucking plague!

Before my time at the Hard Rock and Las Vegas had come to a close I'd had one fucking hell of a great time, and I was lucky enough to realize how special it was. Back stage at the Hard Rock I'd had the opportunity to see dozens of shows as the concerts would finish on the weekends, and 30 minutes after they broke the club would open, meaning the back of the house was mine to wander.

I had the opportunity to not only see but actually meet Sheryl Crow, Carlos Santana on the Supernatural tour, Dwight Yoakam, Linkin Park, Smashmouth, The mother fucking Rolling Stones, Jewel and many more. I performed in a stage show with the one and only Rupaul, drag queen extraordinaire, Danced my ass off not only for New Year 1999, but for Y2K itself with a literal sea of human beings spread out before me so tightly that I could have walked across them without stumbling, all while I and my five co-workers jammed to our hearts content with the Hard Rocks massive stage all to ourselves. When that ride finally came to and end and they decided to move the club to a much smaller space upstairs they also decided to cut the dancers, and that was that.

By the time Vegas and I were ready to part ways, I'd worked on and off at The Olympic Garden for eight years, become father to an amazing daughter, worked at or helped establish every dropzone in the city, been fired from two apartment management firms, made more than three thousand skydives, become a tandem instructor, jumped out of a hot air ballon directly over the State Line casinos (illegally), done a thirty-thousand foot bandit jump out of a King Air with the transponder turned off (illegally), worked for two years as a go-go dancer in the largest nightclub in Vegas, skydived naked, film porn stars in free fall (naked of course), competed in the US Nationals with a fellow Vegas tunnel flyer and actually manage to walk away with an Open class Silver medal, had two motorcycle crashes and three more surgeries, two girlfriends, countless random passionate encounters, two malfunctions that required using my second parachute, slept with more than my share of tourist tandem students, pissed off every DZO (Drop Zone Owner) I worked for, and walked away from the City of Sin truly believing that I hadn't left a single fucking thing undone in that town. At least nothing that interested me.

With my acceptance to a phone call job offer as a camera flyer and instructor at a place called CrossKeys in New Jersey, I waved goodbye to Las Vegas in the rear view mirror of the pick-up truck and pop-up trailer I'd bought, and found myself honestly wondering if anything I'd experienced there had actually happened.

The Responsible Choice

When I had decided it was time to go, I'd started looking around to see what might be out there on the horizon for me. My first choice, really my only choice if truth be told was CrossKeys. I didn't exactly have any desperate desire to move to New Jersey, but CrossKeys reputation preceded itself in a major way. It was at the time, pretty much the busiest dropzone in the entire country and perhaps the busiest in the world back then.

To get a job with CK was to hit the top of the pyramid, and when that call came through, I was bouncing off the walls! There was only one hitch to the job offer though, and it was a fucking whopper!

"So all of our staff is multi-rated. We really aren't looking for anyone that can't fall into rotation wherever we need it, so you're gonna have to have your AFF instructors rating as well. Oh fuck me sideways... That was one tall damn order.

AFF, which stands for Accelerated Free Fall is the instructor rating needed to teach non-jumpers how to become licensed skydivers. It is by and large the most difficult and challenging rating in skydiving to earn, and I had no choice. I'd managed to find an AFF course being held in Arizona by a guy named Billy Rhodes, who was by and large considered to be one of the biggest hard ass evaluators in the sport. His was the only one I could manage to get enrolled in before I had to head to CK to start the season, and as I pulled away from Vegas it was with the understanding that if I didn't have the rating, I didn't have the job.

"So its nice to meet ya thar Dean" He said with the thickest southern drawl I'd ever heard. The man was absolutely massive. He had bear paws for hands and a huge grin on his face, but behind that smile... "So I don't believe I saw you in my pre-course last week, now did I?" He asked the question but he knew damn well I hadn't been there. "No Mr. Rhodes, I was stuck trying to finish up things before I moved, so I wasn't able to make it. "Well that's aaaright Dean... Although I don't believe I've ever passed anyone who didn't take my pre-course... Well, nice ta meecha." and strolled away from me with that shit-eating grin on his face. What a mind fuck!

The goal with the AFF course wasn't just to see if you could physically manage another human being in free fall while flying yourself. It was to see if you could manage the mental game of it all too. Could you handle yourself, as well as keep another person calm and focused durning one of the most stressful situations a human being could put themselves through? The AFF course was designed specifically to make sure if you couldn't then you didn't get the rating. It was by and large the least enjoyable skydiving experience of my entire career, and I can't say that I enjoyed a single bit of the course, right up until my last jump.

I'd made it through all the role playing that was required (where the "Student" would do things like try and put their gear on wrong or walk through a spinning propeller), and made it past all the jump levels I'd needed, but it had all come down to one last jump. One pass or fail shot to get through the course, and I drew the big straw. Big as in massive Billy himself. I had to do a one on one jump with him as my student, and he was going to do everything within the limits of the course to fuck me up.

"Tell you what Billy, fuck it! Lets just go have some fun up there no matter what!" He had to smile a little bit despite himself, and up we went for my only shot. I'd never seen a man that big fly like he did. The son of a bitch seemed to flat out be defying the law of gravity with the way he could float, but I'll be fucked senseless if I was gonna let that man beat me. I nailed that jump from start to finish, and when we hit the hard deck for the jump and I pulled both his and my parachute, I was told they could hear me screaming from the ground.

I stood with Billy in the classroom posing for a picture, the only one of six people in the course to actually be given the rating, and as I shook his hand on camera, I thanked him and sincerely told him I hoped I never saw him again! As I hit the road again in what promised to be about a four day drive, my rockstar Jack Russell Terrier Diego passed out in the seat next to me, I had to admit I was pretty damn proud of myself. I'd gone into the course giving myself a 50/50 shot at passing, and had turned out to be the only one to do so. The drive went by without my smile fading a bit.

Leaving Las Vegas meant a whole lot of things. It meant leaving behind the clubs, it meant leaving behind the reputation, and best of all it meant leaving behind Dales fucked up nickname!

"HEY! Are you Princess? The stripper from Vegas??" Oh fuck me.... So much for a blank slate! The person on the other end of the voice was named Kim. She was a Brit AFF instructor that had been at CK for a few years by then, and was anything but reserved (while at dinner once with my mother in attendance, she actually leaned back, rubbed her belly and loudly proclaimed "UUAH! I'm as full as a sluts cunt!). As it had turned out, when I had originally applied for the job, a few calls had been made to check out my references, and being the good friends they were, they made damn sure that my "new" dropzone was well aware of who they'd hired. The truth of the matter is, if you don't have a thick skin in skydiving, you sure as fuck better grow one if you're gonna last!

Paperwork, bullshit, and cross training for new gear aside, the first week went by at CK without a hitch, and I was put in rotation and jumping my ass off in no time. By jumping my ass off, I couldn't be more serious about it! I had come from a dropzone where a crazy busy day meant doing between 8 and

10 jumps, and moved all the way across the country to a dropzone where a normal day meant doing 25. Exhaustion at the end of each weekend didn't even begin to cover it.

On any given Saturday or Sunday, the only meal you ate until sundown was breakfast, unless you counted Snickers Bars and Redbull a meal, and the pace was break-neck from 8am until sunset every damn day. Weekdays were a little better for sure, and If you had a Tuesday where you only had eight jumps, you almost felt lazy. And on the one day off a week you had? Well damn. It was downright decadent!

Just like ninety percent of the staff at the time, I lived on the dropzone. The seventeen-foot pop-up trailer I'd purchased in Las Vegas ended up in a wooded area across the massive parking lot of the grounds, surrounded by about a dozen other trailers in various stages of decay. They called the spot that I had picked "The Maxi Pad" because the majority of the trailers there were occupied by women, but it was by far the quietest place to relax anywhere on the DZ, and when it was time to crash, it was perfect.

What I hadn't known when I took the job over the phone was the real reputation of CrossKeys. It was by and large the hardest partying DZ on the god damn planet, and I'd managed to land myself smack in the middle of the peak of it's popularity. There was simply no way to avoid it, and about the time my birthday rolled around, it grabbed me by the balls and squeezed.

One of the greatest things about skydiving and those that are in it is their ability to form friendships and bonds quicker than I'd ever experienced before. I always imagined it was a bit like the whole "Band of Brothers" military mentality, in that, when you spend your time putting yourself in harms way day in and day out with the same group of people, you learn quite quickly who you can count on. Once you've figured that out, the friendships fall into place almost as an afterthought.

A month had gone by for me at CK, and I considered quite a few of these people close friends already. As June 21st and my 33rd birthday rolled around, it was just another good excuse for a party, and damn did these people know how to go big!

At the time I still didn't drink. Not a drop. Just like my old crew in Vegas, my new crew in Jersey didn't like it anymore than they had, but weren't yet to the point where they found the need to push it on me. Instead, they did things like dose me up on LSD. Yeah, I fucking know!

My new, and by then very good friend Simeon and his girl Jory had decided that since I didn't drink, grabbing me a sugar cube laced with a drip of acid from the "Naughty Bottle" a packer named Chet kept around his throat was a great idea! I'd swallowed it before I really processed what they'd just done. Luckily for me, the one thing I'd learned since my horrendous acid trip so long before was how to keep a much tighter reign on my emotions, So I figured I'd be fine.

Then about two hours later, as the acid was kicking hard, in a thankfully pleasant way, Chet himself found me, dragged me into the bathroom, had me open my mouth, and say "Happy fuckin' Birthday Princess" as I felt two drops of something hit my tongue. Already being pretty damn high it took me a minute to process what had just happened, but as soon as the realization hit me, I was wiping my tongue with a wad of toilet paper and gargling water by the bucket loads! No way did I want three doses down me, and I sincerely hoped that I'd managed to get a fair bit out of my mouth before it was too late.

As it ended up, the remainder of the night went by colorfully, but thankfully without anything too out of control and as I climbed into my trailer some time before sunrise, I had to laugh at myself. This had been the responsible choice… I had taken the job because of the volume of work to be done, not the level of partying to be had!

Now I know people that have said they've seen video. I know people that say they've known people that have seen it. I, on the other hand, can name more than a dozen people with video cameras and still cameras that were there with me.

It was the morning after my birthday. Lots of drugs had been taken by a whole lot more people than just me. Lots of alcohol had been consumed, and when I say lots, I mean stadium size baseball game lots. Mr. Craig Kusky, one of the packers and fun jumpers at the dropzone had elected to take my place as the most fucked up person after the night's festivities, and was currently reaping the rewards. Now being the most fucked up in the group was not exactly a new thing for Craig, but on this particular occasion he had outdone himself to say the least.

Now to paint the picture properly for you, all of what you're about to read took place on a relatively busy weekday at close to 11am. Staff and customers alike meandered on to the back deck to be greeted with quite sight. First, pictures of him from every angle, passed out cold on the back deck of the landing area were taken. Then pictures of him surrounded with beer bottles. Then one of his closer friends decided cutting his shorts off, only after nicking his smokes, was a good idea, leaving him completely stark ass naked in the middle of a rather large deck, still sound asleep. Then of course, painted toe and finger nails, etc... I, and I dare say most of the other people watching had ever seen someone so completely passed out, and it actually wasn't until later when I wondered if anyone had bothered to see if he even had a pulse! When none of the shenanigans did anything to rouse poor Mr. Kusky, the ante was upped to a level none of us were totally prepared for.

As we watched in rapt horror, Marley, the oldest and nastiest DZ dog you've ever seen came hobbling from around the corner, following the container of melted peanut butter being led straight toward Craig. None of us really seemed to believe that it was actually going to happen. Yet the next thing we knew, we were face to face with the image of Craig lying naked and spread eagle on his back, cock and balls completely soaked in creamy melted peanut butter as Marley hungrily licked every bit of Peter Pan from his junk. He woke up only for a moment, raised his head to look down at the dog hungrily licking away at his balls, let out one "HA", and passed right the fuck back out. This was my new home.

All of about a week after my birthday, the most important visitor I'd ever had came to stay with me all by herself for the very first time. Not only was it was her first time visiting me at a dropzone, it was her first time away from Ohio with me, and I was way past nervous. I had driven all night from Jersey to Canton, Ohio to pick up my daughter Bailey, and think I managed all of about three hours sleep before she and I hit the road our way back for her week long stay with Dad.

I was nervous for a few really good reasons. First off, the entire last week prior to her arrival had been manic to say the least. Second off, Dad was living in a seventeen foot pop-up trailer in the camping area in a residential neighborhood in fucking Jersey. Third, CrossKeys was the party dropzone at the time, and the place was just cool as hell, which when I was taking her into consideration was not a positive thing.

I was worried that at seven, and coming from a very nice large suburban house in an upscale neighborhood in Ohio, it wouldn't so much feel to her like a camping trip with Dad as having to cope with the fact that Pop lived in a tiny trailer. I was worried that being the total party dropzone, she may unwittingly witness some seriously inappropriate behavior for a seven year old to see, and I was borderline frantic that she would on some level realize just how fucking awesome that place was. I had a very real fear that somehow her experience at CrossKeys would instill in her a deep, almost subliminal desire for exactly that lifestyle, and that thought kept me up at night!

I know all too well not only how fun a lifestyle it is, but how easy it is for people, both men and women to get caught up in the whole thing. So half way thru our week, when my adorable little seven year old wouldn't stop talking about "Jackson", the handsome and charming Englishman that every girl (and some of the guys) wanted to bang, the realization that every father of a girl must have at some point in his life slammed into me face first like a brick. Every girl out there that I had done unspeakably fun things with was somebody's... Daughter!

All of the sudden, every guy on the DZ was nothing but a slobbering, throbbing cock, staring at my little girl like she was on a shelf labeled "layaway". Every guy clearly had bad intentions, and I couldn't wait to get my little baby off that damn drop zone! I even ushered her out of New Jersey at break neck speed a day earlier than planned, taking her to an insanely busy amusement park just so I could relax a little!

Hard lessons

Less than 30 days later "Peanut Butter" Kusky was dead. Although up till this point in my career I'd been around for fatalities and even lost someone I had known, this was the first time I'd been witness to the loss of a friend.

When I'd been first introduced to Kusky about two months prior by Miss "Aren't you that stripper" Kim, the very first thing she told me about him to his face no less, was that he would most likely be the next person to "go in" at CK. To my surprise, he laughed and shrugged it off almost as if he either agreed with her assessment, or had just heard it that many times. Although simply by definition skydivers are risk takers, they are most certainly calculated risks. Kusky on the other hand… Well, in the two or so short months that we were friends, I'd heard both by story and seen in person that he was just a risky fucker!

On the day that Craig died, I had actually had the day off. In any normal circumstances having the day off work for most people means not being anywhere close to work, but since I not only lived on the DZ with most of the other staff and since everyone I knew and had become friends with did as well, there just wasn't anywhere else to be! That, and if I'm being honest, Williamstown New Jersey isn't exactly a hot spot for entertainment and activity. The closest place worth checking out was most certainly Philadelphia, but getting to and from was an event you'd take on with friends, not on your own.

Strolling lazily through the hanger at just past noon, I was still wiping the sleep from my eyes when I crossed the packing mat, a large open area dedicated to the packing and maintenance of parachutes and rigs. Kusky, along with a few other jumpers was flopped in a bit of a pile in the corner of the mat with a glazed look in his eyes and hazy demeanor.

"Hey Princess" He slurred at me from the floor "Hey… hey… would you do this, this swipe thing for me? I really wanna jump!" I remember not being surprised that he was hammered and completely off his ass at lunchtime, nor surprised that he wanted to go jump, even though it appeared he probably couldn't manage to get up off the floor unassisted. What surprised me was that the dropzone actually had alcohol test swabs to administer to check to see if someone was over the limit!

Back then, CrossKeys was widely known as '"The" party DZ, and a lot of the normal "rules" observed at other large dropzone's didn't seem to quite apply. It was a terribly normal thing to see someone drunk mid-day on a Tuesday, or running around higher than the parachutes overhead. Hell I once had one of my fellow jumpers plop down and tell me all about the time he was arrested for being hit by a bus in downtown London at around 2am while on acid, dressed up as a Native American Indian. Of course he told me this story in the middle of the day on the back deck at CK while high on acid…

On that particular day though, we had a pretty large number of visiting jumpers around, as It was CrossKeys work-ups to a big professional canopy competition called the PST tour (Pro Swooping Tour), and in town were more than a few people that I'd known from out West. One in particular, a good friend who'd been part of my very beginnings in the sport was doing practice training jumps before he was to compete, I hadn't seen Kevin in years, so later that afternoon I found myself enjoying catching up with him in front of one of the team rooms in the main courtyard of the DZ. With what I can only call really bad timing on my part, I turned from Kevin to look up the main road leading through a residential neighborhood up to the parking lot of the dropzone, just in time to see Craig rolling over from his back at about treetop level. In a millisecond my mind registered what my consciousness refused. I shouldn't have been able to recognize Kusky. I shouldn't have been able to tell he was falling on his back. I'd seen no parachute.

The sound that I heard next just didn't sink in. The group of about twenty people who'd been milling around and chatting all froze in an instant. Still confused over what I had just watched, and even more confused over what had sounded like a stick of dynamite, literally so loud that I could feel the sound waves bounce off the sheet metal wall next to me, I had to turn to a fellow instructor and ask "What the hell was that noise?" With an expression that displayed as much confusion as I felt, his one and only word reply was "Kusky".

I snapped out of whatever daze I was in, sprinted to my truck about fifty yards away, and raced off in the direction I'd seen him hit. I wasn't thinking if I'm being honest, because if I had been I would have sat right where I was, already knowing what I'd find. As I raced up the avenue, I could see sitting in the yard of one of the neighboring houses Craig's friend that had been on the jump with him, clearly out of sorts, but alive and well. Stomping on the gas pedal to drive the four or five houses further down the road, I found Mr. Craig Kusky.

Laying on the driveway of an otherwise normal little rural Jersey home was Craig. His reserve parachute had literally exploded off his back when he'd hit the ground, and bouncing back up in the air as he must have, the cloth from the parachute had unfurled and was almost completely covering him.

As I ran to his side, the first responder training I'd taken a few times in the past kicked in to some degree, and I attempted to at least check his pulse. Reaching for his hand and taking him by the wrist I instantly knew I'd find no pulse because when I lifted his arm toward me, there was nothing rigid left inside and it simply folded and bent around in completely unnatural ways. I was ready to walk away right then, but at that same instant one of his close personal friends ran up and begged me, pleaded with me to help him do CPR. What was I suppose to do?

As we pulled the reserve canopy off of him so that we could make the attempt, I was struck instantly by the fact that there was no blood anywhere. Other than a small scratch on the side of his face, Kusky didn't seem to have a single visible injury. As I positioned myself to begin chest compressions, I watched as his friend turned Craig's head to face up so that he could sweep his tongue before he started breathing for him, and as he did, I watched in horror as Kusky's entire face went flat like a pancake. The one and only chest compression I did had my hands quite easily feeling the flat concrete behind him, and as I looked up to see two young children peeking out the screen door of the house where he had landed, I knew it was finished. Grabbing his friend and dragging him away, I only said lightly in his ear "we're done man…He's gone" and draped the reserve back over him as I turned away.

I think I managed to keep it together across about half of the parking lot. My truck parked in a ditch and running was completely forgotten, and as one of my friends came to me to see how I was I simply buckled. Its one thing to see someone die. We've all been so desensitize by movies and television to the visuals that violence and death can bring that even when we see it firsthand it doesn't shock like it could, but that sound…

In the first weeks that followed Kusky's death, something I never would have expected happened. Business spiked! We found ourselves overbooked almost every day, and we ended up jumping like mad. It seemed there was a phenomenon I was previously unaware of that many of my brethren knew all too well. Death brings advertising and business. Craig's impact at CK had actually managed to make the ticker on CNN that night, and for the briefest of moments, CrossKeys was launched into the spotlight. People who had long ago decided that skydiving was just too mainstream these days all of the sudden realized "Hey! That shit actually is dangerous? Lets go!"

Climbing back in the plane and jumping hadn't been a problem for me or anyone else that I'd known, mostly because of how Craig had died. When the toxicology report came out from the coroner, his blood alcohol level was close to four times the legal limit. It seemed someone had gone ahead and done the alcohol swab for him… Kusky had also long before decided that a CYPRES, a computer system most skydivers use that will automatically deploy the reserve parachute if you're still in freefall at a pre-set altitude was something that he didn't need. If he'd had one, well, he'd probably still be dead, but not from that jump anyway.

Still, as things do, life started to get back to normal quite quickly, and although Kusky was a topic of conversation regularly, It was usually to laugh about all the stupid or crazy shit he'd managed to get up to. Skydivers have an amazing ability to just get on with it, like any extreme sports athlete I assume, or even like a soldier I suppose. Shit happens, people die, mourn the loss and move the fuck on.

It wasn't all that long afterward that I started flying planes. On the same field that CK operated was a flight school run by the assistant manager of the dropzone. A fellow co-worker and the owner of the rigging loft where all the maintenance and repairs of the skydiving equipment was done had been taking flying lessons, and in random conversation with me I revealed that back when I was 16 years old, I'd wracked up 36 hours of flight time in a Cessna 152.

When I was a little pain in the ass spoiled 16 year old my parents, in a sincere attempt to get me to stop being such a dick had enrolled me in a local flight school in Sacramento after I had expressed an interest in learning to fly. It turned out that I took to flying an aircraft quite quickly, and the actual handling of the little Cessna's I trained in was a very natural thing for me. The ground school on the other hand… By the time I'd logged my time in the aircraft, I was so desperately behind in book work and general knowledge that I decided like the asshole that I was to just quit.

My desire to fly though never really did leave me, and the next thing I knew I'd been talked into taking a "first flight" introduction to aviation at the school and just like that, I was signed up for the course to try and earn my private pilots license.

I had long before lost track of my logbook which contained all the proof I needed to show the hours I had flown as that asshole kid, but it turned out I was in luck! The hours that a pilot fly's never expire or become invalid, and if I could prove that I'd flown those hours way back when, it would go a long way toward saving me a shit load of both time and money.

After about a week of trying, I actually managed to track down my old flight instructor who as it turned out, had ended up working for the FAA. Happily for me, she not only remembered me, but had kept every logbook for her entire flying career, and was able to recreate all the flights she and I had done. As I presented my official FAA stamped letter from her verifying all 36 hours I'd spent crammed into a tiny little Cessna 152 with her, my instructor, a kid of all of 23 years old laughed, and said "shit man! You're gonna be the quickest student I ever had!"

All of a month or so later, to my and my families great surprise, I was a fucking licensed pilot! CrossKeys, in all of just a few months had provided me with more twists and turns than I could have ever expected. From the stress of my AFF course just to get the job, to the party atmosphere I hadn't expected, to Kusky's dramatic departure and now this, I was having a hard time keeping up!

When I'd left Las Vegas, I remember wondering if somehow the whole thing hadn't just been some kind of a crazy dream, but as I climbed into the beautiful little 172 I'd rented from the flight school to go on my very first flying "Date", I figured if it all had been a dream back then, I most certainly hadn't woken up. Then my date projectile vomited all over the panel of the airplane, and I decided that I most certainly must be awake after all. "Yes" I thought, "this absolutely is your fucking life."

East Coast vs. West Coast

New Jersey is absolutely no place to spend the winter. Under any circumstances. As I packed up the truck and trailer and headed off down the road on my way to Sacramento, I thought back about what had been one of the craziest summers of my life. I'd be seeing New Jersey and CrossKeys again come the spring thaw, but if I was gonna go broke not jumping I was going to do it somewhere a hell of a lot warmer than there.

I'd managed not only to secure a slot with a Skydance Skydiving just about thirty minutes outside Sacramento, but I'd enrolled in an IFR (Instrument Flight Rules) course in the same flight school that I'd attended as a kid all those years before. I had decided that just having my private pilots license wasn't gonna cut it after I'd managed to scare the living shit out of myself a few months before.

After I'd gotten my license, I was asked on a few different occasions by the owner of CrossKeys if I wouldn't mind ferrying equipment and staff back and forth between CK and our sister dropzone in Sussex up by the city in a little 172. It was a great deal for both of us really, as I wanted to fly but didn't want to spend $100 bucks an hour, and he didn't want to pay any of his pilots to do it. The few times that I'd made the trip it had been pretty straightforward, and as I was flying through my first one hundred hours I was getting pretty comfortable with being the pilot-in-command, if not just a touch cocky. But as life will do if you're fortunate, I was given a pretty solid reality check.

Mother Nature, clearly seeing that I was getting a bit of an attitude in the air decided that I needed to be taken down a peg or two. After departing Sussex on my way back to CK late one afternoon I managed to put quite a scare into myself. I'd been running late when I departed Sussex and already knew that I'd be flirting with arriving back at CrossKeys after dark, which in itself wasn't a huge deal. What was a huge deal was the weather.

A solid overcast layer that had been sitting a good six-thousand feet off the ground when I left Sussex had slowly drifted down to five, then four, then three thousand feet, and then just for good measure it started to rain. As the ceiling continued to drop and visibility got worse and worse, I was starting to get more than a little nervous. You see, as a private pilot not only are you not allowed to fly in bad weather below certain minimums, you aren't even trained for it. All of my navigational training up to that point was based on visual rules, and if I couldn't see where I was going... Well, you get the point.

By the time I finally managed to turn onto my final approach to the little strip at CK, the ceiling had dropped to less than a thousand feet, the rain which had been only inclement up until then was now a steady drizzle, and the very last light of the day was all but gone. As I tied the aircraft down and walked back toward my car, my back was soaked with the cold sweat that had been pouring down me, my head and shoulders were soaked with rain, and I swore to myself that I'd never let that happen again. Skill or training had nothing to do with my safe landing back home. It had been pure luck that the weather didn't deteriorate quicker than it had. If it had gotten the least bit worse, I could have ended up just another NTSB report. So with my IFR training well in hand, I spent as much time as I could hitting the books and flying as much as possible, as well as jumping as much as a Northern California winter would allow.

Skydance had been around for quite some time by the time I joined the team, and the owner and crew were a pretty great fit for me. Unlike CrossKeys, it was a much more low-key dropzone, but the gang out there still managed to have a pretty great time both in and out of the air. Between the tandems, video and AFF jumps I was managing to at least earn enough money to get by, and just as I had in CK I was making some really solid friends.

One of the other tandem instructors by the name of Dan became the "R" rated Laurel to my Hardy in very short order, and if we were working together, you could damn well bet we were having a good time. The time in an aircraft as its climbing to altitude can be dead time for sure. You've more than likely got a nervous student with nothing to do but think about whats coming, and a bored tandem instructor who not only doesn't want a freaked out student on his hands, but will do just about anything to keep themselves entertained. It was that reason, and our matching senses of humor that Dan and I worked so well together. We'd fall into a bit of a back and forth every time our asses hit the bench in the airplane, and it usually worked out really well! Unfortunately, that wasn't always the case…

"So I'm fuckin' this guy in the ass the other night, and he gets a God damn hard on, so I say get the fuck outta here you fag!"

It was quite possibly my favorite gay joke ever, but more than likely one of the most inappropriate ones ever told. Even more so when you consider that when I told it, it was while jumping at a Bay Area DZ onboard a jump plane that just happened to have a gay couple onboard… Now its not like I just up and decided to blurt this horrible joke out for no particular reason, but still.

Dan and I had started trading jokes back and forth on the ride to altitude that day, and for some reasons they turned to our favorite prods at the gay community. He'd tell a joke, then I would. He'd up the anti by telling one a little less appropriate, then I'd take my shot. When Dan uncorked the worst one he could think of, what was I to do?

These two poor guys didn't know that I'd made a CrossKeys comedy film festival winner just a few months prior featuring me running all around New Jersey in fish net stockings, hot pants, high heels and a push-up bra . They knew nothing of all my time spent in San Francisco partying with the likes of Dee, my favorite drag queen, or my stage show with Rupaul. They only knew that I appeared to be a gay bashing bastard that had one of their lives in my hands. Neither Dan nor I had any idea that the two we were taking were even a couple, right up until just prior to exit they leaned in for a very romantic goodbye kiss.

Even as I was busy making a complete ass out of myself at work, and ruining some poor guys skydive by unintentionally bashing his entire lifestyle, I was keeping even busier flying.

IFR training was intense to say the least, especially because of the weather that Northern California can bring during the winter months. At least three or four days a week there would be a low overcast layer across the entire valley, which meant that the majority of my training took place in actual IFR conditions. It was a humbling time to say the least, but with the help of a great and very patient instructor, I was managing to get through things pretty well and learn a whole lot along the way. I remember thinking shortly after my first required "Cross-country" IFR flight, if I'd managed to end up in "the soup" as they called in on that flight from Sussex, I probably would have crashed.

As that first winter in Sacramento came to a close, I'd managed to make a few hundred skydives, a bunch of new great friends, and to my thrill my IFR rating! I'd also learned some very important lessons along the way as well. Some good, and some not so good. First off, I leaned that perhaps not telling fucked up gay jokes quite literally within reach of San Francisco, the gay capitol of the US was probably a damn good idea. I also learned another very important one that winter, this time about myself.

Shortly after earning my IFR rating, I'd flown up North to Oregon to visit a close friend I'd known in Las Vegas. My great friend Jim had moved back home to pursue a new career on his own, and when I'd found out he was just a few hours flight from me, I decided it was a great excuse to continue building hours as my next step in flying was to get my Commercial license. I'd come so far with my training in airplanes now, that I was pretty sure I knew I wanted flying in my life on more than a casual basis.

This time, armed with the ability to navigate through bad weather, I hopped in the beautiful little Piper Archer I'd flown for my entire instrument course, and headed off and what was suppose to be a nice relaxing day trip. Relaxing it most certainly was, on the way there anyway.

Jim and I grabbed a nice bite to eat, shot the shit for a few hours, and just enjoyed having a nice catch-up before I looked at my watch and decided it was probably time for me to hit the air. After hopping online to the NOAA (National Oceanic and Atmospheric Administration) website to check the weather heading back home, I noticed that and Airmet (Airmens' Meteorological Information) had been release for what was being called mild to moderate turbulence along the route that I would be flying home. Not exactly what I had wanted to see, but now coming up on 200 hours of flight time I'd been bounced around a fair amount, so not a huge deal.

The first time my head slammed into the roof of the plane I realized I was in a bit of trouble. Sometime between the time I had checked the weather, and the time I arrived at the leeward side of Mount Shasta, the Airmet announcing mild turbulence had flipped to a Sigmet (Significant Meteorological Information) and was now warning of severe to extreme turbulence along a substantial portion of my route. I'd wrenched my seatbelt down as tight as I possibly could, wiped the sweat from my hands and face, and decided that my best course of action would be to turn around and go back to Medford and wait it out. The instant I lifted my left wing and began the turn, I was almost flipped upside down by a massive gust, and it was everything I could do to get the wings back to level before I ended up inverted.

As the terrain continued to climb up toward me along the route, I was being bashed about by up and down drafts of wind that had me struggling just to keep my plane aimed in the same direction. I was acutely aware that if I ended up in a strong enough down-draft, I simply didn't have enough horsepower at my disposal to keep the plane off the side of the mountain. At least three times during the course of my forty-five minute crossing through the affected area I was within two hundred feet of the tree tops, and as I finally broached the final pass and across and into the San Joaquin Valley, I was literally shaking with adrenaline and fear.

"November 5391A, you are cleared into controlled airspace. Information Quebec is current. Enter a right downwind for runway 34 and report mid field".

I managed to make my voice sound as calm as I possibly could, but the truth was I was completely shot. As I repeated back the instructions tower had given me, they had to have heard just how shaky my voice was.

"You just flew over the pass from Medford 91A? Must have been a pretty bumpy ride...". "Oh yeah" I croaked. "All I need right now is a cigarette and some fucking toilet paper."

I must have been lying face down on the pavement next to the plane for a good ten minutes. I'd taxied and parked on the ramp where I'd been instructed, shut off the engine, climbed out the door and stretched out spread eagle face-down on the tarmac. I'd never suffered through such a sustained level of fear for such a long period of time in my life, and my mind flat out shut down with the engine of the Piper.

"Uh HUM…" I heard from somewhere over my shoulder, and lifted my head up off the ground, face covered in bits of black-top to see a rather heavy set middle-aged man looking down at me, lit cigarette in one hand, and a roll of toilet paper in the other. I started laughing so fucking hard I was in tears!

Climbing back into that fucking plane a few hours later was one of the hardest things I'd ever done, but at the end of that day, when the airplane had been tied down safely back in Sacramento I knew one thing. If I could get back into a plane after that terrifying flight, I was a fucking pilot.

The next season at CrossKeys saw a number of things. It saw me earn my Commercial Pilots License, it saw parties, it saw hard work, a dropzone world record for the most tandem skydives ever done in a day, sex, drugs, friendship and fights; and unfortunately, almost a year to the day later, it saw more serious injury and even death.

This time I wasn't there. I was jumping out of helicopters for CrossKeys down in Wildwood New Jersey for the PST tour when it happened. Sister Sarah we called her. A very religious yet very liberal girl, Sarah was a friend to everyone she ever met. One of the sweetest demeanors I'd ever encountered, when she gave you a hug and said "I love you", you knew damn well she meant it.

On what should have been just another fun skydive on her day off, she'd made the mistake of turning her parachute into the path of another canopy in a steep dive for landing, and the two collided about three hundred feet off the ground. She died there on the field, as did the pilot of the second canopy who as it turned out was her boyfriend. When the staff down in Wildwood were given the news, we weren't given the luxury of staying on the ground to let it all sink in. We were told to keep on jumping…

Although CrossKeys still held quite a few good times in store for most of us, the truth was, it never quite was the same. Over the almost three years that I worked at CK there were seven separate fatalities either during skydives, or simply of people attached in some way to the place, countless minor injuries (myself included) and a few major ones, and it almost felt as if a dark cloud had settled over us. For every amazing time we had, we ended up suffering through something dramatically worse. When I hopped back in my truck once again to make the 4 day drive back to California, I was pretty sure it would be the last time I'd see the place.

Back in California, I found myself not only continuing to jump as an instructor at Skydance, but flying their Cessna 182 for jump operations on days when there wasn't enough business to take the 15 seat turbine PAC750 aircraft up. Flight time, when one load takes 45 minutes round trip can add up quite quickly, and I was filling up my logbook at a pace I had never thought possible.

After taking a few months to go and work abroad jumping over the islands as an instructor in Fiji, I returned to California with only one goal in mind. Turn full-time pilot and leave the work jumps for someone else. The very moment my logbook reflected the flight hours I needed to qualify for the PAC, I hounded Ray the owner until he finally gave me a shot. As soon as my training was done, and I was release to fly solo jump operations in the PAC, that was that. I had become a full-time working jump pilot, and was moving on to yet another chapter in my life.

As the Turbine Spins

Flying, the condensed version.

From 36 hours to almost three thousand in four years. Turned out I had been as serious about flying as I thought I was. From the first flight on my own in the PAC750 I was hooked! With a stick instead of a yoke, 750 horsepower in a Pratt turbine engine and a super light airframe, that fucker could fly like a bat out of hell, and damned if I wasn't having a blast!

When I'd first started flying jumpers for Ray, I was lucky if I'd manage to fly four or five loads a day because it took so much time to get to altitude and back down, but in the PAC? Fuck me, I was turning more than twenty loads a day on the weekends, and loving it. Of course there were a few occasions when Skydance was beating my like a damn dog for sure, and on those days, no matter how much I loved flying that thing I wanted out. And unfortunately, even some nights.

Most pilots that end up flying skydivers do so simply as a way to build up a massive amount of hours quite quickly. Under the types of regulations that airline pilots have to follow, there are very strict rules about how hard you can work your pilot. With skydiving though, the rules that governed that kind of flight were dramatically more relaxed, and as I would learn very early on, there was no limit to the number of hours you could fly. It meant that at times, I was pushed crazy hard. One particular night my first full season stood out more than any other.

Load one had fired up at 8am. It was the first load on the second day of The American Boogie which was the biggest event for the year at Skydance. I'd flown the entire first day for a total of thirteen hours in the seat without a single engine shut down. I was tired, but I'd managed a good night sleep after day one so I wasn't destroyed. As I hit the half way point of the second day, the fatigue that I was feeling wasn't over the top. It was at around load twenty that I was ready to be done with it all and go home. On load twenty-two I got the horrible radio call that reminded me that we were flying night loads as well. When I finally shut down the plane from load twenty-six as the sun was starting to dip below the horizon, and I was seriously worn.

I had enough time to drink a couple of Red Bulls, eat my first real meal of the day, and stretch out just a little before it was time for me to give the pilot briefing on night jumps. There were going to be three or four loads maximum. I could do this. Push on!

On the sixth night load I asked manifest to start sending me an observer on each load to keep me company. On the ninth load the drop zone manager radioed up, slurring his words from enjoying too many of the liquid party favors, saying "hey maaaan, they wanna, they wanna keep jumping!" As I contemplated the brutality of continuing the torture I glanced down for a look at my watch. It was just past midnight, and I couldn't quite remember how the day had started. As I thought about it more, I couldn't remember any of the jump runs I'd made that night, and even had to turn around just to see if the load I was busy flying had even jumped out or not. When I keyed up the microphone I actually had to concentrate hard just to think of what to say. "Look... None of these gauges make sense. I don't know if if I'm going up or down right now, and if I survive this flight and they still want to jump, you fly the fucking plane, cause I'm DONE!" Thirty-seven loads in one twenty-four hour go is just too fucking much, no matter how important the flight hours were!

Fortunately, days and nights like that at Skydance were few and far between. For the most part, I loved flying the PAC, loved flying at that dropzone, and really enjoyed all the people I worked with. But as I started wracking up some serious hours, not only in general, but in the Turbine PAC specifically, I started to realized that I could and should do better.

Once I had rolled through more that fifteen-hundred hours in the PAC, I knew it was time to move on yet again. The pay at Skydance just wasn't nearly enough for the level of work I was having to sustain, and I started actively keeping my eyes and ears open for other opportunities.

Chicago came to my attention through one of the mechanics that worked for the company that serviced Ray's aircraft. He had worked the previous season in the midwest with a company he knew was looking for a new pilot for their Twin Otter, and figured it would be worth it for me to shoot over my resume. So, with about as much thought as I seem to give anything in my life, I hit "Send" on the keyboard, and then promptly forgot all about it.

"No, I don't have any Multi-time, but I actually just signed up to get the rating, and should hopefully be through the course in a few weeks."

The owner of the dropzone, a guy by the name of Doug had taken a look at my resume, and although he was looking for a twin pilot, was impressed with not only the amount of time I had flying the PAC, one of which he operated, but of my time flying jumpers. He decided that it would be a relatively easy thing to teach my to fly the Otter as a high time jump pilot than it would be to teach an Otter pilot how to fly skydivers. I was offered the job as the full-time pilot for his dropzone, contingent of course on my passing the multiengine course and earning my rating. So, just like it had been when I took the job in CrossKeys, my immediate future all rested on my ability to get through yet another, shall we call it trial?

I'm not going to lie. The multi course was not nearly as easy as I had expected it to be. I had gone into it wondering just how much harder a plane with two engines could be over a plane with only one. In all honesty, the actual flying of the aircraft wasn't terribly hard, but the theory behind it, and how to handle potential emergencies was a fuck load more in-depth than I would have ever imagined.

When the time came to take my check-ride with my FAA examiner, I was as ready as I could be, but the two and a half hour oral exam, followed by a ninety minute flight was enough to leave me exhausted! I'd managed to pass ride though, and now found myself holding an FAA Commercial Multi-Engine Instrument rated pilots license.

Flying from the left seat of a Twin Otter is simply a joy. Actually, saying flying it is a joy is a massive understatement. It's so damn pilot friendly and well designed that its just flat out sexy! The first time I sat down in the left seat, to say that I was intimidated wouldn't even come close. The Twin Otter is one big girl. She'll hold 20+ skydivers inside, and a pilot and co-pilot on top of it, and most certainly makes her presence known. But when I started to train in her, and learn to break down the systems and learn my way around, she became an absolutely wonderful beast!

In the Otter, everything is easily within reach, usually without ever having to look, allowing maximum concentration for the job at hand, which in an Otter's case is flying a 12,500 pound aircraft full of your friends and co workers. When I'd first begun training, my new boss had told me about his winter commitment for the aircraft, which was a four month gig flying in Southern Mexico. He was hoping that once the season was over in Chicago, I might want to take on that job as well.

Still having next to no time in the Otter, and only thirty hours of multiengine time under my belt, I asked him if he wouldn't mind waiting until after I'd been flying her long enough to decide if both he and I thought I could handle it. Thirty seconds into my very first solo flight, and I was on the radio. "Doug? Yeah… Count me in for Mexico!" I was in love. If the

PAC had been love, it was puppy love for sure. The Otter…
Oh she stole my heart from that first solo flight.

Chicago was a pretty decent fit starting out, and there were
quite a few cool people working there. I'd known one or two of
them from my time jumping at CK, and a few that had come
through out West, so it wasn't like it was a complete fresh
start. And, as it was with every DZ I went to, not only were you
able to make friends pretty quickly, but as every past dropzone
had done, Skydance made damn sure that Chicago knew all
about my stripper days, and of course, Princess.

About the time mid June rolled around that first season in
Chicago, I'd managed to talk the boss into giving me a couple
of weeks off so that I could take off to Australia for a very
special 40th birthday celebration. Turning 40 was a pretty epic
occasion for me, seeing as how I was officially turning middle
aged but still one of the most immature people around, and I
had no intention of ringing in such an event in my life
(especially since actually turning 40 had looked quite doubtful
at times) in some damn bar in Aurora Illinois.

As I headed Down Under to celebrate with two of my closest
and dearest friends, I had two goals in mind. Have an
absolutely amazing time with Derick and Mandy for my
birthday, then upon my return home, banging the living fuck
out of the cutest large breasted little 20 year old blonde who'd
started working at the DZ and had been shamelessly flirting
with me since day one. Both Australia and my goal upon
returning were raging successes.

As I turned Chicago into my home, I brought with me the same
level of hard work that I'd given to Ray when I flew for him.
Both the aircraft that I flew for Doug, being both the Otter and
a PAC were kept meticulously clean by me. Once a week not
only would both aircraft get a top to bottom scrubbing, but
when I had the time, they'd end up getting waxed as well. My
entire life revolved around that dropzone, those planes, and

when I had the time, banging blondie. It was a pretty great season.

As the season started winding down and the weather started getting cold, the planning for Mexico began. I was going to a place that was a good hour South of Mexico City, and would for all intents and purposes be completely on my own. I had to take all of the spare parts, tools and equipment I could possibly need for that period of time with me, and when the Otter was finally fully loaded and ready to go, it was literally stuffed top to bottom.

Chicago to far Southern Mexico is no small trip. Flying your own aircraft internationally is no little deal. Doing it with nothing but a few notes from a jump pilot buddy named Kro, the first flight plan I'd made in more than two years, an outdated GPS database and non-pilot co-pilot is just, well fucking stupid.

Hinckley to Texarkana to Brownsville went without a hitch. My close long time friend Mandy who'd celebrated my birthday in OZ with me was kicked back in the co-pilot seat listening to music and enjoying the view, while I sat wondering if the cloud layer we'd been over for the last two hundred miles was going to break before we got to Texas and had to shoot an approach I was completely unprepared to make. Once the Otter was firmly planted on the ground in Brownsville Texas (thru clear skies), and the prevailing weather had been checked (fucking crap), I let the boss know that I wouldn't be continuing on into Mexico until the next day (even though Brownsville Texas was the biggest shit-hole town I'd ever been in) because the thought of trying to land at some random field in Mexico in the forecast bad weather ahead scared the living fuck out of me. I'd learned long ago, don't fuck with Mother Nature.

Two days later… Puebla Mexico was in sight. It was a pretty straight forward flight, other than the fact that it didn't appear that Mexico had an Air Traffic System (that I could identify anyway). I believe after having crossed the international line, I spoke to only one Mexican controller, and he basically told me he didn't care what I did. Once I was on the ground in Puebla I started their version of clearing customs which involved spending a lot of money on paperwork I wasn't told I'd need and going back and forth between two counters filled with people who's apparent job was to make the whole experience as difficult as possible. I made contact with the owner of the DZ, Tony, who told me he was about an hours flight South of Puebla, just around the back side of the big fucking volcano. He said that Pepe, his "Guy" on the ground would be waiting for us.

A day and a half later, the plane had been emptied, and happily parked on the newly paved dropzone runway, all ready to go for the operations annual Halloween boogie. The dropzone owner had quite the reputation as a total party animal, and fuck me, it was true. I was to be a guest at Tony's house for the first week or so that I was in country, which unfortunately for Mandy, I, and a couple other visiting jumpers, meant we couldn't get away from the damn music raging at Tony's house long enough to get any rest. As I began flying on Saturday, it was only the mood of the jumpers that was keeping me awake.

Besides my Otter, the DZ had a King Air that they had leased from a dropzone in Colorado that was being flown by a local pilot by the name of Cesar. I'd heard about Cesar from Kro, the pilot that had flown the Mexico gig before me and was warned quite firmly to keep and eye out. At first Cesar didn't seem to be much of a concern. He didn't speak English, and didn't seem to have any desire to get to know the Gringo pilot in the flash Otter. I'd almost decided not to give Cesar a second thought till I watched him taxi the King Air down a hill and hitting one of the props on the runway, sending sparks and a few chunks of pavement flying! I was floored almost to inaction by what had happened, but after what I'd seen soaked in, I ran in front of the King Air as the jumpers began loading the plane screaming "shut this fucking thing down! Shut it down!" Not only had Cesar known he had a prop strike, but the fucker was still intending fly the load, putting not only himself but everyone onboard at serious risk! There was just now way in hell I was gonna let that happen.

After I'd finally managed to get the attention of Cesar, as well as Tony, I was able to get the load transferred over to the Otter while they "inspected" the King Air. I didn't really know what type of inspection they were doing, but as I pulled up to load the third group since the prop strike I saw some really stupid shit. The King Air was chalked on all three tires and completely un-attended with both engines running. I can only assume that Cesar must have decided that doing a run-up from a safe distance would be a good idea. The next thing you know... He also decided that taking a quick flight was a good idea as well. A quick flight that involved buzzing me in the Otter at high speed! I just about lost my fucking mind.

I was so mad I couldn't see straight, and ended up happy that I had another 2 hours of flying before I was able to shut down, giving me a good chance to cool off before I could confront Fuck Stick for his actions. With Tony interpreting, I told Cesar that he had absolutely no business being a pilot. I made it very clear to him that in no uncertain terms was he to go anywhere near the Otter either in the air OR on the ground, and that he should stay the hell away from me as well. As it turns out, considering I was basically all alone in far Southern Mexico right around the time the drug cartels were really getting the hang of killing people and cutting off their heads, calling Cesar out in that way may not have been the wisest of choices.

It was almost twenty-four hours later that I climbed out of the plane after a beautiful flyby that I found myself approached by six different men. I guess it had been a really good day, full of fun jumps and happy people, because the previous day's excitement wasn't even remotely in my mind when the first guy walked up and said "We have a problem".

That's just about the time I swallowed half of my tooth. The smallest of the six, who probably stood no more than about five foot five, walked up from beside me and threw a sucker punch from my blind spot that confused me more than anything else, because my first reaction was to laugh and bark out the word "what??" It wasn't until he came in for punch number two and I'd shoved him away that I saw the baseball bats. As he came in for number three, I got my first view of the gun barrel pointed straight at my chest, and just let the little shit swing away.

Cesar, being the big man that he was, stood a safe twenty feet back from the action, letting his boy's prove how rugged and tough he was. The gang clearly saw that I saw the gun CLEARLY, and slowed the pace a bit, I assume to savor what was to come. "This is MEXICO" came from the mouth of Mr. "We have problem". He had clearly been voted the spokesman for the group, and was taking his job quite seriously, using the full weight of the situation to really put some impact behind his words. And then... My savior!

Mandy had been watching the situation unfold, and according to her, screaming her fucking head off (although to this day I don't recall hearing a sound) loud enough to attract the attention of the military on the field. It didn't appear that the military intended to do a damn thing about the attack, but they did stand up and look our way (I assume to get a better view), which turned out to be just enough to back my new friends off a touch. The Spokesman looked to the military, then to me and said, in his most ominous tone "Eeef you are here Saturday, you go home in a box".

"Doug, if I'm here on Saturday, the fuckin' guy say's I go home in a box! So... Either I leave Mexico with the Otter, or I leave without it! Your choice!"

Tony, the owner of the DZ, had quickly gone into damage control mode, and was busy telling his entire staff that there had been no gun, and that for some unknown reason I was making the entire story up. It wasn't until one of the visiting jumpers stood up and called bullshit. Luckily for me, she had seen the guy with the gun (who turned out to be a fucking federale`) and told the entire staff right then and there what she had seen. Between her, Mandy, and a staff that wasn't blind or stupid, everyone got a pretty good picture of what had transpired.

As I crossed the border from Mexico back to the USA and Brownsville Texas, I remember thinking that it was just about the most beautiful place I'd ever seen. I had lasted a total of four days in Mexico.

I could say a lot of things about that first season in the Otter, but the one thing I sure as hell couldn't say was that it had been boring!

Blown Home

Landing back on our little grass strip back in Chicago was about the greatest feeling ever. After the winter I'd had, I didn't want to be anywhere else. I'd slept in trailers and vans, decent hotels and fucking shitty motels, and even two full weeks on an inflatable mattress in the back of the Otter.

My flight back home over the Rockies was one of the only truly entertaining parts of the entire winter! With Diego curled up in the co-pilot seat, and my good friend Zach and his girlfriend in the back, I was just happy to be on my way. That, and having fun enjoying messing with them in the back of the plane.

We were flying somewhere over the Rockies at 17,500 feet. Both Zach and his girl had made their way to the back of the aircraft by the jump door behind the cargo that would obscure most if any view I might have of their antics. One of the reasons they had wanted to make the trip to Chicago with me was specifically so they could join the coveted "Mile-High" club, which I had happily agreed to let them do. I'd had them take their oxygen tubes with them to plug in to the jacks in the back of the plane and told them that if they "chose" to remove their masks or their seat belts for any reason, it was "against" my wishes as Captain. They of course both assured me that they would never think of such a thing…

I guess it had been about twenty minutes. The fact that I had previous experience with high altitude hypoxia made me start to wonder if the fact that I'd not heard a thing in quite some time might not just be because they'd both passed out cold. I had a difficult time imagining they were up to anything terribly energetic with so much time having gone by. But how to check that they were good?

I tried using the PA system to get their attention, but it was difficult to hear near the door even if you weren't all fucked up on a lack of gas, so when I didn't get a reaction from my yelling I wasn't terribly surprised. I thought about descending to a much lower altitude to see if that my get a response but I couldn't justify burring all the extra gas getting back up, nor did I want to give up the monster tail wind I had going in my favor (245 knots groundspeed in an Otter!) So, with no other ideas I could think of, I went about the only good plan I had.

After getting clearance for a short, quick decent from ATC, I trimmed the Otter to about a 10 degree pitch up as slowly as I could without a noticeable change. As soon as I had I had a nice little climb going I started adding a fair amount of forward pressure to the controls and…

As I began my "Rapid decent" down to 16,500 feet, the only things that weren't strapped down to the floor (namely Zach and his girl), gently began to rise towards the ceiling of the main cabin, confirming two things for me. One, that they were both clearly conscious, and two, that they were now absolutely card carrying members of the Mile High club. The brief but very entertaining view I got staring into the mirror on the instrument panel also confirmed that sex in a weightless environment looks pretty fucking uncoordinated, but must be a hell of a lot of fun, because other than looking really surprised to find themselves floating in mid-air, they looked positively giddy!

Season two in Chicago was pretty much like season one. Fucking busy. Lots of flying, lots of washing and waxing, and thankfully a decent amount of fucking around as well. What there still wasn't a whole lot of though was money, and being constantly just above broke was starting to put quite a strain on me. When I finally approached Doug about some kind of a pay increase, I was met with excuses and reasons why, but no real bump in pay. With over a thousand hours in the Otter now, I had honestly hoped to get at least a little bump…

A few unfortunate things did take place during season two that managed to put a real fucking damper on my life, the worst of which was completely tearing my left bicep completely off during a drunken water skiing accident during the staff getaway and Drugs family lake house. I think by this time I was up to surgery number eight, and this one not only cost a stinking fortune, it sidelined me from flying for over a month, leaving me more broke than I'd been working the Holiday Inn all those years ago. Luckily, with the help of family and some really good friends, both in Chicago and all around I managed to get by, and after a pretty difficult rehab to get healthy again.

As season two and close to another thousand hours came to a close in Chicago, I was crossing the Rocky Mountains in the Otter once again, my dog Diego sitting this one out this time in Chicago while I flew back to California for a gig flying with Skydive San Diego in the Chicago Otter. It was a contract working primarily for the part of the operation that trained the US Navy Seals in their high altitude jump training, and turned out to be exciting and challenging flying to say the least.

Being in California again offered benefits not only to Doug, as his primary mechanic for the Otter was based out of San Jose, but for me as well, seeing as how I had close friends all over the state. This time, there were no trailers and no shitty vans to sleep in, but a whole lot of couch surfing.

Unfortunately that winter, the Otter was plagued with mechanical issues continually, and I found myself sidelined in San Jose quite a few times. Still, it didn't keep me from having some seriously interesting and borderline twisted times, as was the case with one flight back from San Diego that Zach once again joined me on.

We were leveled off at 17,000 feet, sucking down the O2 and enjoying the view. As we crossed over the beginnings of Los Angeles County, I told Zach how much I despised the LA area(except Skydive Perris of course) and that even the thought of spending time there again made me sick to my stomach. Then, I got sick to my stomach.

Well let me clarify. I didn't exactly get sick to my stomach. I got sick to my ass... Having been a self proclaimed professional flatchulator, I'm use to a fair amount of discomfort from time to time, but this... Well this was no case of gas. It seems that the dinner, drinks and desert from the night before, were not nearly as happy with me as I had been with them, and it all wanted to part ways with me IMMEDIATELY.

It was an emergency shit of epic proportions. And it was going to happen. Right then. My options were quite few really. I was 17,000 feet over Los Angeles California, and below us was some of the busiest airspace in the entire country. I was at that altitude because from there, I was able to easily bypass all the bullshit involved in the normal lower altitude crossings. Normally it was no issue what so ever, but in this instance, it was huge. There was simply no way that I could justify to my boss why I had descended so many thousands of feet down into crazy airspace, landed at a field that would undoubtedly charge a fortune in landing fees and burn a ton of gas in the process, all so I could go take a poo.

Luckily for me, not only was Zach able to fly the Otter, but was as was his habit, always overstocked with supplies for his day. His supplies usually involving a large amount of fresh fruit, some type of grain or healthy so and so alternative, water, no sugar added juice, etc... All of which he always always carried around in a plastic shopping bag. There in lie my salvation! Well, that and the fact that Zach quickly understood how truly dire the situation really was.

I quickly briefed him on all the different scenarios that had gone thru my mind in the five or so seconds since the sensation hit. The instant I had the bubbleguts, I knew it was going to be bad. I also knew I had a very limited time with which to deal with the potential disaster, so I wasted no time. As I pulled off the oxygen tube and dumped the contents of Z Safeway bag out on the cockpit floor, I knew I had to not only move quickly, but carefully as well, knowing full well that any misstep could have serious ramifications.

As the lack of oxygen at 17,000 feet began to take effect not only from the loss of the hose, but from the exertion of removing my shorts as I worked my way towards the rear of the cabin, I started to get the warm, fuzzy and familiar feeling that hypoxia brings. I almost happily thought "If I stay next to the door, then perhaps Zach won't have to deal with what could be a rather unsavory odor.

While on my way towards the tail, I'd come up with what I thought would be a pretty good plan for how to most effectively use the Safeway bag, and quickly put that exact plan into action!

One handle in front to not only to allow easy placement of the bag, but allow the "equipment" not currently being used to stay out of the danger zone. One handle in the back, again for bag placement but also to act as a "relief valve" for said destruction and...

"OH MY GOD!! DUDE!! WHAT THE...(gag) Pa-please STOP! FOR THE LOVE OF (gurgle) GOD!!!" The PA system speaker which sat directly above my head quite clearly conveyed the urgency and borderline panic in Zach's voice. He was clearly freaking out with images of my rotting corpse wracked with the Ebola virus acting at super speed, yet there was simply nothing I could do. I had completely surrendered to what was now an all encompassing evacuation of what felt like every liquid and at least half of the solid mass that made up my body, and was almost completely deaf to Zach's begging and pleading for mercy.

With hypoxia now in full effect, I found that I was actually even mildly amused at his increased suffering, and realized that he had made the ultimate rookie Otter mistake by pulling down the side window next to him. unfortunately, instead of filling the cockpit with the fresh air he so desperately wanted, all opening the side window of the Otter did was draw the air surrounding my explosive ass straight toward that open window and right across his pain stricken face. The giggling fit I was starting to have was doing nothing to make the situation easier, but somehow I managed to keep the bag in place and all the shit where it belonged.

Time had all but stopped for me. It could have been two minutes, it could have been three years. Zach's sobs of misery were barely audible over the buzz in my head, and it took almost all my remaining faculties to put the old load sheets to proper use. When I was finally satisfied that I'd managed to wipe all of the destruction off my own ass, I tossed the last of the load sheets into the bag, double and then triple knotted the top, and pulled my skivvies up over my shaking legs.

Standing next to the closed jump door, listening to the air blowing past and watching the scenery flying by miles below; happily relieved, ten pounds lighter and way beyond drunk on a massive lack of oxygen, what to do with the bag that helped save Zach and I from a fate much much worse seemed completely obvious.

"Dude... Dude. That was probably the worst thing I've ever smelled in my entire life! I seriously thought I might pass out!" It still smells SO FUCKING BAD in this plane, it's like everything I can do not to jump out!"

I was still working the rest of the giggles out of my system as I approached the cockpit, but when I saw his face, and heard what he had to say, they came back with a vengeance! As I poured my way back into the seat, and tried to remember exactly what part of my body I was suppose to put the oxygen tube in, I managed to calm myself down just enough to answer his question.

"Dude, what the fuck did you do with the bag man? It still smells like holy hell!" After a few seconds of formulating the answer I replied very matter of factly, "I threw it out of the fucking plane, of course!" "Oh. My. God. you just shit bombed Beverly Hills."

By the time that second winter on "The Road" in the Otter came to a close, I was pretty sure I didn't want to do it again. And as it turned out, I wouldn't. Season three was pretty much a carbon copy of one and two there in Chi-town. It was busy, it was happy, it was energetic and I flew my ever loving ass off. Other than going steadily broke and working really hard, I didn't have any major complaints in life. I was moderately happy, but as the months went by I couldn't help but start wondering if there just wasn't something more I should be doing. Was I actually starting to think about my long-term future?

As my third season in the windy city came and went, I let Doug know that this year I wasn't going to be available to fly for him during the off season. The prospect of another winter flying the Otter wherever the wind blew was just too much.

 Through one of the staff in Chicago, I'd managed to get a gig working as an instructor in a little town on the North Island of New Zealand, a tropical little place called Paihia. It was exactly the break that I needed after what had been three very busy years. As I boarded the plane to NZ, It was with more than 3,000 hours in the Twin Otter alone, and I decided that a bit of a break from the front seat was exactly what I needed. Boy was I right!

I spent the winter flat out loving life. My days were filled filled taking happy people on skydives, and my nights were filled hanging out with good friends, both new and old. I'd entered myself in a long distance open water swim race, I'd become friends with a local Maori tribes woman who'd not only done the swim with me, but had given me the gift of an amazing tattoo for taking her son on a skydive and bringing him back home to her safely, I'd been scuba diving, raced sailboats around the bay with my then girlfriend from Chicago, gotten ragingly drunk at least a few times a week (Oh yeah, I became one hell of a drinker somewhere along the way. Big surprise I know) and had managed to get the big reset I felt I needed to make season four in Chicago a good one. At least I thought it had been…

The Ultimate Goal?

As I entered into my fourth season in Chicago, it had officially become the longest single run I'd had for any one skydiving operation. I tried as things got underway to keep a good outlook on what the season might have in store, and approached my boss in a very positive way with a few things I was going to need to happen in order to keep me happy and satisfied. As it turned out, a meeting of the minds just wasn't in the cards, and I sadly went about beginning the search for my next chapter. Still, even though I was leaving Chi-Town with a bit of a bad taste in my mouth, I had a lot of great memories, both good and bad to look back on. As is my style, in no particular order. Here's my Chicago's greatest hits:

One.

Over four thousand hours as single pilot-in-command of my beloved De Havilland Twin Otter. Never in my life would I have ever expected…

Two.

We'd left at about four in the afternoon for the four plus hour flight from Chicago to North Carolina where the maintenance facility we were using was located. I'd be dropping the plane off there, waiting the two days needed to get the required inspections done, and then head on back . My girl at the time who I'd been dating for about six months had decided she wanted to come along, and I happily welcomed the company, as I'd discovered that time on the road in the Otter could be beyond boring. It was perhaps all of 30 minutes into the flight when she came up with the idea.

As I may have said before, the Twin Otter is the most well thought out and ergonomically designed cockpit in any aircraft I've ever flown, and is absolutely perfect for single, or even dual pilot situations. What it's not perfect for, is having both people in the cockpit in the left seat at the same time.

"Just don't fucking lean back no matter what!" As she looked down at me trying to understand the instructions I was giving her in-between my responses to Air Traffic Control who had been asking about my constant altitude changes, it was clear that we hadn't thought this thing through very well. As she slid me inside her, with more than a little difficulty I might add, I was having to crane my neck over her shoulder to see not only the GPS on the panel as well as all the other important instruments, but to see out the windscreen as well! It was both our official entries into the Mile-High club for sure, but as it turned out, it was far from what could be considered "engaging" sex! After about ten minutes of struggling to balance my concentration between fucking her, and not crashing the plane, I put her safely back in the right seat with a massive pout on her face.

"But you didn't cum!" About half way through explaining to her that I'd been just a touch too distracted to get that far I gave up and said "Honey, if it makes you feel any better, I'll cum all over anything you want once were there!"

Three.

On a random weekday without too much business, I ended up flying the PAC750 as we always did on slower days. On that particular day, the upper winds at the altitude which we normally dropped from was quite literally insane! The ground winds themselves were quite mild which meant that there was no reason we couldn't jump, but if the weather report I had brought up was even close to accurate, I was flying into 80 plus knot winds at the top and as I lined myself up on the first load the PAC most definitely confirmed that the reports had been dead on. Now flying in high upper winds poses no problems for an aircraft in a safety sense, as the airplane only knows how fast it's going through the air. The wings don't give a good god damn how fast they're going over the ground, as long as the airspeed is enough to keep them flying. So my only issue was trying to figure out how damn far away from home I was going to have to drop these guys to get them back home safely.

Flying the opposite direction from the dropzone, almost a full three miles from the field, I turned on the light for the door to be opened. When the second group of jumpers onboard asked me how long they should wait to exit so that they wouldn't risk a collision with the previous jumpers I yelled back "wait till you see them landing!"

"ATC, 902ST with request...". "Go head with request 2ST" came the standard response. After as long as I'd been flying in Chicago, the controllers on the other end of the radio had long before not only learned to recognize my voice, but knew exactly what they could usually expect from my flying, and I had cultivated a very cordial and casual working relationship with most of them. It allowed me a certain level of "familiarity" you wouldn't normally get if you were in strange airspace.

"Could you tell me what you're showing as my current groundspeed. I'm not really sure I can believe my GPS...". Silence.... Then the crack of the a microphone being keyed up, then silence again. Finally, "Ahhh, 2ST, I currently show your groundspeed at 2 knots. Ahh, correction, make that 1 knot. Wait.... 2ST, have you reversed course?"

I was giggling so hard that I could barely get my transmission across. "No Sir... I actually believe I am currently flying BACKWARD!"

Four.

Another weekday in the PAC, and although it was steady, it was far from crazy. As was the policy of the DZ, we would allow people to do observation rides in the aircraft from time to time as long as I didn't have a problem with it, and this time I most certainly did not! She was fucking adorable. This bouncy little blonde with perky everything, including her attitude had come out to the dropzone to check out the operation in an attempt to decide if she wanted to make a skydive. When she found out that she could ride along in the airplane, she signed up as quickly as she could.

By load four of shameless flirting on my part, with absolutely no intention of asking her to get out of the plane, I got a few radio calls from manifest asking what was going on. By the time I shut the airplane down for fuel on load five, I'd managed a pretty decent bit of headway with her, and had already invited her to continue flying with me. Manifest had different ideas.

"C'mon Dean, you can't have her just flying around with you all damn day! She only paid for one ride, and I know she's not gonna pay for all the ones you've taken her on, now is she!"

As I explained that I wasn't going to have her onboard for anymore of the flights, the disappointment in her eyes was obvious. "It's too bad you're not making a jump" I joked, "Cause then I'd just tell you to jump naked, because anyone that jumps naked jumps for free!" She looked at me, gave a bit of a sideways grin and said "Well what if I'm naked while I'm flying with you?"

For the next five loads every single male jumper in the PAC sat facing the cockpit, basically spending the ten minute climb to altitude having to do abdominal crunches the entire time, so that they could stare at my buck naked passenger, clad only in an emergency bail out rig, headset and a grin.

Five.

It was our annual staff getaway to the bosses Lake House. For three days each season, we would load up staff, food and booze in the Otter and make the relatively short flight to Indiana for a few days of utter drunken fun.

By the time day two rolled around, most of us, myself included had been raging drunk for most of our time there, and as we pulled the boat away from the dock at all of ten in the morning, we were already back at it! By noon, I'd already been up on skis two times, and was not only getting pretty worn, but was way past just a little buzzed. Buzzed enough it seemed, to think that round three in the water was a damn good idea.

As I managed to get the slalom ski on with more than a little difficulty, I signaled to the driver that I was all set. Unfortunately for me, both of us were way too far gone to notice the almost three feet of slack in the tow rope as he hammered the throttle. As the line went taught with me still holding on, the only thing there was to take the jolt to the handle was my arms.

With an audible POP and a brief but insanely intense jolt of pain, I was launched a few feet into the air before my grip gave way, and I found myself floating in the water with my left bicep curled up into a knotted ball, pinned just under the life vest I was wearing. By the time the group in the boat had struggled to help me back onboard I had managed to massage my brutally torn bicep into a relaxed state, but it now simply hung weakly as it was no longer attached inside by the tendon near my elbow.

$30,000 worth of surgery and rehab later I was back flying the Otter, with an empty bank account, another surgery under my belt and a whole bunch of new scars, but hey, this time I knew how to jerk off right handed!

Six.

We'd been planning if for weeks, and the load had not only been fully booked within an hour of announcing it was going to take place, but we had almost a dozen people as a "backup" in case any of those who got the slots weren't able to make it. Air Traffic Control had taken a fair bit of convincing, because in their estimation, a 30,000 foot jump was a monumental undertaking, but after a whole lot of time and planning, we finally got their approval.

Flying a load that high posed a number of unusual problems for us, but in regard to the jump itself, we had enough information from other operations that had done them to set up our aircraft and brief and train our jumpers accordingly. The biggest problem came not only in working out the timing and logistics with Air Traffic, but even with filing a flight plan for the load, as we would be twelve-thousand feet up into Class A controlled airspace.

As I climbed up through 18,000, for the first time in my career I was flipped over to "Center" for control on an IFR flight plan, with jumpers onboard no less. Other than talking to different controllers and having an O2 mask covering my face, it was just another flight really. One that just so happened to be really fucking high and take a long damn time to complete. As I turned onto jump run, asked for clearance from Center to drop jumpers, then requested permission to descend it all seemed to go as smooth as could be.

As I descended back down through 18,000 feet and was instructed to go back to my normal controllers, I was met on the radio with the shocked voice of one of the girls that had been handing me in Chicago skies for a couple of years by then.

"What in the world did you do up there Dean?" I didn't have a clue what she was talking about, and said as much. "Well I just got off the phone with Center, and they were freaking out the entire time you were up there! You're never gonna believe this, but the held all departures and arrivals for a solid ten minutes!" At least three other aircraft that had overheard her statement to me keyed up their microphones to blurt out some version of "whoa". As it turned out, I had been single handedly responsible for what I have to imagine were thousands of delayed travelers, and probably more than a few missed connections. FUCK. YEAH!

Seven.

I was already a full day late returning from North Carolina with the Otter due to weather, and Doug was loosing his fucking mind. I had told him when he first hired me that he had to make a choice. He could either pay to keep me current and up to date flying IFR (Instrument Flight Rules), in which case, I would be able to perform cross-country flights for him even in bad weather, OR, he could save himself that cost, but run the risk of my sitting on the ground if the weather wouldn't allow me to fly. He had gone with the second option, and this was one of the half-dozen times that the choice bit him quite solidly in the ass. I had learned my fucking lesson when it came to weather, and call me a pussy if you want but if I wasn't current with my IFR flying, I didn't fly.

As I finally hit the air again, having been stuck somewhere midway between NC and Chicago, it was with bad weather still looming all around, but enough gaps in the "green" on the weather radar I'd pulled up online that I was wiling to at least give it a shot. I'd made sure not to get his hopes up too much by telling him there was still a decent possibility I may not make it all the way, but he seemed at least satisfied that I was willing to take the chance.

The rain started about 30 minutes into the fight, but it wasn't terribly strong, and although it obscured my forward vision out the windscreen, the ground was still clearly visible with a ceiling a good 4,000 feet above me, and in a legal sense it was still very much VFR (Visual Flight Rules). Then the rain got stronger. And stronger… No gusts of wind, no thunder storm warnings, and according to the radar controller on the other end of the radio, no significant weather other than the solid lake of water I seemed to find myself flying through. For about an hour, I used the small side window next to me to ensure I had good visibility below, so I could easily land on one of the many airports I flew over along the way. I used the GPS to stay on course, and I used a very agreeable controller to make sure I wasn't going to inadvertently fly into some serious shit.

When I was just about to land back on the field in Chicago about mid day, they were thrilled to hear me on the radio about ten minutes out, and asked if I had enough gas to leave the engines running and fly a load or two in what for them had been blue skies all day long. As I pulled up to the loading area, the look on not only Doug's but all the jumpers faces as well were frozen in clear confusion. When I got the signal from Doug to cut the engines and hopped out of the Otter, the only thing I could manage to say was "damn!"

Every leading edge of the aircraft was stripped down either to fiberglass or bare metal. The rainstorm it seemed had been so strong as I flew along, that it managed to blast more than a fair amount of the paint off the plane along with it. The only thing I could say to Doug was "guess I should have waited a little longer!"

Eight.

Mexico

Nine.

It was once again time to get all the inspections done and unfortunately, that for me meant one more flea bag motel in the middle of nowhere. But luck would have it, I was within a few hours driving distance to what was then the biggest wind tunnel around. As it happened, one of them was an old friend of mine from my Cross keys days. As soon as I let him know I was heading that way, he managed to get me all sorted out with a good chunk of time in the tunnel, and an invite to dinner with the wife and relatively new baby. I was thrilled!

The tunnel time was a blast, if not a bit humbling, and I had fun regardless of how badly I was performing. As we wrapped up flying, he told me to just follow him over to where we'd meet the wife (whom was also from my CK days) and the new baby for a nice dinner. As dinner finished up and the bill came, I was more than pleasantly surprised when I was told that no way was I going to drive all the way back to the hotel that was hours away, but that I would come back home with them, have another drink, and crash out on the floor for the evening. Awesome.

One or two drinks later, and my gracious hosts put the baby down, told me to make myself completely at home, and retired for the evening, but not before telling me they had great WiFi and giving me the password so I could check up on the world, as I'd bitched that for months it seemed I hadn't been able to do more than occasionally check my email. Check up on my email was exactly what I did. Then I got on Facebook for the first time in ages to find out what everyone had been up to while I'd been "away", and then I got an all too familiar inclination...

Here I was, comfy as can be. All stretched out on the couch cushions they'd laid out on the floor for me, glass of wine by my side, lightning fast internet connection and the realization that I not only hadn't been laid in months, but had been forced to suffer through the same half dozen adult movies on my laptop for ages. I mean c'mon, what would you do? Three o'clock in the morning and the house completely quiet. Slightly drunk, terminally horny and all alone... So, www."insert porn site here".com it was, and off to the races! The setting never really crossed my mind if truth be told. Straight down to business it was, and coming along just fine if I do say so, right up until...

"OH SHIT!!! SSS...Sorry Mate!"

The living room lights had come on, and gone off so fast that they hardly even registered with my eyes! I was completely frozen, even though the couple on my laptop were most certainly not! I couldn't quite comprehend what had just happened, and then slowly but surely, it sunk in.

My old friend, who had just shown me the most entertaining evening I'd had in months, flown me in the tunnel, taken me out for a great meal, and then invited me into his home out of the kindness of his own heart had just walked into his own living room to find a middle aged man masturbating on the floor, surrounded by plush stuffed animals, baby toys and a play pen unmercifully lit momentarily by the rather bright light that hung directly above where I was lying.

As I surveyed the scene, now only lit by the flickering images screwing their brains out on the screen, I tried to think of what I could possibly do now (other than finish, of course! which I totally did.) The thing was, for as bad as I suppose it looked just catching a guest goin' at it in your living room was, when you added to that the fact that everything the poor man directly associated with his kid was strewn all around me, it was downright shocking! I couldn't possibly imagine in my embarrassed state how I was even going to begin to apologize, so, I didn't!

I did what any self respecting deviant with a bit of a porn habit would do. I woke up really fucking early, wrote a quick "Thanks for everything" note, and got the fuck out of there before the sun came up! It was the worst possible end to a horrible winter season I could have possibly imagined, and probably the worst beginning to a season he never would have imagined! I actually haven't spoken to the poor bastard since.

Ten.

It was my first season in Chicago, and although I was new to the DZ, I certainly wasn't new to the sport anymore. Facebook being what it was even then had made it extremely easy to keep in touch with friends from all around the world, and although common in skydiving circles, it was always nice to hear from old friends. Kolbrún, a.k.a Kolla was an old friend from my CK days that had gone from working for one of the sports largest gear manufacturers to diving into a venture with a good friend of hers named Lara. They had decided that the magazine Parachutist which dominated the sport simply didn't represent a large portion of the skydiving community, and started up Blue Skies Mag as an alternative.

When I was approached to write an article for the new magazine on the pilots perspective of day to day operations, both Kolla, and Lara who was to be the editor of the magazine went out of their way to tell me to avoid political correctness like the plague! They wanted articles written by skydivers, for skydivers, who were by and large not the most P.C. people on the planet. So when I sat down to write my very first article ever, it was with the idea that it should be at least a little over the top.

When I was finished, I'd ended up with a seventeen-hundred word article entitled "Pissed off Pilot? What your pilot may be thinking and why." I assumed when I hit the send button, that I would eventually receive a chopped up version of my writing, with a lot less "Fucks" and the language toned down quite a bit. To my amazement, when the article went to print, it was word for word exactly as I'd sent it to them.

After that first submission, I was asked by Lara if I would like to me a monthly columnist for Blue Skies, and I jumped at the chance! She had loved the first article, and wanted me to pretty much continue to do the same. What started out as an article I assumed would be diced up to hell for being a bit over the top now seemed to be exactly what they wanted, and an unspoken little competition (at least in my mind) was started. Every time I'd write an article, I would try and be just a little more over the top, a little more racy, and a touch more offensive just to see which one of us would blink first.

When I wrote an article for the magazine entitled "PC Line Dancing" that started out with that same horrible gay joke "So I'm fuckin' this guy in the ass…" and it went to print without a single word changed, I knew I'd met my match! If she let that go to print, there was simply nothing I was ever going to write that would be too far. (As a side note, I didn't find out until years later that the entire time, her poor mother had been proof reading all my work. Poor poor woman!)

All and all, for good and bad, the Windy City had been one hell of an interesting time in a life thus far filled with them! As I said goodbye to the Midwest and headed off to the Caribbean, it was most certainly with more good memories than bad.

A Long Overdue Puberty

And so it came to pass, somewhere in the neighborhood of my 43rd birthday I decided to enter the real world for the first time in my adult life. I'd managed (with a fair amount of help from a Skydance Jump pilot friend named Kris) to be offered a slot in the upcoming training class as a First Officer for Seaborne Airlines, based out of St. Croix in the United States Virgin Islands.

Real world it might be, but it seemed that the same old rules applied. The offer wasn't for a job. Not exactly anyway. It was an offer for a "chance" at a job. I'd accepted the challenge, packed up all my belongings in little boxes which were left with my girlfriend who would bring them along if I got to stay, and hopped on a flight to San Juan Puerto Rico where I'd be flown to my new home in the first commercially operated passenger Otter I'd ever seen. Just like it had been so many times before in my life, this was a deal or no deal shot. One chance.

The next month of my life sucked serious fucking ass. I'd gone into the course thinking that I knew a fair amount about not only flying, but about the Twin Otter specifically, and found to my chagrin that in fact, I knew jack shit! The real airline world was vastly different than anything I had ever experienced and was full of ridiculous regulations and rules, required knowledge that didn't seem as though anyone would ever need to know it; chain's of command, terms, phrases, acronyms for fucking acronyms.... All of which I had to know just long enough to get me through the course.

And the Twin Otter? Why in the fucking hell did I need to know that the gas generator spun at thirty five thousand RPM's a second? Was it really necessary for me to be able to list the three different components of an Otter that were made of wood? Was being able to list the names of the different internal sections of the engines really going to make me a better pilot? Who in fucking hell gave a damn if I knew how tall the tail was, or what power source the coffee pot (we had a fucking coffee pot?) ran off of? I was dumbfounded at the ridiculous things I was required to learn.

By the time the ground school had ended I'd managed to get through it all, but not without losing a fair chunk of weight and stressing massively. As it turned out, in both airline flying and in Twin Otter systems I did have a lot to learn, and even with the huge amount of bullshit I was required to retain I ended up learning a shit load of very "real world" valuable things. It hadn't been easy by any stretch though. Having a ridiculously insecure girlfriend back Stateside that seemed to think I was living the party life on a tropical island didn't help the situation much either, as I was just as busy trying to calm her jealous nerves as I was trying to pass my courses.

By the time I was flying to Toronto for my week of sim training, I just wanted it over. What I discovered quite quickly was that having a Twin Otter as an airline passenger aircraft was a horrible idea! They had taken what was to me one of the easiest single-pilot planes that had ever been made, and completely ruined it by forcing two pilots to try and multi task the items that one good pilot could do alone almost by reflex. Even though I managed to get past the sim training without any real problems and should have been both relieved and thrilled, I flew back to St. Croix without any real sense of excitement. Was this how all grown up's felt?

About the time I had been hired, Seaborne was pretty short on first officers, of which I was one. What that meant was that I was constantly on the schedule from the word go, and as soon as I was cleared off IOE (Initial Operating Experience) and put on the line, I was pulling fourteen hour days pretty regularly. All of the first officers were being scheduled literally as much as the law would allow, and it was brutal. In relatively short order, simply because of the amount I was working I had become quite use to the way things were done around the place and although I was a zombie most of the time, I had no real issues at work and was generally considered a good addition to the team.

By the time the girlfriend moved to the island, I had managed to rent us a beautiful little furnished house in a gated community on the island, get both her and both her's and my dogs happily situated, and then promptly worked my ass off. All of six months into the job I knew it wasn't for me, but this was my shot. I was earning just enough in my position at Seaborne to be able to afford to pay the rent and eat and that was about it. I'd rolled the dice on become a contributing member of society, and like it or not, I was gonna stick this shit out! My girlfriend though was having an amazing time. Working very part time as a waitress at one of the more popular bars in town, she enjoyed spending her days either tossing back shots and smoking blunts at work, or tossing back shots and smoking blunts on the beach.

If truth be told, I was crazy jealous of her time on the island. She got to enjoy it in all the ways that I didn't. As an airline pilot on a very small island, going and getting into "trouble" just wasn't something you could get away with unless you didn't mind it getting back to all the wrong people, and for the first time I minded.

I managed just over two years with Seaborne. Just over two years in a first officer slot flying with Captains, some of which had thousands of hours less flying than I did. Just over two years of fourteen hour shifts, followed by a few hours sleep before I was right back on the line to do it all again. Just over two years of watching my girl have the time of her life while I worked my ever loving ass off to finance it. Two years of being an adult in the real world that was now in my opinion two fucking years too many.

It was a random Facebook conversation that did it. I'd been running a "Fuckin' Pilot" page for Blue Skies Magazine for quite a few years by this time, and because of it, and the monthly articles I'd been writing for them for almost four years I had a long list of skydiver followers and friends, a lot of whom I'd never even met. My chat that day was with one of them.

"Yeah man... The whole airline thing really just hasn't turned out to be what I expected. It's just not the lifestyle I thought it would be".

"Really?" He replied, "I've got a few friends now flying for the majors, and the love it! It's kind of my next move I think." "Well Jeff I wish you all the best of luck! I know we're aways looking here, but I'd never recommend you coming out this way! Hell, I don't suppose you guys are looking for any Otter drivers there are ya?"

It was meant more as a joke than anything. I might have been hating life in St. Croix, but it was exactly what I was suppose to want, right? I might have had a girlfriend I just fought with all the time, but it had to get better at some point, didn't it? I was just about to receive my upgrade to Captain, having recently passed my check ride to become a real life licensed mother fucking Airline Transport Pilot for fuck sake! Of course I was kidding when I asked.

"Dude, I'm seriously looking to leave and they know it, and they're gonna want someone to take my place the minute I do. You should totally send me you're resume!"

Fuck it. It couldn't hurt to just send one out and see. I mean the odds that they were going to be able to beat what I'd be getting as a Captain for an airline was super slim cause really it was just a dropzone after all, not to mention I hadn't flown jumpers in over two years so I really doubted anything would come of it anyway. I spent all of about thirty minutes updating my resume to add my Seaborne time and qualifications to it, and hit the "Send" button, pretty damn sure not one thing would come of it.

When I woke up the next morning and heard the "Ding" of my inbox while I was drinking a cup of coffee I didn't think much of it. I didn't recognize the email address, and it wasn't one of my contacts, so I was mildly interested in what it might be, but just assumed it would turn out to be more spam. What it was, to my shock and surprise was not only a very brief email from Jeff's boss offering me a position as one of the Captains for the dropzone he was the Chief Pilot of, but an attachment that turned out to be a full blown contract for me to review.

I had to read it twice. Then I had to google the exchange rate from there to the US to find out what all the funky numbers meant. Then I had to pull out my calculator and double, and then triple check the numbers…

"Really nice to receive your email. As you know, I'm currently employed with Seaborne Airlines, and if I were to decided to take the position with you, I'd need to give them a minimum of thirty days notice before I could leave. If you don't mind, I'd like to take a few days to think this over, as I've just started training for my Captain upgrade, and leaving at this juncture would be quite a big decision."

His email reply, which came back in less than five minutes told me to take as much time as I needed to think things over, and that of course he understood needing to give proper notice, and that in fact if I didn't give it, he wouldn't want me.

That whole day of flying went by in a blur. I couldn't recall a single leg of a single flight, couldn't remember any of the conversations I'd had with the Captain I was flying with, and in fact couldn't even remember the Captain! As I went to bed that night, I had managed to not tell a single soul about the choice that had been laid out before me, not even the girl sound asleep in my bed. I fell into one of the most fitful sleeps of my entire life and eventually ended up sitting bolt upright in bed at about 3:12am, never more instantly awake. One last flash of the contract popped into my mind, along with all that the last two years had brought, and I knew in that very second.

"So Heath! Glad I was able to catch you. This time difference is crazy!" It was 3:18am, and I'd been awake for six minutes, and It took me four of those minutes just to find his phone number. "This is Dean out here with Seaborne… So yeah, If you're offer is legitimate and on the level, I'm in!"

Shawn, the then Director of Operations for Seaborne looked at me like I'd just walked in the office wearing a leopard skin tutu and a dildo glued to my forehead. "Dean… you're on the books to start your Captain upgrade training in less than two weeks! What in the hell are you thinking??"

I just kind of shook my head slowly and responded "That's why I'm telling you now Shawn. I didn't want you guys to pay for all the training and SIM time". He just sat there looking back and forth between me and the resignation letter I'd placed on his desk. "I just… I just don't get it man. Why on earth would you want to throw the left seat away after all this?"

Without saying a word, I slid a copy of the contract I'd been sent across the desk, the conversions for my pay and other allowances to US dollars noted down the side, and waited while he read. As he reached the bottom of the contract, finished it and slowly slid it back across his desk to me, he stood, extended his right hand, and in the most sincere way possible said "Good luck to you my friend! It's been a pleasure working with you."

As I boarded the first of three flights bound happily outside the shores of the United States, I couldn't help but think back about all the things I'd been through. All the things I had seen and done over the years that had continued to lead me exactly to places just like this, being whisked away on yet another adventure who's outcome was impossible to predict.

That lie. That one little white lie to try and get laid. Actually following through with a show that never EVER should have happened. My time as the token white boy, the inexplicable success with telegrams, and then on stage. The raves, the drugs, my own real awakening and the beginning of knowing myself. Wild times in Sin City from the OG to the Hard Rock, all the stage shows, all the girls. That very first jump, and knowing that very instant that I'd found another path. Death and drama. Life jumping out of, and then flying airplanes. Traveling all over the U.S. and the world. Australia, Fiji, New Zealand, Mexico, the Caribbean, and now...

I couldn't help but sit there and wonder as I sipped on a shitty glass of airline wine just what on Earth might be waiting for a guy named Princess in the Land of Sand...

Stripper Wisdom

So, Were at the ass end of what can only be considered one hell of a ride, and it's time to figure out what I may or may not have learned through it all. Over these past years I have managed to form some rather unique opinions, as well as picking up a few from other people that I've adopted as my own. I'll see if I can't convey them to you now. And once again, just like my life, in no particular order…

- Generally, I have found that most women are twice as horny and perverted as men are, they are just twice as good at controlling it. They have learned either through years of practice, or by some genetic trait in them that the best way to rule the world is to hold back most of their urges and desires until the time is right. When that time is right though, hold on brotha cause it's gonna be a hell of a ride. I have personally witnessed your average every day straight laced women get a few drinks in them in a provocative atmosphere and loose their fucking minds. I can easily imagine the stories that have been told in confessionals around the country, and the millions of Rosaries counted out all over the world over the things I have seen. Those perverted traits have shown themselves to be evident in every single woman I have ever met, and I'll be hard pressed to believe that there's even one out there past puberty that doesn't contain them.

- I have come to the honest and informed conclusion that under most circumstances, men are complete idiots. Most of the time they operate under good, or at least not bad intentions, but they have the uncanny ability to completely ignore their own common sense in favor of what looks to be more fun. The misconception that women are more -emotional than men is a bunch of crap. Men are just as emotional in most cases, and even more so in others, but we have been trained over the years that we aren't suppose to show any of it. Being emotional is a sign of weakness and makes us appear needy, and fuck if any man ever appear to need anybody. In my experience, when emotions finally get the best of a man, it's over. Emotionally I can be more of a basket case than any woman I have ever met, but it's usually much more short lived, and almost never in front of anyone else.

- The idiot part of most men generally takes place below the waist as most of you would assume. That all comes back to that whole control thing. Us guys are so use to attempting to be in control, that as soon as a piece of tail comes along that makes us feel "funny", we loose our fucking minds and do all the things we know we shouldn't just so we can get a bit. Idiot's! You really wouldn't believe some of the things us guys do in regard to women.

- I have discovered over the years that generally, the preconceived notions that people carry around about others are usually so far out of whack that they almost defy definition. All men are pigs. All women are bitches. All male strippers are gay. All female strippers are hookers. People with money are simply better than people without. It's these kinds of things that never cease to amaze me. To honestly believe that all black people are dishonest thieves, all Asian people are terrible drivers, all Italians are in the mafia…it's ludicrous, but people believe these things none the less. Even crazier than the fact that people run around believing these things, is that the rest of us actually care what they think. The way it should really work is quite easy. If you don't mean anything to me, then neither does your opinion. Why on earth would it.

- No matter what you say, sex is probably the single most important ingredient in a relationship. Without good sex, your screwed. You could get along better than anyone in the history of man. You could have everything in common, and everything going for you, but if you don't have that chemistry, what you have is a wonderful friendship. Don't get me wrong, I'm not knocking friendship, but I don't generally want to fuck the hell out of my friends, and if I don't want to fuck the hell out of my girl, she's probably not going to be my girl for long.

- If your going to go out and have a great night whacked out of your mind on Ecstasy, don't do it with someone your trying to screw. Trust me when I say from personal experience, and from those that I know very well that it's just not worth it. The last time I tried having sex with someone while we were on Ecstasy, we ended up going at it like porn stars for ten straight hours. Now when I say we went at it for ten hours, I don't mean we hit it for a few then rested, then went at it again, I mean we went at it for ten hours. We didn't even bother getting up for water, she and I simply had our bottles close enough to us that we could drink without stopping. The recovery time for a marathon like that is one thing, but the fact that in that ten hours I never managed to reach a climax because of the drugs made the whole thing absurd. I ended up having to wear loose fitting shorts for two days afterward, and have a feeling I may have done some long term nerve damage.

- We all know that the bad boys seem to do much better where women are concerned. We all know that nice guys almost always seem to finish last, and I know that having an equal mix of the two never seemed to do me much good either way. The girls that went after the bad boys loved me right up till they got to know me, and the girls that wanted the good guys never even bothered to give me a chance. What I've learned in regard to that is that no matter what, you have to be true to yourself. If you try to play a part to attract someone else, your never going to be able to stop playing it. If you do, then it almost goes without saying that your gonna loose 'em.

- Thong underwear sucks. No matter how they are cut, no matter how they fit, no matter how they look they are simply the most uncomfortable piece of clothing ever made. If you then take into consideration that for a man at least, wearing one means letting everyone who sees you in it know everything there is to know about you, it can be even worse. I haven't considered myself anything but average, and for me average was always good enough. But for some of the guys I've seen in my business, average must have been on a radically different scale. When average covers less distance than, oh let's say, a healthy green bean, then you really should consider another line of work. On the other side of that coin, when average is measured using your forearm for scale, your gonna scare people. To take either of those two extremes and strap them into a thong then plop them down in public can be terribly traumatic.

- FUCK POLITICAL CORRECTNESS! So sorry somebody said something unkind about you. Sorry you had to listen to a joke you found offensive. Bummer that some people don't like the color of your skin, or you political affiliation, your religion or the size of your tits or cock. Sorry somebody said you weren't attractive enough, or that the newscasters opinion on the Oscars really upset you cause "Leo should have won years ago"... Toughen the fuck up Cupcake! Stop being such a pussy! And by pussy I mean weak and overly sensitive... You over the top feminists who find the word "pussy" to describe weakness offensive are just a bunch of dicks... At the end of the day, who really gives a fuck! Say what you feel, cause the only person you betray by being "politically correct" is yourself.

- This one leads me to the whole size doesn't matter thing. Women seem to have become very fond of telling men that size really doesn't matter, it's what you do with it that counts. Well, to that I say bullshit. That's just like me saying it really doesn't matter just how loose a girl is, as long as she can wiggle nicely. Trust me when I say occasionally grazing the sides won't really do much for your average guy, and I'm guessing that a needle dick, no matter how masterfully it's swished around, isn't going to cut it for a woman. Let's just agree that each woman will consider a different size dick acceptable, with dick's on either end of the scale simply out of the question.

- "Foreplay's nice, but having a man inside me is simply the best". I've actually heard women say this. Yes, penetration is wonderful, and it feels great if everything fits and it's done right, but if you haven't gotten a bit worked up before you stick it in, it's just mechanical. Any woman that isn't a fan of foreplay has never dated a guy that's really good at eating pussy! Excuse my crudeness, but that's the honest to goodness truth in my opinion. Any guy out there that either won't munch, or isn't any good at it simply doesn't know what the hell he's missing. There is simply nothing better than sliding down between a woman's legs, and quite quickly gaining total control. You just can't imagine how wonderful it is to truly make a woman climb the walls, then beg you, not ask but beg you for more. What a power trip. It's the same on the flip side as well. There isn't a guy out there that can say that a good blow job isn't one of his favorite things in the world, and not one that I've ever met that would pass one up if given a good opportunity. If a guy doesn't want to get blown before sex, it's cause he's gonna end up shooting his load before things can ever get started, and he can't stand the thought of looking like a fool.

- Kids are the most amazing thing in the entire world. Forget how they got here, forget what's going on between the parents, forget all the bullshit. They are quite simply the best. There is nothing in the world that could ever make me regret anything I ever did because it all led up to my becoming a father. A father is the greatest title anyone could ever give me, and it's truly all that I could ever ask for. If when it's all said and done, I am simply known as Bailey Jessica Ricci's dad, then I'll be buried a famous man indeed. That being said, now that she's an adult I am happily back to hating kids. Bunch of little assholes, the lot of them.

- Overcoming shyness is not a prerequisite to stripping. I and most of the dancers that I've met over the years are really very shy and self conscious people. The fact that we have ended up in a profession that forces us to toss those fears out the window on a daily basis simply helps to enforce the belief that there's something seriously wrong with all of us.

- I'm totally pro gay marriage. You should be able to marry who ever the fuck you want, regardless of gender or race or nationality, or... Fuck, marry a chez lounge if it makes you happy! Who the fuck is anyone else to judge, but seriously, how is this even an issue anymore?

- I'm an Atheist. Pretty sure that shows, but just in case, Yet... I one-hundred percent support any and all religions and peoples ability to worship anything or anyone they choose, as long as not one single soul is hurt while doing so or in the name of that religion. I'll admit I find I'm jealous of people with faith, as I have no doubt that they sleep much better at night than I do, but hey, you believe what you believe...

- Back to the men are stupid thing. The guys that go to strip clubs on a regular basis honestly believe that if they spend enough time and money on a girl, there gonna get what they want. By want I don't necessarily mean sex either. Some of the fellas that hang out in the clubs are there looking for love. They don't seem to realize as this beautiful busty blonde dances all over him that she is more than likely trying to remember what bills still need to be paid, or what time she told the sitter she was going to be home. Just in case your one of those guys...it's all about the money son!

- Skydivers aren't crazy, nor do they have death wishes. They are just a group of people that have discovered that life on mother earth isn't always what it's cracked up to be, and they need a bit of an escape, even if it is only a few minutes at a time.

- The single best blonde joke I ever heard was told to be by a very straight laced and proper looking forty-five year old Midwest blonde on the ride to altitude one day. "What's the difference between a mosquito and a blonde?…The Mosquito stops sucking when you smack it!" Just goes to show that you can never ever judge a book by it's cover.

- Along those same lines as stereotypes are all the macho guys that strut on to the drop zone figuring there's nothing we can do to scare them, and walk off the drop zone having peed themselves, or at least cried a bit after having faced their mortality. Ball's are almost always bigger than brains.

- Ladies, please, for goodness sake, always play with the balls…

- Sex is really fucking cool, but cool just isn't enough. The hardest lesson I've ever learned, and one that I still don't seem to be able to follow is that sex isn't much without real feeling, and it's no replacement for loneliness. Going out and getting laid cause your feeling lost and alone only helps when your deep in it. Once it's over, you end up feeling even more alone than you did before.

- If you don't have guts anywhere else in your life, make sure you have it in the sack. If you can't tell the person your with what you want and what you like, your never going to be fulfilled. Sex shouldn't be selfish, but it should be what you want it to, and the only way your ever gonna get what you really want is to open up your mouth and ask. Ladies, that means you! Never in my life have I met a straight man that wouldn't do what ever it took to get a girl off. It's not even that we have some deep desire to give pleasure or anything like that, we just like knowing that when it's all said and done, you're gonna walk away thinking we are the shit! Who knows, you may even tell a friend, and I don't know of any guy who wouldn't want to be known as a dynamo in bed.

- That one leads into a theory I've held for quite some time, and one that's started it's fare share of arguments. If there was ever a time that I was bad in bed, it was the woman's fault! Ohhh, tough one to swallow now isn't it. What's my justification for such a bold statement, I already told you. Ask me for it, tell me it gets you off, and it shall be done, simple as that.

- The simple pleasures in life seem to be the ones that count the most. Soak it all in, every day. The whole smell the roses thing might sound corny, but a truer statement has never been made. Live your life any way that you choose to, and no matter what happens, or what anyone else says or does, be happy.

- I completely support the legalization of marijuana and a complete end to its prohibition, as well as the release of any and all people currently incarcerated for non violent drug offenses. I also completely support the de criminalization of ALL other illegal drugs, so that those suffering through addiction can seek help instead of hiding... Why? is it because I've done a fair amount of drugs in my time? that may have a bit to do with it... That, and it would make trips home a fuck load more entertaining! Along with ending the National Debt, stoping the "war on drugs" and making the States a much less violent place.

- I honestly believe that activities like skydiving, rock climbing, surfing, BASE jumping, and anything else that can push someone near to and or past their personal limits is a must for anyone looking to grow as an individual. It's one of the reasons why I have such a high level of respect for my skydiving counterparts world wide. Even if I disagree with their positions on different subjects, I believe their position comes from a life lived with much more personal reflection than the average man or woman.

- And finally… Totally pro porn.

This book is sincerely dedicated to (In no particular order):

Nancy Ricci, Bailey Ricci, Derick Massey, Jim Lindstrom, Patrick Middleton, Diego Ricci, Simon Wade, Dale Hinton, Jim Dolan, J.J. Jaworski, Zach Kimsey, Sara Losche, Kim Worthington, Mark, Donnie, Vince, Kory Dudgeon, Paul Joseph, Thumper, Corvette, Twila, Ray Ferrell, Donny Brown, Perry and Zinda Colburn, Crystal, Shelby, Mandy O'farrell, Gloria, Robert Browning, Craig Kusky, AJ Moller, Joe Herbst, Allison Martinez, Mary Tortomasi, Barbara Carqueville, CJ Freeman, Wes, Shea, Tui and Jeff, Rene Heather Sabala, Eric Volcano, Brandi, Incognito, Brett Racine, Chris Bozeal, Courtney Boast, Danny Koon, Hector Hoya, Steve and Jenny Verner, Range Luda, Micah Couch, Paul Wetzel, Kris Hackler, Rosala, Egon Sussman, Donna Crose, Lara Kjensen, Kolbrún Knotachance, Jamiroquai, David Junior Ludvic, Steve and Jenny Verner, Eli Thompson, Heather Bock, Irving Clifford, Steven Jackson, Rob Stanley, Johno Gordon, Heather Bock, Mark Norman, Paul Ericksmon, Jerry Fox, Jill Kusman, Jim Matthews, Christina Rodriquez, Ben Collier, Margret Ricci, Robert Ricci, Hot Wheels, Kro Cox, Val, Heath Hayley, Chemical Brothers, Vanessa, Liz Mann, The Brand New Heavies, Dave Pancake, Mallory McCormick, Kelsey Mizure, Ryan Zebro, Ammon Mcneely, Nick Martinez, Ivo Ninov, Nick Armstrong, Nikki Colon, Paul Piccalo, Paul Patterson, Ryan Arnold, Sammy Popov, Simeon Lott, Selwyn and Melody Facey, Stephanie Eggum, Tom and Tracy Bohm, Tommy Cahill, Vic Pappadado, Brad Wedge, Dan, Billy Sharman, German nanny 1, German nanny 2, Stripper's 1-362, Every fucking skydiver I've ever jumped with or flown, Every woman I ever danced for...

Blue Skies,

Dean 'Princess" Ricci